EXCELLENCE IN THE WORKPLACE:

LEGAL AND LIFE SKILLS

IN A NUTSHELL®

SECOND EDITION

KAY KAVANAGH
Professor of Law Emerita
University of Arizona
James E. Rogers College of Law
Tucson, AZ

PAULA NAILON
Assistant Dean for Career and
Professional Development, Retired
University of Arizona
James E. Rogers College of Law
Tucson, AZ

WEST
ACADEMIC
PUBLISHING

Nutshell Series, In a Nutshell and the Nutshell Logo are trademarks registered in the U.S. Patent and Trademark Office.

© 2007 Thomson/West
© 2018 LEG, Inc. d/b/a West Academic
            444 Cedar Street, Suite 700
            St. Paul, MN 55101
            1-877-888-1330

West, West Academic Publishing, and West Academic are trademarks of West Publishing Corporation, used under license.

Printed in the United States of America

ISBN: 978-1-63460-776-6

INTRODUCTION

We were gratified to receive West's invitation to prepare a second edition of this Nutshell. Over the decade since the first edition, we've heard from readers who continue to refer to the book long after their first few months on the job. What could we add?

One of our fundamental assumptions in both editions has been that change is inevitable—within ourselves, in others, and in our professional and personal worlds. In the legal profession, changes are occurring too quickly to be usefully documented here, as our observations would likely be obsolete by printing. But what hasn't changed, and in fact has become more urgent, is the need for greater attention to lawyers' and law students' lives. Where is the help for new (and old) lawyers to manage the challenges that lawyers face in trying to solve other people's problems?

In our second edition, we have emphasized even more than in the first the soft skills of self-awareness, emotional intelligence, awareness of differences, and conflict resolution. Throughout, we have focused on reflection, flexibility, resilience, and self reliance supported, as always, by the need to develop a solid set of skills and abilities. Our goal is simple: to provide you with the practical tools, suggestions, and support you need as you meet the challenges of solving other people's problems.

ACKNOWLEDGMENTS TO THE SECOND EDITION

We reiterate our thanks to all who inspired and supported us in writing the First Edition, and add our thanks to J. Randall Harris Design for the tables in Chapters 22, 24, and 27.

In addition to the sources that influenced us and upon which we relied for the First Edition, we add the following: American Bar Association, *ABA Model Rules of Professional Conduct* (as amended through August 2016) (www.americanbar.org); American Bar Association National Task Force on Lawyer Well-Being, *The Path to Lawyer Well Being: Practical Recommendations for Positive Change* (2017) (www.americanbar.org); American Bar Association Section on Legal Education and Admissions to the Bar, *2017–2018 ABA Standards for Approval of Law Schools* (www.americanbar.org); American Bar Association Section of Legal Education and Admissions to the Bar, Catherine L. Carpenter, Editor, *A Survey of Law School Curricula: 2002–2010* (www.americanbar.org); American Bar Association Section on Legal Education and Admissions to the Bar, Robert MacCrate, chair, *Report of the Task Force on Law Schools and the Profession: Narrowing the Gap* (aka the MacCrate Report) (1992) (www.americanbar.org); Dana Caspersen and Joost Elffers, *Changing the Conversation* (Penguin Books 2015); CEO Action for Diversity and Inclusion, *The Pledge* (www.ceoaction.com); Roger Fisher, William Ury, and Bruce

Patton, *Getting to YES (2d ed.* Random House 1991); Terri LeClercq, *Expert Legal Writing* (University of Texas Press 2002); National Conference of Bar Examiners, *NCBE Job Analysis: A Study of the Newly Licensed Lawyer* (January 2013) (www.ncbex. org); John Perry, *The Art of Procrastination* (Workman Publishing 2012); M. Shultz and S. Zedeck, *Predicting Lawyer Effectiveness; Broadening the Basis for Law School Admission Decisions* (Law & Social Inquiry, Vol. 36, no. 3, 2011); and Gregory Urban, *The Power of Team Culture* (Penn Online Learning Initiative website, www.onlinelearning. upenn.edu/courses/).

ACKNOWLEDGMENTS TO THE FIRST EDITION

We could not have written this book without the energy, wisdom and inspiration of our students. We offer a special thanks to the following students, from the graduating classes of 2003–2009, for the professionalism and insight they shared with us (and with you), some through their discussions with us; others through their journals: Tyler Abrahams; Andrew Barbour; Michael Bird; Sarah Bradley; Christopher Breitkreitz; Amber Byers; Amy Chapman; Alison Christian; Jessica Christensen; Matthew Clark; Tom Collins; Laura Winsky Conover; Jennifer N. Copenhaver-Celi; Shaun Courtney; Kate DeAngelis; Angela K. DeMarse; Devon Doane; Ben Durie; Josh Estavillo; Jesse Evans-Schroeder; Rob Ferrier; Nick Frey; Melody Gilkey; Gregory Gills; Laura Nelson Hale; David Harlow; Kami Hoskins; Marina Hadjioannou; Karen Hobbs; Christopher Ingle; Bryn Jones; Stefanie Jones-Campbell; Naomi Jorgensen; Magdalena Jorquez; Julia Kim; Jim Kirchoff; Kara Klima; Karen Komrada; Renee Kuhn; Annette Kundelius; Heather Lane; Mary LaPaglia; Amanda Lueders; Frances Maffetone; Lorinda Mall; Matt Marner; Pauline Meola; Christine Nguyen; Kevin L. Nguyen; Chris Pastore; Jonathan Pinkney-Baird; Amanda Ortiz; Robin Quarrier; Erin Raden; Rebecca Reed; Lindsay Rich; Amy Robinson; Justin Sabin; Billy Santoro;

Benjamin Schachter; Carol Shegog; Nonnie Shivers; James Sowka; Autumn Spritzer; Lindsay St. John; Joshua Steinlage; James Strong; Fred Urbina; Mary-Carol Wagner; Graham Waring; Ian Wilson; Bruce Weisenberg; Jennifer Wolfsong; Anna Wright; and Juan Pablo Zaragoza.

Nor would this book be possible without the generosity of the judges and legal employers from Arizona and around the United States (private firm, government, public interest and others), who continue to give our students and graduates the benefit of their knowledge and experience, and the opportunity to hone their skills in the workplace. We appreciate, too, their willingness to share their insights with us about professional skill building.

We are particularly grateful to our Dean, Toni Massaro, for encouraging us to share our message with law students and the legal community, and for fostering an environment that supports personal and professional growth.

We are indebted to Professors Arthur Andrews, Charles Ares, and Dan Dobbs. We hope that each of our readers is as fortunate as we are in having such inspiring and encouraging models and mentors.

Colby Pfeil Kavanagh has spent *countless* hours reading and re-reading chapters, paragraphs, and sentences at a moment's notice; we thank her for her encouragement, enthusiasm, and enduring support.

We want to thank the following friends and colleagues who have helped us put these ideas into shape: Karen Adam; Barbara Atwood; Graeme Austin; Paul Bennett; Mary Birmingham; Elizabeth Bushell; Lissette Calderon; Barbara Carlson; Kim DeMarchi; Jenny Flynn; Kristie Gallardo; Cynthia Ginnetti; Holly Gwaltney; Kenney Hegland; Zhanna Spektor Helwig; Eileen Hollowell; Margaret Mary Kavanagh; Charlie Kleiner; Jane Korn; Martha A. Lavaty; Barbara Lopez; Peggy Lundquist; Sue Mahon; Anne Kavanagh Moshtael; Cordell Parvin; Nancy Reeder; Sally Rider; Debbie Roller; Lana Ryan; Alicia Saposnik; Barbara Sattler; Keri Silvyn; Sally Simmons; Anita Stafford; Elizabeth Strange; Jeanne Svikhart; Lee Tucker; Randy Wagner; Sierra Wolter; Lisa Waggenheim; and Rose Weston.

Thanks also to members of the following groups: The Board of Visitors of the University of Arizona James E. Rogers College of Law; Tucson Paralegal Association; members of NALP, the National Association for Law Placement; NIFTEP, the National Institute for Teaching Ethics & Professionalism; and the Tucson Transpersonal Group.

We want to recognize the influence of and our reliance upon the following sources: Alan L. Dworsky, *The Little Book on Legal Writing* (Fred B. Rothman & Co. 1992); American Bar Association, ABA Model Rules of Professional Conduct (2002); Mahatma Gandhi, *An Autobiography: The Story of My Experiments with Truth* (Washington: Public Affairs Press 1948, Dover Publications

1983); Bryan Garner, *The Redbook: A Manual on Legal Style* (West Group 2002); Cathy Glaser, Jethro Lieberman, Robert Ruescher & Lynn Su, *The Lawyer's Craft* (2002 Anderson Publishing Co.); Daniel Goleman, *Emotional Intelligence* (1995 Bantam Books); Charles Kostelnick & David Roberts, *Designing Visual Language* (1998 Allyn & Bacon); Terri LeClercq, *Expert Legal Writing* (1995 University of Texas Press); Steven D. Stark, *Writing to Win* (1999 Main Street Books, Doubleday); The NALP Foundation, *Keeping the Keepers II: Mobility and Management of Associates* (2003); Theodore Voorhees, *On Training Associates* (1989 ALI ABA); and Richard C. Wydick, *Plain English for Lawyers* (5th ed. 2005 Carolina Academic Press).

OUTLINE

SECTION 1. FIRST THINGS FIRST

SECTION 2. NOW THAT YOU'RE ON THE JOB

SECTION 3. SELF AND OTHERS

SECTION 4. PRACTICAL TOOLS FOR CAREER PLANNING

EXCELLENCE IN THE WORKPLACE:

LEGAL AND LIFE SKILLS

IN A NUTSHELL®

SECOND EDITION

SECTION 1
FIRST THINGS FIRST

CHAPTER 1
HOW TO USE THIS BOOK

This is the book we both wish we'd had when we started working in our first law jobs. It's intended as a safety net, to help you with challenges you'll likely face in your first days, weeks, and months on the job—whether as a lawyer, law clerk, intern, or law-trained person in a non-legal setting. Most of the principles we discuss apply to any professional setting or position, and we have heard from non-lawyers working in law, as well as professionals in non-legal settings, that they have found much in our previous edition helpful.

The book arose from our experiences in a course we co-taught for many years designed to help students in summer law jobs get up and running and excelling from day one. This is a practical book designed to help you use the skills you have and to develop new ones you'll discover you need. We also address these concerns you might have:

"How can I thrive, not just survive, in a life in law?"

You can answer the question for yourself **by reflecting on your experiences, including your responses to those experiences, so that you can consciously learn from them and set your own course.** In fact, reflection is so central to answering this question that we've included liberally edited excerpts from student journals illustrating how their reflections enriched and improved their experiences.

You'll find them indented and in *italics* throughout the book.

We address issues such as emotional intelligence, effective interpersonal communication, cultural differences, and learning styles (why they matter, and how to tune in to them). Within these broader contexts, we give practical advice about further developing the critical skills of oral communication, writing in a professional setting, and time management.

This book is intended to help you find your own way of developing a life in law that allows you to breathe fully and be comfortable with your choices. We don't suggest that all professional settings are appropriate for everyone, nor is this book designed to help you fit a certain mold. Our goal is to help you create professional and personal lives that are fulfilling and that reflect your unique interests, talents, and aspirations.

We've seen many people thrive at work—taking everything they can from the possibilities offered to them, contributing as much as they can, and embracing their work lives. We've seen others suffer at work unnecessarily—with their work environments, with the quality of their own performance, with the criticism they receive, and with dampened expectations. **There is a difference that can be articulated between those who thrive and those who suffer.** Put simply, it is possible to transform one's work life from an experience of "holding one's breath until it is over" to an experience of breathing deeply and energetically.

Here are some **fundamental assumptions that inform the book:**

- Different parts of the book will be relevant at different times. **Our message is "take what you need."**

- **Productive reflection** on your experiences makes future experiences less charged with irrelevant influences or seemingly unsolvable problems. It can help you understand your responses to people and situations and allow you to *choose* your responses more consciously.

- **Change is inevitable**—change in ourselves and our preferences, change in other people, technology, organizational practices, expectations, and environment, to name a few. By recognizing and accepting the reality of change, you'll manage your responses better.

- **Flexibility is usually a virtue, and is often necessary for survival. This follows from the inevitability of change.** The ability to adapt to new circumstances, and to adapt quickly to circumstances that cannot be changed, is important both to professional competence and personal comfort.

- **Learning is a lifetime necessity. Assume responsibility for your own growth. No one else will.** You'll gain more control over your experiences and your life.

- **Law students, lawyers, and those with whom they work, come from a variety of backgrounds and life experiences,** all with unique strengths, assumptions, and unconscious limitations. One of our goals is to help you recognize your strengths, develop additional skills, and remove unnecessary barriers to the choices your talent and inclinations allow. Another goal is to help you realize the strengths and abilities of others, regardless of their training or title.

- **Many of us avoid certain professional settings because we are uncomfortable in them, or because they simply don't appeal to us.** Whatever your reason for avoidance, we hope to offer you skills to be able to overcome discomfort so you can choose your own professional settings and not be deterred by superficial dislikes or unexamined preconceptions.

- A great deal of **early professional training and development is about becoming competent in certain areas and developing skills that you may now have little interest in developing.** One example of this is competence and confidence in formal and informal professional/social situations; closely related are matters like "networking," and appropriate attire. We address these, as well as other very practical issues, to widen your choices and to lessen your vulnerability in situations that at least for now, may not appeal to you.

We hope that some of the ideas in this book will enrich your professional and personal lives and that as a result, you'll find your work and your lives as lawyers to be as satisfying as they can be.

And now to your first day on the job . . .

CHAPTER 2

EVERYTHING YOU NEED TO KNOW

"Eighty percent of success is showing up."
Woody Allen

During your first days at a new job, information will be coming at you fast and furiously. Adding to the tension is the knowledge that you will be asked to produce high quality work. It makes for a very stressful time.

As the first day approached, I began to get nervous. My fear was that everyone would find out how little I knew about anything legal. It was generalized apprehension mixed with terror. I knew there was no way I could learn enough to make myself look good to a bunch of lawyers by the middle of May.

The Friday before I started work I realized that the problem was pride. That helped, because I know the antidote to pride is humility. I decided to try to be humble. I was not going to work to impress anyone; I was just there to help with the work. I know how to work. I don't know everything about the law or government, but I know how to work. I felt a lot better.

Student Journal

As the writer quoted above realized, it's helpful to look beyond your anxiety to the broader picture. The attorneys in your office understand that this may be your first time in the legal workplace—and it's probably not their first time working with beginners. They expect you to produce useful work, and to give your best efforts, but they also know you're new to the field. Start with the understanding that your first days on the job will present a steep learning curve and will have uncomfortable moments. At some point (perhaps several weeks into your new job), you'll suddenly realize that you've absorbed a lot of information that seemed so strange initially.

> *Monday, I was clueless and felt like the worst choice they could have made; Tuesday was a little better; Wednesday I was convinced that I was just slightly below average; by Thursday I was feeling somewhat intelligent; finally, on Friday, I started to believe that the hiring attorney might have known what he was doing when he hired me.*

> Student Journal

This section offers advice about how to cope with some initial on-the-job challenges.

A.   BEFORE THE FIRST DAY

Even if you've carefully read your workplace's website, read it again. This will help you get a feel for the level of organization of the office, and may give you a good picture of the people you'll be working with and the kind of projects you may be working on.

You might think that your new workplace is well-organized and that someone will tell you the essentials about reporting to work, but that's not always the case. The person who hired you may not be the person who will be responsible for your arrival and may not even be in the office the day you arrive. Especially if your first day is a Monday or the day after a holiday or long weekend, your arrival may catch someone by surprise. **So, take the initiative and anticipate as much as you can about the first day.**

- **They are expecting me, right?** A few weeks, or even months, may have passed between the time you accepted the job offer and your first day of work. If you haven't spoken recently with someone at your new job, touch base at least a few days before your start date, to be sure that you are expected. If your new employer has a formalized recruiting process, your call or e-mail will be appreciated but unnecessary. But in other settings it could mean the difference between finding a workspace and office supplies ready and waiting for you, or having a flustered administrator confess that he inadvertently forgot that today is your first day of work.

- **Where should I go?** Don't assume, and don't just look up the address—employers frequently have satellite offices or offices on multiple floors in one or more buildings, all with the same mailing address. Some have moved and not yet changed their address on their website. If possible, before your first day, make the trip to your office on a weekday during rush hour, to confirm the exact

location and know how long your commute
will take.

- **Whom should I see, and at what time?**
Before the working part of your first day
begins, you may need to fill out paperwork,
participate in an orientation, take a tour of
the office, and get settled in your work space.
Someone other than an attorney will probably
assist you with these administrative details.
**Find out whom you should see first, and
at what time.** Ask whether you should bring
along any paperwork (such as driver's license
or proof of citizenship or immigration status).
On your first day, plan to arrive in the vicinity
of your office ahead of time, so that you can
report to work punctually at the "appointed
time." Don't be *too* early. They may not be
ready for you yet. Find a coffee shop to visit
while you wait and try to arrive only 5 or 10
minutes early.

- **Where should I park if I'm driving to
work?** Depending on the location, parking
might be a very big issue. Don't forget to ask
about it, especially if you're working in an
unfamiliar city or town. Find out, too, if there
are mass transportation alternatives.

- **What should I wear?** Don't hesitate to ask.
You'll feel out of place if you show up in a suit
and the entire office is dressed in business
casual, or vice versa. Find out what people
wear who work in positions similar to yours.

I was glad to be wearing a nice suit, because everyone here is formally dressed, despite my boss telling me that the office dressed in "business casual." Next time I will ask a woman how the law clerks and attorneys dress. I wear suits every day now.

Student Journal (female)

- **What about lunch?** Are there restaurants nearby? (Be sure to bring enough cash, so you're not caught short or left frantically looking for an ATM machine.) Do people usually bring their lunch? Are there facilities for eating in?

- **What time do folks generally leave, and when are the doors locked at night?** Several years ago, one of our students was working on her first day with great concentration, with her office door closed. Eventually she realized it was after 5:00 p.m., everybody had gone home, and she was locked in the office. She had to call the sheriff to come get her out. The next day, an attorney in the office said the same thing happened on *her* first day, and she had had to crawl out a very small window. Be safe, and double-check!

Despite your best plans, things may still go awry. Sometimes you'll have to be resilient and figure things out on your own.

My welcome wagon was a frazzled administrative assistant who didn't have time for a proper orientation. By the second day, I met my coworker and we began exchanging whatever pieces of knowledge we could acquire to help orient each other. I am taking opportunities to meet people in the elevator, copy room, or at lunch time. This effort is paying off—I am finally becoming oriented.

Student Journal

And sometimes, when things go wrong, a little humor will get you through the embarrassment, as one student found on his first day at work.

Day 1: I make my lunch, pack my bag, and hop on the bike. I pedal my way to the office, meet up with one of the clerks in our office (who mistakes me for a bike messenger), and head off to change. I have packed everything that I need except my dress shirt! I had my belt, socks, undershirt, but no dress shirt. Oh, the horror!

Student Journal

B.   THE FIRST WEEK

You'll feel a bit lost until you get everything figured out, so find out ahead of time the name and phone number of the "go to" person for non-legal issues. This is likely to be the office manager, a paralegal, legal assistant, or administrative assistant. Ask about other information and resources that will help get you off to a good start before you need them urgently.

- If not part of a formal orientation, **arrange to meet the IT person as soon as possible.** If there is no formal IT department, find out who the default IT person is. **Find out what the IT policies are. Is there a policy about using personal e-mail? Will you have a work e-mail address? Make no assumptions about your IT privileges. You know the questions you need to ask. Ask them early.**

- Even if you have a knack for remembering names and faces, you'll be meeting a lot of people. Ask for a copy of the **internal phone directory,** and make notes about who works where. This may be on paper or on an office **intranet.**

- Find out if **Lexis or Westlaw or other online research sources** are available and, if so, what the **policies** are concerning their use. Unlike law school, where you have unlimited access, in most employment settings (even large firms) there are likely to be restrictions. If necessary, brush up on your skills so you can make the most of your time online. **Many firms and offices routinely use public access databases for most of their legal research.** Find out whether this is so for your office.

- Attorneys often keep the most **frequently used legal reference materials** in an easily accessible location. See if this is the case in your office. Even with almost everything accessible online, most attorneys have a few key printed references on hand. Find out what they are and how to use them. If you will be working in a specialized area, find out the key government and other websites and sources for research that everyone uses.

- Ask whether the office keeps a file, containing **previous projects, research, and memoranda** about issues that frequently arise. Ask whether there are **templates or samples of standardized formats** that you should use, where appropriate.

- If there is a **law library** on site or nearby, check it out and become familiar with its contents and layout. Introduce yourself to the **law librarians.** Find out, **before you need help,** what services they provide.

C.   WHAT TO WATCH FOR

Besides honing your developing legal skills, each on-the-job experience will help you learn more about different employment settings and your own personal preferences for the ideal work environment. Here are some questions to get the thought process started.

- Does the office have a **formal, or informal, mission?**

- Can you identify other, more **implicit goals** of the people working there?

- **What kinds of decisions** are the attorneys making? What kind of tasks are they doing?

- **Who makes up the rest of the team** and what kind of work is each person doing?

- **What is the level of formality** in speech and behavior?

- **How do people interact** with each other, on all levels of the organizational chart? What kinds of **interpersonal relationships** have developed?

- **Who are the clients?**

- Do there seem to be any **unique obligations or interesting challenges** in the office?

The first two weeks of work, you engage in cordial, polite, but short conversations with people around the office. It takes a while for people to size you up. You eat lunch alone for the first few days, try to smile at everyone. Eventually, as people begin to recognize some consistency in your greetings and your personality, they begin to let down their guard. They ask you to remind them of your name, since they've clearly forgotten from your first introduction. You realize that you'll probably fit in well enough by the time you leave.

                                Student Journal

CHAPTER 3

DRESSING THE PART

"Beware of all enterprises
that require new clothes."
Henry David Thoreau

As an enlightened society, I think it's high time
that we dispensed with ties. They're expensive,
hard to actually tie, and restrictive.

Student Journal (male)

In a profession where maturity and wisdom are essential, wouldn't you rather stand out because of your skills and potential, instead of your nervousness, clothing, or behavior?

Your personal appearance and demeanor send positive—or negative—messages about you, about your employer, and the respect that you have for the situations and the people around you. Whether your job is paid or unpaid, high-profile or low-level, with a private firm, government or public interest agency or something different entirely, your appearance matters. You'll see this fact reflected in the attitudes of your supervisors, other attorneys, and co-workers, and in opportunities that are (or are not) extended to you, such as invitations to go to court, meet clients, and attend meetings.

Like it or not, some type of professional clothing will be in your future. While we don't want to over-emphasize the issue of fashion and wardrobes, we do want you to be comfortable and feel that you are appropriately attired.

Professional styles vary depending on geographic location, as well as on the size and type of your employment setting. For example, in some offices only a suit will do; in others, you'll feel overdressed and uncomfortable if you go to work in a suit. In some offices, jeans are strictly taboo, while in others they might be perfectly appropriate on days you aren't meeting clients or going to court. Notice what attorneys and other professionals are wearing, and dress accordingly. If in doubt, check with your employer, or someone in your school's Career Office.

I'm not entirely comfortable dressing the part of a business woman. I thought I looked professional, but was still apprehensive until I met my supervisor and the law clerks I'll be working with this summer. All four of us were wearing a skirt or a dress! So, I let myself relax while still paying attention to what other people were wearing around the office.

Student Journal (female)

Attorneys know that students and new graduates have limited finances and don't expect you to wear expensive clothes or a different outfit every day. **Take advantage of sales, and buy a few well-chosen simple, conservative pieces.** You'll find that you can dress appropriately without straining your budget.

To get maximum mileage from your wardrobe, stay away from fads and trends, and buy in one or two complementary color palettes. There is no need to restrict yourself to black, gray and navy, but do use good judgment in your choice of color. To create different outfits, mix and match separates, and accent with accessories (like ties for men, and belts and jewelry for women).

"Business casual" causes a great deal of unnecessary confusion for students *and* lawyers. A safe bet for both men and women is slacks or khakis (but not blue jeans), and a long-sleeved shirt, blouse, polo, or golf shirt. Some women prefer sweater sets, skirts or dresses. A tie for men is not necessary. Be sure to keep a jacket handy, in case the opportunity arises to go to court or a client meeting.

Your clothing should fit well, be comfortable and allow you to move without exposing too much. Double check the fit by sitting down, standing, bending over, and using a mirror to make sure you look okay from behind.

Fashion taboos for women include tight clothing, open midriffs, short skirts, spaghetti straps, cleavage, lingerie looks, and excessive jewelry. Other "don'ts" for everyone are sandals and scuffed or open-toed shoes. Men, make sure your socks match the trousers and, until you've established yourself, think twice about unusual touches like bow ties, suspenders and double-breasted suits.

Finally, in all but a few settings, **being well groomed involves** covering visible tattoos, removing jewelry from facial piercings, and trimming or possibly shaving facial hair (depending on your employer's preferences). It also means not wearing excessive makeup, perfume, or after shave. This has become more important lately, as the number of people allergic to various fragrances has risen. If you smoke, be sure that your breath and clothing are clean-smelling. Non-smokers are becoming more accustomed to smoke-free environments, and the smell of smoke is not only increasingly noticeable, but actually repels many people. Over time, with patience and by making wise decisions, you'll eventually accumulate a professional wardrobe that you feel comfortable with. At least as comfortable as a person wearing a suit can feel!

Don't get too comfortable. Remember that you are in a professional setting.

Advice from an Employer

Trying to avoid wearing pantyhose or heels is my most important goal of the day. I go to sleep at night and wake up in the morning thinking about it. Probably, I should be thinking about more important things.

Student Journal (female)

I look really young and started paying close attention to what made other women in the office look so polished. I finally spent the money to buy a set of work clothes that were really me and FIT! This way, all my clothes will never go "out of style." I hope to use them forever!

Student Journal (female)

I am jealous that my friend doesn't have to wear a suit every day—though I am getting eerily comfortable in one these days.

Student Journal (male)

CHAPTER 4
THE SOCIAL GRACES

*"Does anybody really know where
the bread plate goes anymore?"*
The Authors

We've known students who were so anxious about picking up the wrong fork or saying the wrong thing at a social event that they couldn't enjoy any part of the experience. Others were so shy that they could hardly speak. In contrast, we've known students who relaxed a little too much and, oblivious to social convention, embarrassed themselves and/or their employers.

Polish and good manners will never substitute for good performance but, rightly or wrongly, people do make assumptions about you every day based on your behavior and appearance. We are not implying that you must sacrifice your individuality to become a lawyer. However, to get settled or established in most professional environments, one must dress and act the part—at least at first.

Fortunately, faux pas are mostly avoidable. If you want to learn about the topic of etiquette in detail, Miss Manners offers over 800 pages devoted to "excruciatingly correct behavior." Otherwise, presented here are a few simple suggestions to help you handle professional and social situations with ease. You'll learn how to handle introductions, navigate the buffet table, and sail through sit-down meals with style.

A. MAKING INTRODUCTIONS

In addition to a smile and a handshake (firm, but not knuckle-crushing, and not limp like a noodle), the basic how-to's of introductions are relatively simple.

- **When making introductions,** start first with the oldest, most senior (e.g., the managing partner), or more influential (e.g., a judge) person. Include a brief explanation to get the conversation started. "Mr. Smith, this is Chuck Jones, a law school classmate. Chuck, Mr. Smith is my supervising attorney at Lowell Ritchey, the firm where I'm clerking this summer."

- You may find yourself in a conversation where you don't know one or more people in the group. In that case, **introduce yourself** in the same way you would introduce another person. "Hello, I'm Mary Albright. I'm co-chair of the Environmental Law Society at the law school."

- **When being introduced,** volunteer your name if the person introducing you hesitates. Don't take personally anybody's forgetfulness—attorneys meet so many people and juggle so many projects every day, that they should be forgiven for the occasional slip of memory. (There are tips for remembering names, but that's a different book entirely.)

If you feel a bit tongue-tied once the introductions have been made, you'll find some practical suggestions about how to strike up a conversation and keep it going in Chapter 6, "The Art (or Horror) of Networking."

B. NAVIGATING RECEPTIONS

Remember that the main purpose of this type of event is to socialize and network, so don't head directly to the buffet table for food and drinks. Instead, **spend some time moving about the room and chatting with other attendees.** Resist the urge to socialize primarily with fellow law students; this is not a good use of your time and will dramatically reduce your chances of meeting new people.

Reception fare is rarely meant to substitute for a meal; in fact, your host probably created the menu in quantities sufficient only for light eating. Once you do make your way to the buffet table, avoid overloading your plate with too much food. After you've "filled" your plate, move away from the table, so you can talk with other attendees and allow others to help themselves to refreshments.

Most people find it awkward to juggle a plate in one hand and glass in another, so you may want to eat and drink at separate times. Along these same lines, many women slip their keys and a few dollars into their pocket, and leave their purses behind, so they don't have so many things to hold.

If waiters are circulating around the room with trays of food, use a toothpick or napkin to take just one serving or bite. No double-dipping into the salsa or sauce, either, and limit yourself to just one alcoholic beverage. Hold the glass in your left hand, so you have a dry hand available for shaking hands.

C.   ENJOYING SIT-DOWN MEALS

Formal Dinners
"Not for the novice to attempt."
Emily Post, "Etiquette" 1922

While we don't want to dwell on table manners too much, we know that many people have grown up with casual family meals, and may not have a great deal of experience with formal dining. You'll be relieved to know that it's not complicated. By remembering a few simple guidelines and knowing what to expect in the way of table service, you can focus on the pleasures of good company, good conversation, and good food.

- **Food allergies and dietary restrictions.** At restaurants, most dietary needs can be easily accommodated, but there are no established "rules" about whether and how to notify your host if invited to someone's home. You could briefly explain in advance and offer suggestions about how to accommodate them (e.g., "I'm allergic to eggs, but it's an easy problem for me to handle. If you'll just let me know what items I should stay away from, I'll be fine."). On the other hand, most vegetarians are adept at navigating around a menu on their own.

- **Arrivals.** Whether you are being entertained in a restaurant or at someone's home, the meal has been carefully planned. In your personal life, it may be appropriate to be "fashionably late," but in a business setting, 7:00 p.m. means 7:00 p.m. If you arrive late, you run the risk of making people wait for the first course or arriving after the meal has started. Either way, others will view your behavior as discourteous, and you're likely to be embarrassed. If for some reason you can't be on time, call your host with an explanation. Upon arriving, greet your host at once and then, time permitting, mix and mingle with the other guests.

- **Napkin etiquette.** Never place a napkin on top of your plate. Once everyone is seated, place the napkin on your lap. If you leave the table for any reason, place it on your chair or folded beside your plate. Once the meal is over, place it beside your plate.

- **Ordering from the menu.** Look to your host or hostess for cues about whether to order an appetizer and/or dessert, but don't order more than you can eat. You probably shouldn't order the most expensive thing on the menu either, unless you're certain you're in the right setting. Do order something relatively easy to eat, instead of something like spare ribs or a sloppy cheeseburger.

- **A word about alcohol.** Make it a personal rule not to drink alcohol at lunch and, at dinner, to be conservative about your consumption. You don't want to be "the law student or new associate who had one too many and . . . ."

- **Shared items.** "Community food," like bread baskets, cream and sugar, and salt and pepper shakers (always together) are passed to the right. Like every good connoisseur, taste your food before seasoning it, too. If you can't reach something on the table, ask someone nearby to pass it to you, instead of going for the long reach.

- **The mysterious bread plate.** Which bread plate is yours? Here's an easy way to remember. Hold your hands out in front, palms down, with thumbs and forefingers together in circles. Notice that your right hand forms a "d" (drink) and left hand forms a "b" (bread). Set the bread on your plate, along with a pat of butter. Then, break and butter only a few small pieces at a time, and set your bread knife on the plate in between bites.

- **Food service.** The wait staff will serve your food from the left, and remove it from the right. Wait for all at your table to receive their meals before beginning to eat unless the person waiting requests that you begin.

- **Silverware.** Forks are on your left, knives and spoons on your right, but don't worry too much about which implement is for which course. Simply begin with the utensil on the outside and work your way towards the plate with each course. Cut a few small pieces of food at a time (including large pieces of salad). In between bites, place the fork and knife (blade facing in) on your plate. When you're finished eating, place them diagonally on your plate as a signal to the wait staff that they can be removed.

- **Manners.** You might think it goes without saying, but we do hear from recruiters and attorneys that students occasionally forget their manners. Don't take large bites, don't chew with your mouth open, or talk with your mouth full. Also, keep one hand in your lap while eating, and keep your elbows off the table.

- **Awkward moments.** If you drop a piece of food, just leave it where it fell, unless it is too obvious. If necessary, pick it up and place it on the edge of your plate. If you need to remove something from your mouth like a piece of bone or olive pit, don't spit it into your napkin. Instead, remove it with the same utensil that put it in, and place it on the edge of your plate.

- **Departures.** Just as your arrival at a social event should be timely, so should your departure. Unfortunately, knowing when to leave can be a bit tricky. If after-dinner coffee is being served, you should plan to leave shortly thereafter. Otherwise, your host may send subtle signals that it's time to wrap up the evening. Frequently glancing at her watch, beginning to clean up and/or remove items from the table, and switching off some of the lights are all tactful cues that it will soon be time to politely thank your host for the evening and take your leave.

A short hand-written thank you note sent within a day or two of the event is always appreciated.

CHAPTER 5

OVERCOMING SHYNESS

"The shell must break before the bird can fly."
Lord Alfred Tennyson

You are not alone if you feel nervous in social settings. In fact, the percentage of Americans reporting that shyness presents a problem in their lives now hovers around 50%. Some people may have been introverts since birth and perhaps others developed shyness as they began to rely more heavily on technology as a substitute for face-to-face communication. Whatever its cause, as those who have experienced it know, the feeling of being "alone in a crowd" is not pleasant.

There is an even bigger problem—shyness can cause people to avoid their coworkers, colleagues, and others. **Shy people are also often assumed by others to have bad attitudes and to be haughty, rude, or even condescending.** Although this is not generally accurate, initial perceptions are difficult to overcome.

I know I have a lot to learn about how to send just the right message at just the right time in this new legal environment.

Student Journal

Our conversational abilities can smooth things along in seemingly small, but important, ways. For example, a pre-meeting cup of coffee and casual conversation can often pave the way for a productive settlement conference afterwards. Similarly, a few minutes of conversation can help relieve a client's nervousness before a deposition, or provide an enjoyable way of passing time before and after a closing or court appearance.

Even in business settings, it is through casual, informal conversation that we build relationships and come to know, and trust, one another. Lawyers and other professionals are invited to a long list of activities and events that have "social overtones," including firm luncheons, bar association meetings, and receptions.

If shyness interferes with your interactions and your behavior, it could make the difference between getting a client, resolving a conflict, or being given the responsibilities and opportunities you desire. In the courts, law firms, and other places where lawyers are working, **the art of conversation is a necessity, not a luxury.** Fortunately, if shyness is a problem that you are ready to tackle, there are specific steps you can take to help boost your "sociability factor."

1. First, examine your inclinations and preferences for both casual conversation and for building and maintaining relationships.

2. Then, identify situations that make you feel uncomfortable.

3. Next, notice your reactions when you are placed in uncomfortable situations.

4. Finally, using insights you gained from the exploration process described above, gradually change your behavior, in ways calculated to reduce stress. At the same time, seek out opportunities to increase your social contact with others, so that you can practice your growing skills.

A.   EXAMINE YOUR INCLINATIONS AND PREFERENCES

Think about how you formed relationships as a child, and how you form them now. **In an ideal world, given your personality and personal preferences, what kinds of relationships would you develop, and how would they evolve?**

- How big is your circle of friends, and what is the balance of casual vs. close friendships?

- Who are the people that you feel close to? What are their personalities like, and how would you describe their styles of communication?

- Do you take an active role in making friendships, or do you rely on others to assert themselves?

- Do you share equally in making plans to meet, or do you wait to be contacted?

Answer with as much specificity as possible. There are no right or wrong questions or answers in this process. The goal is not to transform yourself into an extrovert. Rather, it is to become more attuned to and accepting of, your natural inclinations, and learn to work with them as you continue to form informal and professional relationships in the future.

B.   IDENTIFY UNCOMFORTABLE SITUATIONS

You are probably more comfortable in certain social settings than others. To overcome your shyness, try to **develop a better understanding of specific situations that make you feel uncomfortable.**

- Are you equally shy in large and small group settings?

- Are social situations easier to handle after you've gotten to know people better?

- In certain settings, do you find yourself measuring your own social skills against those of people who are (or seem to be) naturally more gregarious than you?

- Are you even more shy in situations where you feel unprepared or where you feel your skills are inadequate?

Some people seem to need more private time than others. Could what you think of as shyness in certain situations actually reflect the need for more time alone? For example, after a very busy week, a Friday evening networking event might be the very last thing you want to attend.

- Do certain situations seem to trigger your shyness more than others?

I'm nervous about meeting new people and being vocal in new situations. I think it's important to be outgoing from the beginning to avoid being overlooked or dismissed as someone who has nothing to contribute.

Student Journal

I'm shy around large groups, but have no problem talking in small groups or one-on-one. I have been working on this and it is getting better, although it's a difficult thing to practice without forcing it.

Student Journal

C.   OBSERVE YOUR REACTIONS

As you identify specific triggers that cause discomfort, try to **gain a better understanding of exactly how shyness affects your behavior** in those settings (beyond things such as the common increased heart rate and excessive perspiration). Don't forget to explore your body language. Whatever your behaviors, be willing to examine them honestly. Once you know what they are, you can take steps to bring them under control.

- Do you make excuses and avoid social occasions altogether?

- Do you try to blend unnoticed into the background?

- Do you wait for people to approach you?

- Do you make awkward attempts to converse, or overcompensate by talking too much?

- Do you find someone you know and stick to them like glue?

- Do you find yourself uncomfortably unable to disengage yourself from conversation with the first, and perhaps only, person you talk to?

I have a difficult time going up to someone and introducing myself. Instead, I stay within my comfort zone and hope to find people I know. If I don't know anyone, I end up sitting at a table, waiting for another person at the table to talk to me. I know this is something I need to get over.

Student Journal

D. GRADUALLY CHANGE YOUR BEHAVIOR

1. One-on-One Situations and Small Groups

Within proper boundaries, a certain amount of **light socializing can be a very productive way for you and your colleagues to get to know and trust one another.** But some people find it difficult to socialize in smaller, more intimate settings. Because conversations are longer, the subject often turns from small talk to more personal topics, and that can make some people uncomfortable. This happens, for example, at events like staff parties which are designed to be fun, but can turn into stressful occasions instead.

As with most things in life, with practice, you can gradually move out of your shyness and learn to feel at ease in informal settings.

- **Try to remember a few personal facts about each person in your office,** on the committee, etc. (e.g., one of the attorneys plays guitar; the secretary just adopted a dog from the animal shelter). These topics will become easy conversation starters and people will appreciate that you remembered something about them.

- Be willing to **share some personal information about yourself, too,** so that people can get to know and become comfortable around you. They don't need to know (and shouldn't) the most intimate details of your life, but do try to find some things to share. Even a trivial fact about yourself can spark conversation (e.g., something you did before law school or a unique talent of yours, like juggling).

- **Look for shared interests** (e.g., musical instruments, children, family, or growing up in the Southwest).

- If you frequently find yourself tongue tied, create an arsenal of **general catch-all questions or comments** that you can use to get a conversation started, such as sports, the weather, the latest book you've read or movie that you've seen. With people you don't know well, it's best to stay away from controversial no-no's like politics, religion, and finances. Gossip should never be part of your conversation.

- **Silence can be an important part of the natural rhythm of conversation,** so avoid the impulse to fill it with discussion. Think of it as a companionable or contemplative, instead of awkward, way to pass a few moments.

- If you must, simply force yourself to **put in an appearance at office functions, even if just for a few minutes.** Change your "no socializing" rule to "light socializing required" when it comes to events like lunches, pot luck dinners and softball games.

2. Large Groups

While you may never be the life of the party (and, in fact, this could be detrimental to your career—but that's another topic), you can take **specific steps to become more comfortable with the art of "mixing and mingling" at social events.**

- Practice your **social skills in "safe" environments,** by joining a club or organization, getting to know your professors better or participating in volunteer opportunities. You will not only begin to overcome your shyness, but will also begin to build relationships with people who could eventually become your future colleagues.

- **Stay up-to-date on current events,** weather, sports, movies, food, celebrities, books, and/or politics. There is no need to read the *Washington Post* or *New York Times* from cover to cover for this purpose. You'll find you can carry on a casual conversation with almost anybody based on what you have read in *People* and *Time Magazine*. Beware of using tidbits from Facebook and other social media, unless you have taken the time to seek out and fully read the original source information.

- If possible, **learn something about the person or group sponsoring the gathering,** to formulate a few questions or generate ideas for starting conversation.

- Should you **arrive "fashionably late" or be on time?** If you are one of just a few invited guests, you should arrive on time. However, if you arrive on time for a larger event, you'll likely find a smaller group of people with whom to socialize. If you come later, the gathering will be more lively. Time your arrival accordingly.

- **Body language can serve as a clue about whom to approach.** Don't interrupt a group of people who appear to be in deep conversation. Instead, look for an "open" group whose participants are clustered loosely together with space for you to join or look for a someone who has made friendly eye contact with you.

- Once you are admitted into a group, **include everyone in your conversation** and be open to allowing another new person to join.

- Resist the urge to stick like glue to people you know. Even though you would rather wait for someone to approach you first, take a deep breath, **walk up to someone who looks interesting, and initiate a conversation.** You can break the ice by introducing yourself as a law student or new attorney. ("This is my first time to attend a CLE presentation." "I just started a new job at the Attorney General's Office.") You'll find that people will pick up the cue and help you move the conversation along.

- **People love to talk about themselves.** Ask a question and watch the conversation take off. ("What kind of law do you practice?" "What did you think of the program?" "Have you had time to go on vacation this summer?")

- **Smile and try not to show your nervousness** via your body language (e.g., crossed arms, hunched shoulders).

- There's **no need to overstay a conversation.** If you notice the other person glancing around the room, or if you begin to feel uncomfortable, politely take your leave. ("I enjoyed talking with you. I hope we can chat again at the next meeting." "I know you need to chat with other people. Thanks for telling me about your practice.")

- **Set a goal to stay for a certain period of time, or speak to a specific number of people.** After that, leave if you must. Eventually, you will find that you can comfortably stay for longer periods of time.

- It may seem as if everyone is having a great time . . . except you. But, as mentioned earlier, the odds are that one out of every two people is feeling shy, too. This is not the time to have a "misery loves company" moment but, rather, an **"if they can do this, so can I"** attitude. In fact, one way to feel more at ease is to reach out to somebody who appears to be equally or even more uncomfortable than you are.

- **Think of the image you want to project, and simply act as if this image were reality.** You may not feel authentic inside but, if your acting skills are good enough, who will know? Eventually, by conditioning yourself from the outside in, you will begin to create your own reality.

- **Don't attempt to mask shyness with alcohol.** It can be a recipe for disaster.

Shyness can be overcome with a little patience and effort. As your social skills improve, you may be surprised to find yourself in the situation of helping others feel more comfortable, too.

I used to be shy and introverted. After assessing, with the help of family and friends, why I always gravitated away from social situations, I decided to make a conscious change. I pushed myself to take the initiative and introduce myself. I found that, once people gain a small amount of comfort, they are eager to continue a conversation.

Student Journal

I was once a very shy person. Over time, I gained more confidence and realized that my voice was as valuable as the next person's.

Student Journal

CHAPTER 6

THE ART (OR HORROR) OF NETWORKING

"Call it a clan, call it a network, call it a tribe,
call it a family: Whatever you call it,
whoever you are, you need one."
Jane Howard

Building friendships is an important aspect of a
job. But, I despise networking just for the sake of
networking. I have no problem with making real
friends or acquaintances, but I will not do certain
things, or talk to certain people, just because
that's the thing to do.

Student Journal

Eventually someone (a professor, law school administrator, or mentor) will bring up the subject of networking. The term has negative connotations for most students and in fact for many lawyers. They are reluctant to try it, and consider networking a superficial and insincere approach to relationships.

Put aside the term itself and think about getting to know people. Law is not a solitary undertaking—attorneys work with people almost all day, every day, on one task or another. Networking, or building relationships, is so fully integrated into the work and lives of lawyers that it is not so much a *separate activity* as it is an *unconscious aspect* of *every* action.

A.   HOW DO WE DEFINE NETWORKING?

Networking is not unique to the practice of law; in fact, professionals in most businesses regularly participate in networking in one way or another. The unspoken "rules" and understandings may vary from discipline to discipline but, generally, **networking is about expanding the circle of people you know,** whether casually or through repeated interactions. It is also about meeting people, often but not always in a "professional social" context, with whom you are likely to work in a professional context in the future.

Some people feel that networking requires you to behave in a friendly manner towards somebody you normally wouldn't choose as a friend. Obviously, nobody is suggesting that you should form relationships with ulterior motives, based solely on the material or professional benefits you might receive as a result.

However, **in a profession built on collegiality, why would you choose to limit your circle of acquaintances, colleagues and, perhaps, even new friends?**

B.   BENEFITS OF NETWORKING

There are many reasons why networking is a valuable skill and, while it does fit into a job search strategy, we will set that issue aside until the end of this section. We hope by that time you will be open to its importance, and more receptive to the idea of developing your abilities in this area.

- **As you know, there is much to learn about law in the early years.** By sharing their opinions and experiences with you, people in your network will greatly expand your base of knowledge.

- As a lawyer, one of your chief responsibilities will be to **seek early and equitable resolution of your clients' problems.** People in your network can often help, by providing information, insight, or introductions. Similarly, you'll be able to do this for others as well.

- At some point, you **might be interested in assuming a leadership position** in your firm or organization, local or state bar association, or in the community. Your success in these efforts will be determined not just by your skills and accomplishments, but also by your relationships and interactions with colleagues (otherwise known as your "network").

- If you go into private practice, your firm will eventually want you to start bringing in new clients (often called "rainmaking"). **Your network will be an important source of referrals** because, as you intuitively know, we are all more willing to refer people to lawyers and other professionals whom we know and trust.

- Through networking, you might **unexpectedly find a mentor and maybe even a new friend.**

- Finally, **networking is a tried-and-true method of finding a job.** Legal jobs are often found through word of mouth. The professionals in your Career Office can explain the process in greater detail, but it entails telling everyone you know that you are looking for a job. It also involves conducting "informational interviews" with lawyers you don't know (not to ask for a job, but to learn about their careers, how they got into their practice areas, and what skills they think are most important). Most experienced attorneys (particularly graduates of your own law school) are delighted to share their ideas with law students. Sometimes (not always, and never to be expected) you'll get a job lead, or a referral to someone who might have one.

C. WHERE TO NETWORK

I feel comfortable in social settings in general— it's just when socializing with lawyers that I start to question myself. I feel a little over my head, since I still have so many questions about the legal system, and have no contacts or ideas about who's who in the legal world.

Student Journal

Even if you don't know *any* attorneys, you should have no trouble finding and getting to know them.

Here are some places to look for the folks that will eventually comprise your "network."

- **The ABA, state and local Young Lawyers Division,** also known as the YLD. For the first five years after graduation, or until you reach age 35 (whichever is later), you will automatically be a member of the YLD—you might as well get involved as soon as possible. The organization has two primary functions. First, as the public service arm of the bar, it organizes programs such as the Disaster Legal Services Program (in concert with the Federal Emergency Management Agency) and the High School Mock Trial Championships. It also facilitates the transition of law students and new lawyers into practice, sponsoring Bridge the Gap continuing education programs, CLE breakfasts, and educational conferences. If you wish to meet some of the lawyers in the YLD, ask your Career Office for contact information.

- **State and local bar associations.** A variety of special interest bar associations are likely active in your community (e.g., family lawyers, criminal defense lawyers, women lawyers, minority lawyers, real estate lawyers, intellectual property lawyers). They, along with your state bar association, hold meetings, luncheons, receptions, etc. With your busy class schedule, you may not feel that you have much time for extracurricular activities. However, if you'll occasionally attend a bar association event, you'll find them to be easy venues to meet attorneys and gain a new perspective on the practice of law.

- **Law school and undergraduate alumni.** Mention your law school or undergraduate university, and doors will open like magic. If your first encounter is not in person, it's generally best to introduce yourself via an e-mail or letter. Many schools have local and out-of-town alumni networking groups that host events periodically. These events are ready-made places to develop your networking skills.

- **Introductions via your mentor.** Many law schools have mentor programs and we hope you are participating. (If not, see if you can get signed up—soon!) You'll find your mentor is more than willing to introduce you to attorneys in the community, through invitations to professional or social events, or upon request. For example, if you want to meet attorneys in a certain area of practice, ask you mentor to facilitate introductions.

- **People you meet through employment, internships or clerkships.** You'll meet lots of attorneys in these settings, and some of them will become part of your network. Take the time, and make the effort, to keep in touch after you finish working together.

D. HOW TO NETWORK

To the uninitiated, and those of us who are not naturally gregarious, networking is awkward. It requires you to "put yourself out there" without knowing how the other person will react to you, or even if your behavior is appropriate in the circumstances. However, most attorneys remember what it was like to be new to the profession. They will want to help, and will feel flattered that you want to get to know them.

To begin forming your network, take the initiative. Be personable. Be respectful of people's time. And stay in touch with them occasionally. As you'll see from the following journals, the art of networking doesn't always come easily, but it is well worth learning.

We'll hear first from those who are not comfortable with networking.

In the evening, I went to another networking event. Like the last schmooze-fest I attended, it took place at a law firm, and was coupled with a reception featuring tasty hors d'oeuvres and cocktails. I made a heroic effort to network, which means that I talked to three people. Being a wallflower by nature, this degree of social interaction completely sapped my small reserve of charm and confidence, and I was happy when the panel discussion began.

Student Journal

One thing I am not doing that could play a role in my future happiness is making connections, and networking more effectively. I haven't made as many contacts as I could and, even with the contacts I have made, I am not sure that I keep in touch with them often enough for it to be advantageous in the future. This is definitely a skill that I plan to work more actively on.

Student Journal

I want to learn how to interact better and more comfortably with people. I'd like to become more proficient in networking. I think forming social relationships with fellow lawyers is an important aspect of practice.

Student Journal

Finally, networking doesn't always involve food or standing around trying to think of something to say. It's not all about receptions, cocktail parties, and meals with people you've never met. And it's not just about meeting and getting to know other attorneys. It can happen anywhere people meet and interact. Networking does come easily for some, while others have to work to acquire the skill. Ultimately, it's about learning how to draw another person out, and about finding out what other people do and what makes them tick.

I've found that people enjoy teaching and gain self-esteem when someone asks for their help or guidance. Additionally, it helps to build closer working relationships.

Student Journal

Often attorneys come to the law clerks' office to drop off work, and take a little break. Everyone realizes this is a good opportunity to network. We hang on their every word, and try to start our own conversations with them. While networking can be awkward, I think it's important that we keep trying.

Student Journal

I've taken time to speak with different attorneys I've observed in court. This has given me networking opportunities, and helped me find out why certain questions were asked or not asked.

Student Journal

SECTION 2

NOW THAT YOU'RE
ON THE JOB

CHAPTER 7

CULTURAL DIFFERENCES

*"Never underestimate the importance
of local knowledge."*

HSBC Advertisement

Throughout this book, we place great emphasis on the importance of positive interpersonal relationships and interactions with others, and encourage you to be open to and accepting of **individual differences.**

In this chapter, we want to emphasize another aspect of interpersonal relationships that you will encounter and benefit from being aware of—that of **cultural differences.**

We make this point for a very practical reason: you will inevitably encounter behavior in others that you find rude, confusing, and frustrating. You may **assume** that the behavior is the result of personal animus directed toward you, or, if not directed toward you, indicative of a personality or character flaw of the other person. Some of these behaviors may in fact be intentionally rude and directed toward you personally. **But other behaviors that you find odd or off-putting or rude may be the result of cultural differences,** and have nothing to do with you, and little to do with the personality of the person exhibiting the behavior.

When we speak of cultural differences, we use the term in the broadest sense possible—that is, differences that result **from patterns of behavior,**

thinking and feeling, and values and goals that are shared among members of a group—in this case, a group to which you don't belong. This group can be based on membership in the same religion, nationality, ethnicity, gender, region, neighborhood, family, company, sports team, school, residence hall, hall in a residence hall, and so on. **The group can also be based on membership in your new workplace.** Most of us belong to many different groups, and thus share cultural attributes of many cultures and subcultures.

In large part, the acquisition of culture is an unconscious process. Many of the shared attributes become "second nature" to us—they become so "natural" that they exist outside of our awareness. Thus, the rules about these attributes are usually hidden—unwritten and unspoken. It is only when someone (usually, but not always, from outside the group) intentionally or inadvertently acts in contrast to the shared attribute or understanding that a particular pattern or attribute becomes fully visible.

Examples of behaviors that are culturally acquired through our families and other groups include such behaviors as how close or far away we stand or sit from our friends and acquaintances (our sense of personal space); how we relate to time, and the value and meaning we place on punctuality; whether and how often we make eye contact with others, and the meaning of making or not making eye contact with others; and how frequently and in what contexts we smile at others. Each of these categories can reflect

possible cultural differences and **possible individual differences.**

Let's look at a few examples. Consider how your response to the same behavior might differ if you know that the unexpected behavior is the result of a cultural difference, rather than the result of an individual's specific motivations.

Eye Contact: A co-worker passes you in the hall daily, and never, ever makes eye contact. Neither does she make eye contact when you are speaking about a shared work project. You may assume that she is intentionally ignoring you in the hall and that she has no respect for your ideas when you discuss work. In fact, her behavior may reflect no more than shyness or social awkwardness. It may also reflect her ethnic culture, where eye contact is considered rude and threatening. If the latter, you would be confusing a behavior that is actually the result of a cultural pattern with an individual trait reflecting a specific intention or motivation that you are inaccurately attributing to your co-worker.

Personal Space: You grew up in a family that is very physically demonstrative and where your large extended family always has room for another around the table. In fact, small children often end up sitting on an adult's lap to make sure everyone can squeeze in. You've become friendly with another co-worker, sharing lunch and talking about office matters informally. You've noticed, though, that when you are with this co-worker, he frequently backs away from you. You know you don't have bad breath, you shower and apply deodorant daily, and your clothes are impeccably laundered. Your feelings are frequently hurt, and you don't understand what the problem is.

Your otherwise friendly co-worker grew up in a family where daily meals were a formal affair, with full place settings and no surprises. To the extent there was an extended family, it extended elsewhere, and drop-in visitors were an unknown. Though your co-worker's family would describe itself as close, they rarely demonstrate affection physically.

Punctuality: You are invited to dinner at 7:00 p.m. at your supervising attorney's home. You are not only new to the workplace, you have moved from a medium-sized city in the Southwest to Manhattan. You arrive at 7:00 p.m. for dinner, and your host greets you in her bathrobe. She is obviously just out of the shower. You are confused and embarrassed and she is equally shocked. You wonder whether you have gotten the date or time wrong. You haven't. What you have gotten wrong is what 7:00 p.m. means for a dinner invitation in Manhattan among your supervising attorney's social group. While dinner at 7:00 p.m. means 7:00 p.m. in your hometown, 7:00 p.m. means no sooner than 7:30 p.m. and not later than 8:00 p.m. to your supervising attorney. It means the same thing to all of her friends. It is so natural to her that it didn't occur to her to clarify the meaning of 7:00 p.m. when she extended the invitation.

As you can see, the impact of **culturally formed behaviors can go both ways: your culturally formed behavior about punctuality might disrupt another's expectations about**

time, and another's failure to make eye contact might disrupt yours about respectful attention.

Cultural understandings can take unexpected forms in the workplace. Example:

Workplace Culture: You are going to your first staff meeting. When you arrive, about two minutes early, almost all of the other participants are already there, seated around the large round table. You take the one seat left at the table, next to one of your co-workers. Everyone gets quiet and looks sideways at you. You check, and see that you haven't spilled your breakfast on yourself and otherwise seem to be in order. Then another of your co-workers walks in; clearly you are sitting in her usual seat. You move to the row of chairs behind the table, and all is well, but you don't understand what you missed. You later learn that she is hard of hearing, and always sits next to the other co-worker, who writes notes to her in the meeting to keep her up to speed. Everyone in the group is aware of this, but the arrangement has not been openly discussed among the staff.

The moral of this chapter is simple:

Don't overlook the possibility that another person's behavior might have nothing to do with you. It may be the result of a culturally acquired behavior or belief or value, and the other person may not even be aware of it. Similarly, you might inadvertently cross a cultural boundary without knowing it. The boundary may be so second-nature to your new group that its members won't be aware of it until you unknowingly cross it. You may not immediately understand why others react to you as they do.

Observe. Reflect. Repeat.

With kudos to Professor Gregory Urban, Chair of the Department of Anthropology, University of Pennsylvania, whose online course, *The Power of Team Culture*, provided many of the basic concepts in this chapter. (See Penn Online Learning Initiative online.)

CHAPTER 8

WORKING WELL WITH OTHERS

*"Consider the rights of others before
your own feelings, and the feelings
of others before your own rights."*
John Wooden, A Lifetime of Observations

New lawyers are surprised to learn that some of their greatest challenges on the job have nothing to do with law.

Rather, they are about dealing with people—all kinds of people. This includes your immediate supervisor, others who may at times supervise your work, and the rest of your colleagues (lawyers and non-lawyers, in and out of your office). You will have daily or almost daily contact with some of these people and only glancing interactions with others. Some will be members of "your team," and others will be passionately opposed to your short- and long-term goals.

In the fast-paced and often emotionally charged atmosphere of law, it is easy to overlook that these people have human sensitivities, as well as personal responsibilities and aspirations independent of the roles they play when interacting with us. In other words, we are working with real people, with real feelings—people in whose shoes we may have been before, and might at some point be again.

This is because, at any given time, each of us could be the boss or underling, the leader or follower, the neophyte or veteran, the most or least knowledgeable, the amateur or professional, the blamer or blamed, the oppressor or victim. Given the variety of tasks we perform and the many contexts within which we perform them, we might be all of these on any single day. This can be overwhelming . . . and a bit intimidating!

You will be relieved to know that many chapters in this book offer quite specific ways to go about working well with others. For example, there are chapters devoted to specific strategies for developing awareness of your own attitudes and actions and their effects on others, as well as awareness of the effects that others have on you. Chapter 9, "The Art of Being Supervised (Gracefully)," Chapter 10, "The Art of Supervising," and Chapter 14, "Feedback," give useful advice about effective supervision in the context of being the giver and the receiver. They also offer a primer on the fundamentals of feedback–how to get it, how to interpret it, and how to make the most of it.

While recognizing the value of specificity, there is another, more fundamental point to keep in mind: **the practice of law, or any profession for that matter, is unavoidably about people.**

When focused intensely on our own projects, it is easy to forget that **we are interacting with people whose lives are as complex and full as ours.** All too often, especially when we are working with non-lawyers, we overlook their contributions to our work. This is unfortunate, because paralegals, legal assistants, and other experienced staff members possess, and are usually willing to share, a wealth of information that can make or break projects, and can certainly make the difference between a pleasant and unpleasant work environment.

While writing this book, we had the benefit of frank discussions with a number of paralegals and other non-lawyers who worked in large and small firms, courts, and offices of corporate counsel. They had a substantial amount of individual and cumulative experience in their jobs. The picture that they presented to us of the life of those who work with lawyers was, at best, a cautionary tale. It was a tale about the importance of humility and courtesy, and the avoidance of arrogance.

The following list, our **Top Ten Rules for Law Clerks, Interns, and New Professionals,** grew out of those discussions. It came from people who have a bird's eye view of everyone who comes in and goes out of a law firm or legal agency's door. For every rule, they gave us a strong and powerful counter example of behavior that we hope you will avoid as you move forward in furtherance of a satisfying "life in the law."

Top Ten Rules

1. Understand that **kindness to others is noticed and repaid.** Disrespectful treatment of others is noted, communicated to others, and consciously or unconsciously translated into less support at crucial times. Small, everyday kindnesses make an enormous difference to everyone.

2. **Admit to yourself and others when you don't know something. Learn how to ask for help.** If you are honest about what you don't know, the chances of someone helping you to learn what you need to know increase exponentially.

3. **Be on the lookout for your own ignorance.** Operate consciously from the assumption that you don't know everything and that you have a lot to learn—not just about "law," but about people, how organizations work, how legal work is managed, and about who might be the most competent person in a given sphere. This increases the likelihood that someone on your team will share something with you that you didn't realize you needed to know.

4. **Don't be misled by titles, status, pay, or place in the hierarchy.** The people who know what you will need to know, and who can help you in ways you will need to be helped, come with all manner of titles, stations, pay grades, and places. You can learn something from almost everyone with whom you interact on the job; each has some area of expertise that you can benefit from, whose insights you will need at some point.

5. **Find out from your immediate supervisor** (or someone who seems to know what's going on) **who is on the "team" for a given project.** If it is a paralegal or legal assistant, he is very likely the "case

manager" and may have the best overall sense of the project—who is working on it, what deadlines exist, where the files can be found, new developments that might have occurred, and other information that you'll likely need to know.

6. **Avoid elitism and arrogance.** This may sound a lot like Rule Number 4. It is.

7. **Be a sponge for information**—about people, procedures, and resources. Ask: What more do I need to know? What am I missing? Think: Who might be able to show or tell me? Try to learn about things and people in your firm or agency before an urgent need for the information arises.

8. **Keep an open mind**—about what you can learn, what you don't know, and about who in the organization might be able to help you.

9. **Take responsibility for your mistakes** and admit them as soon as you notice them. They can usually be fixed, especially if they are addressed quickly.

10. **Don't blame others when problems arise.** Instead, develop the habit of asking immediately, "How can we correct this?" when a mistake is discovered, rather than "whose fault is this?" (Unless the responsibility is yours, per Number 9 above.)

As our Top Ten List illustrates, **it is essential for any successful lawyer to develop respectful**

relationships with support staff. It requires a time and effort to understand and appreciate the varying areas and levels of expertise that they possess, and how their work and yours blend together, but the tangible and intangible benefits make it well worth it.

It's a great relief to a client to see her attorney greeted by everyone from the janitor to the security officers to the judge as they come in and go out of the courtroom. Attorneys who take the time to show kindness to everyone working in the system gain the confidence of their clients. Those who do not face serious problems in the courtroom with clients who do not trust them.

Student Journal

Be a team player and treat everyone with respect.

Advice from an Employer

CHAPTER 9

THE ART OF BEING SUPERVISED
(GRACEFULLY)

*"Tell me and I'll forget; show me and
I may remember; involve me
and I'll understand."*
Chinese Proverb

Let's begin with the work relationship that may
seem the most central at first—that with your
supervising attorney, whom we'll call your "boss." In
the next chapter, we'll talk about another central
relationship—with your key support person. We'll
call *you* the "boss" in that one.

Ideally, your boss is a skilled coach and
conscientious supervisor. He is approachable and is
generous with his time, even when busy. He is
patient and genuinely enjoys working with you. In
contrast, many bosses fall a bit short of the mark.
Perhaps they found themselves in the position of
supervisor without having expressed any particular
interest in the role and without displaying any
natural talent for the task. Complicating the matter,
they may have never received any formal training in
the principles of good supervision.

If this is your situation, where does it leave you?
Over many years of working with law students and
new professionals, we have found that those who
consciously adopt certain key attitudes and
behaviors are more likely to have good experiences
with their supervisors, even those who got off to a

rocky start at first. You see, there is an art to being supervised . . .

A. UNDERSTANDING YOUR BOSS

It's best to take a few minutes to **think about your boss's situation** and how that relates to your situation. Many new professionals find themselves at some point in situations with *some or all* of the following elements. If you can recognize them early, and realize that they are *not about you*, you will be able to respond more productively:

- **Your boss is likely less focused on being your boss** and more focused on the ultimate demands of his job than on how to manage his relationship with you. He may be uncertain about how to manage the competing demands of being both a lawyer and manager.

- **Your boss is overworked** and has less time to devote to interacting with you than you (and he) might prefer.

- Regardless of his best intentions, **your boss may not communicate directly** about what he wants from you, how he wants it, or when he wants it. This may be because of time constraints, stress, or simple oversight.

- While what you do in your job is very important to his success, **your boss has a myriad of other people and priorities he is responsible for.** The better you understand what these priorities are and how they affect you and your job, the more effective you will be.

- **Your boss may not be aware of every project** or every aspect of the projects you are working on, some of which have been assigned by other attorneys. This may even include work that you are doing directly for him. Thus, he will not realize what is realistic for you to handle unless you tell him and, even if you tell him, he may not seem to understand.

- Many people in positions of power are so focused on their own "work," that they are unaware of the effect they have on others. Your boss may be one of these people. In spite of possible evidence to the contrary, **your boss is probably doing the best he can at any given time** and would like to be a good boss.

Even if, from your perspective, your boss's "best" just isn't quite good enough, it might be worth taking the time to **try to understand reality from his point of view.** It's quite possible that you will discover some steps that you can take to improve your working relationship. We have a few thoughts to share, too.

First, if you are new to the job, consider whether some of your discomfort might be related to the stress of settling into a new environment. **First impressions, especially in the early days, may not be accurate.**

Next, explore the possibility that **your perception of your boss's behavior is as much about your own fears** and preconceptions as it is about his perceived unreasonableness.

Finally, try to **break down the *general* difficulties that you are having with your boss into *specific* attitudes, behaviors, and situations that are causing problems.** By doing so, you can more easily develop tangible strategies for coping with and resolving them. Chapter 22, "Handling Conflicts at Work," offers tangible strategies for coping with conflict that you might try.

Unfortunately, even if you take all of the steps described above, you may run into a boss who seems to blame all mistakes on others, makes unreasonable and incomprehensible demands, sets unrealistic deadlines, seems never to listen or read carefully, and who, in general, makes the lives of others miserable.

After reflection and observation, you may conclude that your boss is one of these people. If his behavior is not reflective of the values of the organization, consider discussing your concerns with a trusted, more experienced person in the office who may have suggestions for improving the situation. Alternatively, you might try to find a way to transfer to another area within the organization.

However, if you are in a new permanent job, you might want to find another job as quickly as is realistic. In the meantime, we suggest that you learn more about your boss's situation and ultimate goals, and try to get a sense of where your work fits in that picture.

Initially, much of your time will be devoted to learning your new job. However, no one else will place as high a priority on the process of your learning as you will. Your employer's ultimate goal is the production of work and **you will be expected to produce *useful* work while you are learning.** You'll need to find a way to deal with your boss as best you can while producing that useful work and, towards that end, it will be helpful if you develop . . .

B.   THE ART OF BEING SUPERVISED

If you are blessed with a capable supervisor, you will have the benefit of working with someone who has likely given a lot of thought to the various ways he and others work together—how work is delegated, how feedback is provided, and how a new attorney or law clerk can be supported in learning on the job.

If you have a less capable supervisor or one who is relatively new as an attorney or as a supervisor, you may be working with someone who has not given much thought at all to the dynamics of working together. He may not only be uncomfortable in his role as a supervisor but also still primarily concerned with his development as an attorney. If you are in this situation, be aware of one possibility: when two relatively inexperienced lawyers work together, especially where one is supervising and the other is being supervised, each may (consciously or unconsciously) try to convince the other that he knows what he is doing. **Often this comes across**

as one trying to convince the other that he knows *more* than the other.

How can you tell when you have gotten into this kind of "I know what I'm doing—more than you know what you are doing" interchange? The first hint is usually in your gut, but it sometimes takes a while to recognize what is happening. If you find yourself feeling that, "He doesn't know what he's talking about," and at the same time feeling, "I'm sure I checked everywhere anyone could have checked, and I know I didn't miss anything in my analysis, or at least, I hope that I didn't," you have probably entered this kind of situation.

One way to defuse it is to say something like, "I don't quite understand what you are saying," or "Do you have time to go through the points, so we can get on the same page?" Turn your attention to the task at hand and away from the battle of egos that has developed. As best you can, re-frame the conversation and focus on work rather than on your competing sets of insecurities.

Finally, **once you weather the incident, resist the urge to flee from your boss** every time you meet in the hall. Instead, find a way to initiate positive, more general interactions with your boss; perhaps you can ask for advice in an area where he clearly has more experience and knowledge than you do. Focus on common interests rather than on your recent misunderstanding; you will both be relieved to "clear the air."

As you become more comfortable with the basics of being supervised, turn your attention towards mastering the art of doing it *gracefully*. Your professional relationships and overall learning process will be enhanced exponentially.

So—what goes into the art of being supervised *gracefully*?

- Recognizing and acknowledging that you have entered *a new culture*. **As the newcomer, you must learn the rules of the culture.** This calls for observation, careful listening and reflection, and an open mind. See Chapter 7, "Cultural Differences."

- Realizing that by being hired, you have not been put in charge of managing the organization. Rather, part of your job is learning how organization's practices—at least until you have been there long enough to establish your credibility. This includes learning how your boss likes to work—how your boss likes to be kept informed of progress on projects, whether your boss likes to be consulted along the way or prefers that you get help elsewhere, how and when he best communicates (in the hall, by e-mail, telephone, in person at pre-arranged appointments, or never at the beginning of the day or after a long meeting).

- Asking yourself and your boss, **"How can I help?"**

To develop positive workplace relationships, step up to the plate . . . volunteer!

Advice from an Employer

- **Speaking up when you want to work on certain types of projects.** If you would like to work on a certain case, in a specific area of law, with a certain attorney, or try your hand at writing a motion, ask. Don't expect your boss to be a mind reader. Although you'll be expected to pitch in on your share of less interesting projects, attorneys are generally happy to accommodate your interests when possible.

Be proactive in seeking the assignments that you'd like to have.

Advice from an Employer

- **Making peace with receiving the feedback** we all say we want to receive.

For more specifics on how to solicit and use feedback productively, see Chapter 14, "Feedback." Here, though, it might help to look briefly at the intrapersonal and interpersonal aspects of feedback.

Most of us want to be praised, but prefer not to be criticized. Yet one of the main complaints of interns and new lawyers is that they don't get enough feedback. All we need to do to realize why we might not *get* enough feedback is to reflect on how difficult it is for us to *give* it and how difficult it is for most of us to *receive* it.

Many of us haven't learned how to give direct feedback when it involves pointing out how something could be improved. When we are in the position of *giving* negative feedback, we tend to hold back and give only the slightest suggestion of what the problem is. At the first hint of defensiveness on the part of the receiver, we don't know what to do.

Similarly, when we *receive* feedback, we focus (at least at first) on its negative aspects. This may be one reason we don't *get* enough feedback—our supervising attorneys know that *they* aren't very good at receiving feedback, and so they are *equally reluctant* to give it. **In a world where we defend against criticism, there aren't too many courageous souls interested in taking on the role of inflicting unintended pain.**

So where does that leave the new attorney or law clerk who wants feedback? It leaves you in the position of having to **demonstrate that you will receive feedback gracefully.** When someone suggests a different way of phrasing something, rather than explaining why you said it this way, try to see how the suggested revision might be an improvement. Try not to think that every suggestion for improvement carries an implicit question of "Why did you do it this way?"

Be proactive in seeking feedback, incorporate it into new projects, and try not to make the same mistake twice.

Advice from an Employer

Your supervisor doesn't expect perfection, but he does expect you to be fully prepared and give every project 100% of your effort. Experienced attorneys know that law students and new lawyers face very high learning curves; they will celebrate your successes and be supportive when you make mistakes.

If you **focus on learning in general** rather than on feedback specifically, you'll find that you *can* learn in other ways that might be both easier on your boss and more helpful for you. Ask your boss outside the context of a specific project how *she* learned when she was a new attorney. She may feel more comfortable giving general advice and addressing problems that new attorneys often need to address early in their careers. Ask what her greatest challenges were in learning how to write persuasively and efficiently, and how she overcame them. What advice does she have for you as a new attorney who is anxious to develop excellent skills? By demonstrating your interest in learning from her experience, you may set the stage for future opportunities to receive specific feedback on your work.

Finally, **once you receive feedback, try to view it as centering on the *product,* not on *you.*** The sooner you can view your work product as something distinct from your identity, the sooner you will be able to put feedback to good use. You will be well on your way to being supervised gracefully.

CHAPTER 10

THE ART OF SUPERVISING

"When someone does something good, applaud!
You will make two people happy."
Samuel Goldwyn

In this chapter, we talk about another central work relationship—with your key support person, whom we'll here call your assistant. In many ways, you will work as a team, but **once you are working as a lawyer rather than as a law clerk or intern, your role with your assistant will also be one of delegator and supervisor.** Ready or not, you are then a "boss." This chapter offers some ways for you to begin thinking about how to approach this very important work relationship, one that will be crucial to your having a satisfying and productive work experience.

In the meantime, if you are working as a law clerk or intern, take the opportunity to observe how effective lawyers work with their assistants. Note what kinds of interactions and habits you intend to avoid and best practices you wish to emulate.

A. UNDERSTANDING YOUR ASSISTANT

It's best to take a few minutes to **think about your assistant's situation.** Any of the following could potentially describe your assistant's position:

- Your assistant has **significantly more experience in the organization and in the practice of law than you do,** and is expected, in some ways, to train you. Even if she is not expected to train you, she has knowledge that she could share with you if you were open to learning from her; **or**

- Your assistant is **new to working in law or in your area of practice, and knows little about legal terms or procedures.** In many ways, you will need to teach her about law, as well as about how she can best help you.

- Regardless of both of your best intentions and efforts, **your assistant will often not understand completely what you want done and how you want it done.** Your assistant will often not be clear on what your priorities are or when you need certain projects or tasks completed. She may spend a great deal of time trying to read your mind.

- Unless you've recently done the kind of work or been in a position like that of your assistant, **you probably don't realize how many times she is interrupted or how much time the various tasks she performs take to complete.**

- **Your assistant may be providing support to an entire group of people.** You may not be her first priority.

As improbable as it may seem, you are now in a position of power and may easily become one of those people who are so focused on their work that they are unaware of the effect they have on others. Your moods, stress, and anxiety can communicate to others more than you realize. You might want to review Chapter 9, "The Art of Being Supervised (Gracefully)," to see some of the dangers that are now yours as you try both to do your job and be a good boss. Think about some of the things you wish your own boss would do, about how your boss works, and about some of her preferences that you wish you understood better. In other words, put yourself in the shoes of someone who is working for someone else. **Try to be the boss you wish you had.**

Here are some approaches you might try:

- Realize that **your assistant would like to do a good job,** but to succeed, she needs to know what her job is and what "doing a good job" looks like to you.

- Realize that **your assistant may not understand your concept of time.** For instance, when you hand her a document to be copied, she may not realize that you want or need the copy right now (*unless you tell her*).

- Realize that **the way you like things to be done may not be the way they are universally done,** so that if you have particular ways that you like things done, your assistant may not know what they are (*unless you tell her*).

- Remember that even if you feel the weight of the entire project is on your shoulders, **other people on the team also are invested in the project** and appreciate being told of milestones, setbacks, and challenges along

the way, including the ultimate outcome—
this includes your assistant. She may not
know that priorities have changed (*unless you
tell her*).

Some work situations are like raging rivers: we
have one chance to pull something out of the fast-
moving waters, and then must turn to some other
life-threatening emergency. Relieved that we have
skirted one disaster, we turn to the work that has
been building up in our absence. Often, we neglect a
critical step: letting the others who've been working
on the project know the emergency is over and how it
has been resolved. The case is settled; the hearing
continued; the client has disappeared; and yet our
teammates continue, doggedly, to do their parts of
the project. **They will not know the crisis is over
(*unless you tell them*).** Little do we realize that in
neglecting to tell everyone working on the project
that it's over, especially those with whom we work
most closely, we may be sowing seeds of resentment.

B.   GETTING TO KNOW EACH OTHER

Before too long goes by, it's worth taking the time
to talk directly with each other about how you prefer
to work. It's very helpful to articulate your working
styles at the beginning of your working relationship.

If you are aware of your strong preferences or
idiosyncrasies that would affect how you will be
working together, and don't mind sharing them, it
would be very helpful for your assistant to know what
they are. For instance, if when you arrive in the
morning, the first thing you want to do is check your

e-mail and you prefer not to discuss anything until you've been able to do that, make that clear. Likewise, if you send e-mails to your assistant at night with priorities that need addressing first thing in the morning as soon as your assistant arrives, it's helpful to explain that expectation up front so that you understand each other. You may assume that the first thing everyone does in the morning is check e-mail, but our experience has been, to our surprise, that this is simply not true.

Be tactful in directing staff and don't be high-maintenance.

Advice from an Employer

C. DELEGATING

We all know that we should delegate (or you will soon be told you should), but effective delegation requires an investment of time, careful planning, and consistent follow-up. "Delegation" means turning over responsibility or authority for performing certain work to another. **It does not mean turning over responsibility for making sure that the work is completed, and completed to the standard required, within the time specified.**

What follow are only a few key points to bear in mind when delegating:

- **Give thought to the items that are appropriate for delegation**—are there tasks or projects that you are performing while at the same time saying to yourself, "I shouldn't be doing this" because you know or suspect your assistant or another team member could competently perform them? Caveat: Don't confuse this with receiving a task from someone responsible for your training who has given you the task for your own development, even if someone junior to you could accomplish it as well or better.

- **Once you decide to delegate something, be clear with yourself about what "it" is before delegating it.** Think about and communicate clearly who will make decisions about different aspects of the work, and whether at some point you should also transfer more of the decision-making to your assistant as confidence and trust builds between the two of you.

- With your assistant taking notes, **communicate directly and clearly the elements of the work delegated,** including:

  - any unique aspects of the project,

  - if relevant, how it fits into a bigger picture,

  - where background information can be found,

  - names of any others working on the project and their roles,

  - how long you expect the project to take,

  - where the project fits in with other priorities, and

  - interim and ultimate deadlines.

- **Invite your assistant's questions, contributions, and clarifications,** including whether your expectations about time are realistic and manageable alongside other priorities.

- **Have your assistant confirm explicitly that you share the same understanding of the delegated work and its requirements,** including follow-up dates and deadlines. The best way to do this it to have her summarize in her own words the project and what it entails. Follow up with a written summary prepared by one of you and confirmed by the other, to be sure to avoid misunderstandings.

- **Be clear about how you will communicate with each other** as the work is undertaken, as questions arise, and as new aspects develop.

- **Be clear about what will constitute a job well done.**

- **Establish and communicate checkpoints** for gauging progress, communicate clearly at what stage you want to review various aspects of the project, and indicate what parts of the project you are leaving to your assistant's discretion.

- **Introduce your assistant to other people who are working on the project** and let them know the role she will be playing.

- **Indicate that you are willing to consult about the project.** Adjust responsibilities as you each become more confident with your level of communication, confident in each other's likely responses to actions taken, and confident in your assistant's ability to perform various aspects of the project with less of your involvement.

- **Most people prefer autonomy to subservience.** The more independence a person is allowed, the more pride she takes in her work, the better the work and happier the person is likely to be.

D.   SUPERVISING

Once you have delegated to your assistant, you are now a supervisor. Not only will you be asked from time to time to formally evaluate your assistant, but you will need on a day-to-day basis to interact over priorities, deadlines, and details of how you expect things to be handled versus how your assistant has done the same thing in the past for a previous boss, to name only a few.

In short, you will now be in the position of having to give *feedback*.

Just as we discuss the difficulties of *getting* feedback in Chapter 14, "Feedback," so shall we now step through the challenges of *giving* feedback. Now that the roles are reversed, and you are the feedback giver, it will be a lot easier for you to understand why it is sometimes so difficult to get feedback.

Remember that the person who wants feedback primarily wants reassurance and to develop skills. Remember that the person from whom feedback is sought (this is you) is primarily trying to get the job done and move on to the next catastrophe that's brewing. *You* are now the harried boss who is running into the office to put out three fires, racing past your assistant who stayed until 9:00 p.m. the night before to finalize documents that had to be filed by midnight, not even noticing that she is back again at 8:00 a.m.

Let's track the stages of providing feedback, the same way we track getting feedback in Chapter 9, "The Art of Being Supervised (Gracefully)," and Chapter 14, "Feedback."

1. Preparing the Stage for Useful Feedback

If you haven't already had the experience of discovering, at the end of a project, useful information that would have been helpful at the beginning, you will at some point. It's an object lesson for being a good supervisor: **take the time to give your assistant the information she needs at the *beginning* of the project, to avoid the frustration you both will experience if she completes it under a false impression about a fundamental aspect of the project.**

This really is nothing more than making sure that when you delegate, you provide all the necessary information. But because mere mortals rarely do, **you need to plan for your assistant to ask questions during the project.** This leads to . . .

2.   Providing Feedback During the Project

One of the difficulties new lawyers have with getting feedback and information during their projects is the inaccessibility of the supervising lawyers. If you've ever experienced that inaccessibility, **you'll understand how important it is for you to be accessible to your assistant, or for that matter, to any team member working with you on a project.**

If you have preferred ways of communicating, share them with your assistant. If you meet about the project, make sure your assistant takes notes. Structure the conversation so that by the end of the meeting, you are sure that there has been a full opportunity to explore all the questions either of you has about the goals of the project, any new developments in the project, and any other essential information that either of you should know.

If you feel you are getting peppered with questions at a frequency that is unacceptable, consider whether your initial explanation needs to be re-articulated or clarified. You can also suggest regular times to check in, if you haven't already done so.

If you receive work product from your assistant during the project, give feedback on that work shortly after you receive it. Positive feedback is a strong motivator; negative feedback allows for corrections and improvement on the next part of the project.

3. Providing Feedback After the Project

This is where it gets difficult. The project is over. You've either adjusted to whatever disappointments you had in the work submitted to you, or the project was submitted to you in such good shape that you could keep right on moving without a hiccup. You have now moved to the next project.

At this point, you need at a minimum to acknowledge the work. **If it was well done, say so with specificity.** Say what about it was well done. "The coordination with others was perfect; the documents perfectly formatted; the closing well-planned, and the participants were very complimentary." "Thanks so much for catching my mistake on the X document." "Thanks for staying late to make sure everything would be ready." "Thanks for coming in early to make sure everything would be ready." "Thanks for handling Ms. Y; she was out of control when she arrived, but after she talked to you, she was quite calm and reasonable. I wouldn't have been able to handle her, given what I had going at the time." Don't be afraid to be enthusiastic in your praise. **And if there are things that can be done better next time, a good time to mention it is when the overwhelming result is positive.**

If serious concerns exist with work submitted, arrange for a meeting so that you can discuss them. In doing so, you might do well to consider the "life of the delegated project," so that you can reflect on ways you could have done things differently and ways your assistant could have done things differently. If the work is finished and you are about to meet with your assistant, this should not be the first time your assistant learns of your concerns.

If you pass up the opportunity to discuss early projects, it will become harder and harder to initiate conversations about how things can be improved. So even though you may have very little time to provide feedback, it will benefit you and your assistant to have the conversation.

In having the conversation, remember that most of us react defensively to negative feedback, even when we know the criticisms are justified (maybe especially then). We take it personally, even if we know we are receiving information we should have been provided earlier. **In giving feedback, *specific* suggestions about how and why things should be done differently next time are very helpful.** We want reassurance, and we want to improve. So do most people. Find something to praise. Suggest alternative approaches. Indicate, if it is accurate, that you can understand how your assistant misunderstood the instructions or how she could have made the mistake. Acknowledge any mistakes you may have made during the project. Try to learn how you can communicate more clearly, or check in more frequently, to avoid future similar problems. Make your expectations clear. Give clear and understandable feedback. Make sure it is understood.

4.   Provide Formal Training Opportunities

To the extent possible, encourage your firm or agency to make formal training

opportunities available to support staff.
Encourage your assistant to attend, and discuss
topics covered after the training. This may provide
the opportunity for you to discuss office matters
outside the context of a specific instance where your
feedback would be difficult to give and possibly
harder to receive.

Finally, **show your appreciation frequently.**
Day-to-day kindness is more important than a once-
a-year dramatic gesture. For example, some morning
you might drop off a gift card for her favorite
cappuccino or bring in flowers from your garden to
brighten up her desk. On a busy day, order in and pay
for lunch. Sometimes making sure you are accessible
and attentive is the kindest thing you can do, because
it allows her to do her job well and smoothly.

If your job is stressful, your assistant's job is
stressful. If you are working hard, your assistant is
working hard. Don't underestimate the contributions
that can be made to your professional success and
satisfaction by a competent assistant whose
contributions you demonstrate that you value and
respect, and whose talents and aspirations you are
invested in developing and supporting.

**Finally, don't forget to acknowledge and
thank her for the contributions she has made.**

CHAPTER 11

MANAGING WRITTEN
ASSIGNMENTS

"Less is more. God is in the details."
Mies van der Rohe

A. WRITING IN LAW SCHOOL
AND PRACTICE

It's critical to understand the differences in emphasis between writing in law school and its practical application in the workplace. If you keep these basic differences between law school and practice in mind, your work will be much more useful, much earlier, than it otherwise might be.

The **sheer variety of writing that lawyers produce is a major difference.** Of course, lawyers draft the familiar litigation-related documents most law students are familiar with, including the ubiquitous office memorandum. But lawyers and law clerks also draft letters to clients and opposing parties and their attorneys; opinion letters; legislation; contracts of infinite variety, complexity, and subject matter; judicial orders and opinions; discovery requests and disclosures; motions of every kind; and a wide variety of internal documents, to name only a few. You will have written some of these in law school, but others will be completely new to you.

Even writing that has the same name in law school and in practice differs significantly in

purpose: the office memorandum that is viewed as a "neutral or predictive memorandum" in law school is often viewed in practice as the first step in building a client's case, and is thus the first step in advocacy. An office memorandum in practice almost always is focused on formulating the strongest arguments for the client, in the most persuasive form. **Law clerks and new lawyers who adopt too neutral a tone in practice will quickly find out that neutrality in the context of an ongoing case is rarely acceptable.** New lawyers must learn to maintain the ability to evaluate arguments on both sides while at the same time articulate the client's position in the strongest plausible terms.

Another enormous difference between law school and practice is the importance of fact development. Except in clinical or sophisticated simulation courses, many students have little exposure to fact investigation or discovery. Most law school writing assignments provide a fixed set of facts with no discovery of additional information. Changes or new developments in a client's wishes or goals also rarely occur in law school writing assignments. In practice, law clerks and new lawyers would do well to heed the advice that Gandhi received as a young lawyer, which is to be aware that **"facts are three-fourths of the law."**

In talking with attorneys in firms and agencies about the writing skills that new attorneys need to develop, a clear consensus emerged: **new lawyers need to focus on mastering the facts of their cases. This often means carefully reviewing**

documents for key times, conversations, agreements, actions. Unlike law school assignments, the facts of your clients' cases aren't provided to you in final form. **You will often need to discover facts, consider the implications that new facts have on already-known facts, and then decide whether a given fact has any significance. You will then need to apply the law to the facts—the facts of your real, live, case. Finally, you'll need to be open, always, to learning about additional, previously unknown, facts that come to light unexpectedly.**

Initially and most frequently, the document most new lawyers, law clerks, and interns are asked to write is the **office memorandum.** Most of the principles set forth below apply to all kinds of writing in law practice, but we refer to the office memorandum most frequently to have a shared frame of reference.

B.   AUDIENCE, PURPOSE, CONTEXT

Overview. You need to know the **purpose of the assignment,** its **audience,** and its **context.** In practical terms, you'll need to answer several questions.

- **Who will be the first person to read this,** and who else will likely read it?

- **What do you hope will be accomplished** as a result of the document? What do you hope the reader will do after reading it?

- **What is the situation or problem giving rise to the assignment?**

- **Where will the readers be when they read the document,** and how much time will they have to read it? What other demands will be made on their attention at that time?

The answer to these questions will determine many things, such as:

- **The kind of language and level of detail and formality** you'll use.

- **Whether you are attempting to inform or persuade,** and the tone you'll adopt. If you are attempting to persuade, what, specifically, do you hope your ultimate reader will do as a result of reading your work?

- **The length and organization** of the document, including the use of **summaries, headings, and other signposts** for your readers.

1.   Identify Your Audience

Who your audience is may *seem* self-evident. Your primary audience is likely the person who is assigning you the work (your "assigning attorney."). **But sometimes your audience includes other attorneys, a judge, a client, other law clerks, and possibly members of the public.** Consider what your reader knows or doesn't know about the matter and the field generally; what your reader's main concerns are about the topic; and the importance of the matter to your reader. In other words, think about what your reader needs, and how his perspective may differ from yours. Knowing who your reader is will provide insight into special considerations that you should bear in mind as you draft your document.

If your product is an internal office memo, for instance, you may think you have a pretty good idea of who will be reading your document once it leaves your hands. But it is also true that "remote readers" in time or place may also read your work. For instance, where a matter is large or long-term, many people may work on it over a course of many years. Your memo may be read long after it is written, by people who are not even working for your agency or firm when you write it.

> **Drafting Tip:** The facts section in a memo should be written with the remote and even the unintended reader in mind. **Don't assume that your readers will be familiar with the facts.** Unless instructed otherwise, provide a statement of the relevant facts in your memorandum for someone who has either forgotten, or never known them.

Your work product may be sent directly to a client, without any editing. The ease with which documents can be forwarded electronically makes this even more likely. A law clerk or new lawyer is often surprised to learn that a memo prepared for an attorney has been forwarded, *without any changes*, to a client. Try to find out if the attorneys with whom you are working make a practice of this. If they do, they may not review it first for nuance. As a very broad generalization, your document is being forwarded likely because the attorney is too busy to formulate a personal report, but wants to demonstrate to the client that work is being done on the client's matter. **Consider yourself the final level of quality control: you may be.**

Drafting Tip: You may have readers, such as clients, whose sensitivities about the case are not that of professionals doing a job, but of people who will be directly affected by the outcome. They may respond differently to some of your descriptions of the facts. Draft cautiously to avoid inadvertent insult or unnecessary alarm.

Drafting Tip: If what you have submitted is a "DRAFT," mark clearly and prominently on the document itself that it is a "DRAFT." This way, no one will rely on the document as the "final word." **Don't assume that your transmittal e-mail transmitting will be passed along with the document.**

A "draft" should be neither your "first" nor a "rough" effort. When you are asked for a draft, you are expected to produce your best and most complete effort. Don't rely on your supervisor to supply details (times, places, addresses, etc.) that aren't in the file. If there is relevant information that *you* can track down, do it. **Don't leave for your supervisor work that you can take care of yourself. That's why you've been hired.**

There is no such thing as a rough draft. Don't turn in an assignment until you're certain that your work product is what the assigning attorney requested, is in acceptable format, and is free of analytical, spelling, and grammatical errors.

Advice from an Employer

2. Know Your Purpose

Knowing how your work will be used can significantly affect how you approach researching and writing your document. But exactly how *will* your work be used? For instance, if you're researching an issue so that your firm can advise a client *whether* to bring a suit or not, or whether to defend or offer to settle a suit, your research will be to determine the likelihood of the client's prevailing on an issue. In that case, a thorough analysis of cases pro and con on the issue will be essential. On the other hand, if you are already in litigation and for whatever reasons settlement is not an option, and your task is to find the best arguments that can be made on your client's behalf, your research may be the same, but the emphasis of your writing will change drastically. You are not trying to advise whether the client should sue or defend, but rather preparing for litigation and formulating your client's best arguments and defenses.

Drafting Tip: You need to know how your work will be used to be able to focus your research and writing. Even if you receive an assignment to "research this issue" for future reference it would still be helpful to find out how your agency or firm might expect your work to be used. You will do a better job if you have some context for it.

3. Consider the Context

In what setting will your document be read and used? What else will your reader be doing while reading your document? This information can help you decide how to organize and format your document, which should be easy to navigate, as well as organized in a way that is immediately clear to the reader.

More than likely, your document will be read by one or more busy people who have many other matters lobbying for their attention, and who may be interrupted as they read it. How much time will your reader have to read your document? Will your reader read it once, carefully, and later, rushing into a meeting? Or will your reader read it for the first time as he rushes into a meeting on the topic?

Drafting Tip: Organization and format are crucial and deserve your full attention. Your reader should be able to easily follow the organization of your document, recognize the last place he had been reading before being interrupted, and gather the salient points on a quick re-read.

Knowing the context will help you determine how to **organize your document, how long it** should be, whether to put a **summary at the beginning or end,** and how the use of **headings** and **typeface** might help your reader.

Your need for this basic knowledge about **audience, purpose,** and **context** should inform your search for information as early as possible in your involvement with a project. Now we turn to the specific information you'll need to be able to do an assignment well.

C.   GETTING AND MANAGING THE ASSIGNMENT

- **What *is* the assignment?** This is not as simple as it appears. Re-state and clarify in your own words your understanding of the assignment at the first possible moment— either in the conversation where you receive the assignment, or, if it arrives to you in written form, very shortly after receiving it. If you receive the assignment in an in-person meeting, be as interactive as possible with your assigning attorney. **Ask questions about the facts. Try to extract as much information as possible about the matter as you can.**

- **What will be done with your work?** Where does the assignment fit in the big picture of the project?

- **When is it due? Are there any interim deadlines or checkpoints?**

- **Is there an approximate length expected?**

- **Is there an approximate number of hours you are expected to work on the project?** Bear in mind that your assigning attorney can only provide estimates. If the estimate of hours appears unrealistic once you have begun working on the assignment, consult immediately with your assigning attorney. If you are logging your time to a specific project, avoid the temptation to under-report your time because you are embarrassed that it has taken you longer than expected. **Every new lawyer and law clerk faces this challenge. Most things take longer than you expect.**

- In what **form does your assigning attorney prefer** the project? Sometimes the attorney merely wants a compilation of cases and explanations, rather than a formal memo. Find out.

- **Where can you find an effective sample of similar well-done projects in the expected format?** Is there an associate, fellow clerk, intern, paralegal, legal assistant, or secretary who can provide one?

- **How can you communicate with the attorney** if you have questions along the way—for instance, if you run across a new issue, or a roadblock?

- **Who else is familiar with the file, issues and important details?** Is there someone else who could answer some of your questions?

- **Has a file been created yet?** If so, who has it and do you have access to it? If no file has been created, has a conflicts check been conducted? Who will be opening the file?

- **Who is the client?** The adverse party or parties? What is the case or matter called? Identify the client, case, or matter on everything you do in connection with the project.

- Find out **what suggestions,** if any, the assigning attorney has for you **to begin your research.** Sometimes they will have suggestions; sometimes they won't.

- If you are unclear about any aspect of your assignment in your initial meeting or on receipt of the project, **ask for clarification immediately** while you have your attorney's attention and you both remember what you are talking about.

- **Communicate with your assigning attorneys on your progress on their matters and deadlines,** especially if they are unaware of other projects on which you are working.

D. WHILE WORKING ON THE ASSIGNMENT

Often, you walk out of the initial meeting feeling that you have a good grasp on the assignment, and it's not until you actually begin working on it that you realize you don't fully understand what you've been asked to do. This happens a lot. **Ask for clarification.** Be specific about what is confusing you.

A common error made by law clerks and new lawyers is not speaking to the assigning attorney enough to properly understand the project. If in doubt, ask!

Advice from an Employer

- **Follow up shortly after receiving** the assignment (either orally or in writing) to get additional information that you now see you will need. Do this sooner rather than later. As always, gather your thoughts and questions before meeting with your assigning attorney, especially if it is difficult to find time with her.

- If the project is more than a single, simple matter completed in a brief period of time, there is a good chance that new facts will emerge that may change the legal issues that need to be researched and addressed. Create an orderly way of revising your notes to identify points at which new facts emerge over the course of your work on the project.

- **Organize your thoughts** before beginning to research or write. Formulate the issue or issues so that you have a plan before you begin. Your formulation of the issue may change later because of new facts that emerge, or because after researching you realize that other issues are more critical, but begin with *some* articulation. See Chapter 12, "Research," for suggestions on beginning your research, and Chapter 13, "A Writing Checklist: Remember Your Reader," for writing principles to bear in mind as you write.

- If you are unfamiliar with the field, **begin with a treatise** or other secondary source to obtain an overview. Don't overlook the possibility that **a *person* may be your best initial research resource**—a librarian, a fellow attorney or law clerk, a paralegal, or colleagues in the same field whom you know from other contexts. Before leaving for the summer or after graduation, check with your law school library to see what kind of reference services might be available to you.

- **Keep an accurate research log** and **update all legal and factual research before submitting your final work.** Your employer may have legal software to assist here. If not, develop a comprehensively structured format that works for you. *But do use something.* See the end of Chapter 12, "Research," for more detailed suggestions on developing a Research Checklist.

E.   ORGANIZE AND POLISH

- **Organize your memorandum** so that it is most helpful to your reader. Review the assignment and purpose for which it will be used. **If a specific question was asked, answer it early in the memo** and then give your reasons for the answer.

- **Assume that your reader is very busy,** and does not have much time to read. At the end of your document, include a quick summary of your conclusions with very brief reasons.

- **Assume that your reader will be interrupted while reading your memorandum.** Use headings, frequent paragraph breaks, topic sentences, and transitions to help your reader stay organized.

- **Make your recommendation up front, give your reasons,** and describe the counter arguments. If you are asked to do so, provide a recommendation. If this makes you uncomfortable, **we must emphasize that it's your assigning attorney's job to evaluate your recommendations** based on your reasoning and discussion of the supporting authority for your conclusion. **Your supervisor knows you are new.**

- **Don't assume that your reader (even your assigning attorney) will know or remember the facts.** At a *minimum,* **summarize the facts briefly.**

- Don't assume that your reader will know the law. Attorneys work on many projects at any given time, are often much too busy to do legal research themselves, and rely on you to point them in the right direction. **Often, you will be the first line of legal knowledge on the very particular issue being researched— that is why you are being asked to research the case.** On the other hand, your assigning attorney will likely be generally familiar with the area of law, so **there is no need to provide an encyclopedic description of the general area.**

- **Provide sufficient information about the facts, holding, and reasoning of cases, so that the reader can judge your conclusions independently.** Don't make your reader accept your conclusions or interpretations of cases on faith. Consider attaching key cases, highlighted, to your final memorandum, if this is appropriate in your workplace. **Isolated quotations from cases are useless. Provide specific references to the facts of the quoted case and a description of how they compare to the facts of case.**

- **Make sure that you have fully and accurately described the relevant facts, both favorable and unfavorable to your client.** Assume (because it is often true) that **you responsible for quality control of your document.** You are the person responsible for checking that the facts you describe can be demonstrated to be true and that **your description of the facts is unassailably accurate.**

- **Become a wordsmith.** Add specificity to your work. Be concrete. Be brief. If you must choose between clarity and brevity, though, choose clarity.

- **If you are using stock motions or forms,** as is the case in some offices that file an enormous volume of relatively routine documents, **be sure that all facts are accurate, that all references are to the case you are working on,** and that your document refers completely and accurately to your case, **and not some other case.**

- **Proofread your document.** Don't rely on spell check or grammar software or any other program as a proofreading substitute. Read your document as if you were a new reader, not the writer. Where possible, ask a colleague to read the document as well and provide comments.

- **Don't assume that the assigning attorney is the only person who will read your memorandum.** Other attorneys, future law clerks, and perhaps clients or others may read it, in connection with this or another matter with similar legal issues. Your discussion of the facts and law must be clear to someone unfamiliar with your case.

- Refer to Chapter 13, "A Writing Checklist: Remember Your Reader," one last time before submitting your assignment.

- **Keep a folder of your writing projects** for future reference, for writing samples, to review feedback obtained, and to develop a sense of your work product over time.

F.   PROJECT ASSIGNMENT CHECKLIST

Project Assignment Checklist

Name of Project

Client

Adverse Parties

Conflicts Check Performed

Date Received

Due Date

Interim Checkpoints

Follow-up Appointment: Set This up Now!

Assigning Attorney

Email and Phone

Preferred Way to Communicate

Others Working on Project

Format Suggested

Sample of Format to Use

Sample of Well-Executed Similar Project

Location of File

Copies of Existing Important Documents

Issue to be Researched

Facts

Suggested Research Sources

Standard Secondary Sources in Field

Others to be Copied on Assignment

Ultimate Purpose and Use of Document

Client's Goal or Goals

Particular Concerns/Issues of Emphasis

Suggested Amount of Time, Page Length

Indicate Whether Assigning Attorney Prefers Copies of Cases and Statutes Attached to Submitted Assignment

CHAPTER 12
RESEARCH

A. BE ALERT TO RESOURCES AVAILABLE

Find out as soon as you can what resources will be available, whether any limitations exist to your use of commercial online resources, and where the closest law library is located.

Many law clerks and new attorneys begin their work lives conducting research. For many, the vast and easily accessible resources available while in law school are gone. Commercial online research may be very limited, and preliminary research must be done using free online resources and books. The books available may not be as plentiful as in your law school library.

B. DON'T OVERLOOK THE CENTRALITY OF FACTS

Facts are central to any legal issue. It's critical that you have access to all the relevant facts as you conduct your legal research. What is relevant will change. For example, while you are working on the case, someone else may uncover new facts directly bearing on the legal issues you are researching. **In addition, in researching the law, you may identify the need for additional facts that applicable caselaw and statutes indicate are most relevant.**

C. ORGANIZE YOUR RESEARCH

1. Determine the Relevant Facts

a. Keep a list of questions about the facts of your case, so you can assist in discovery by identifying areas for further fact investigation.

b. Gather known facts, including relevant dates and key documents. Ask questions. Read the file. Keep in touch during your research with those people who know or need to know the facts as they are being uncovered. Share developing information from your research and analysis with them.

c. Note the jurisdiction: federal or state; if state, which state. If federal jurisdiction, and you are responsible for all research on the case, make sure you can affirmatively establish jurisdiction. Note whether there are any international aspects to your case.

d. Formulate the legal issue(s) **in writing** so that you have a research plan **before** you begin. Outline possible approaches and issues—**think first, then research. And then keep thinking.**

2. Find the Applicable Law

Remember that **another person,** including a librarian, your assigning attorney, or other attorneys or law clerks or paralegals in your office, **may be your best resource in beginning your research.**

a. Determine relevant area(s) of law.

b. Especially if you are unfamiliar with the areas of law you're researching, begin with general secondary authorities to get an overview of the law and to find citations to relevant statutes and cases. These include such sources as encyclopedias, ALRs, and other general jurisdiction-based legal resources.

c. If you are somewhat familiar with the area of law, consult specialized treatises. Ask a librarian or attorney practicing in the area for suggestions.

d. Consult jurisdiction-specific practice books and Rules of Court.

e. Find out if your office or subspecialty group in your office routinely uses certain research services or government websites. Ask whether there are specific legal organizations that provide online or other research tools. One example is AILA, American Immigration Lawyers Association, which provides a wealth of resources to new and veteran lawyers.

3.   A Statute or Regulation May Apply

a. Research statutes and regulations independently of case law.

b. Be sure of the precise statutory provision to be applied or interpreted. Check the effective dates of relevant provisions to be sure to apply the correct version of the statute.

c. Even if you know that a specific provision in a statute applies, familiarize yourself with surrounding sections of the statute as well as its overview and applicable definitions (usually at the beginning of the statute) to get the big picture. You may discover other relevant sections or provisions.

4. Find Relevant Cases

a. If your research involves a statute, start with statutory annotations or current secondary sources to find relevant cases.

b. Review case descriptions found in digests to develop a further sense of the law.

c. Conduct online searches and keep a record of your queries, the dates of your searches, databases researched, and results.

d. Pay close attention to the publication dates of cases and effective dates of statutes. If you are working with a statute, make sure to note the **date order of the relevant statutory provision and the cases you cite.**

e. Read cases that appear most relevant. When you find a relevant case, update it to make sure it's is still good law. That way you won't rely on an outdated source only to discover at the end of your research that it's no longer relevant.

5.   Read the Law

a. Think before you print.

b. Pay attention to facts of cases and how they compare to the facts of your own case.

c. Identify the court's holding, including the procedural posture of the case.

d. Identify other issues relevant to the matter, including those negative to your client.

6.   Keep a Research Log

a. Consult with others in your office to see whether the office has conventions or protocols that are generally followed in documenting your research.

b. Develop a system to document your steps, including the dates and details of your sources and the dates you enter them in your log, so that you or anyone inheriting your research can pick up where you have stopped.

c. Keep your Bluebook or ALWD Manual handy so that you can put your sources in proper citation format as you go along. Make sure you note page citations, so you don't need to retrace your steps.

7.   Update the Law While You Research

a. Shepardize, Shepardize, Shepardize.

b. KeyCite, KeyCite, KeyCite.

8.   Develop a Research Checklist

The web is full of excellent examples of research checklists and handbooks. Begin by looking at your law school library's website. Once you've seen four or five others, try your hand at creating your own checklist. **Create a checklist** that will prompt you to take the steps most important to your specific work setting and type of projects you typically work on. **As you become more experienced, you'll want to tweak it, adding some items and deleting others.**

The key to develop an organized approach to your research is to create a checklist

a. you will actually use;

b. will fully memorialize your steps; and

c. **will prompt you to take, and allow you to confirm, all necessary steps to comprehensively research your legal and factual issues.**

CHAPTER 13

A WRITING CHECKLIST: REMEMBER YOUR READER

Before you submit your document, take a few moments to think about your reader. Legal writing should not build suspense. Most readers want to know the answer first, then your reasons. Up until the point of finalizing your writing, your work has entailed mostly research, analysis, reasoning, and synthesis. **Now your writing must be transformed from a *process for you* to a *product for your reader*.**

A document's parts aren't necessarily written in the same order that they appear in the final product. Whether you call it an introduction or a conclusion, your document should usually lead with your conclusion and a recommendation for action, with reasons to follow.

This allows the reader to understand why the rest of the document is there: to support your conclusion and recommendation. This way, your reader will never have to ask, "Why are you telling me this?"

A. FINAL REVIEW BEFORE SUBMISSION

- Place your **conclusion up front**—in the document itself and within each section of your document.

- **Use topic sentences** so your reader knows what each paragraph is about.

- **Use transitions** so your reader will know how ideas and paragraphs relate to each other.

- **Eliminate unnecessary words** and phrases.

- **Eliminate passive voice** unless you intend it for a reason.

- **Refer to parties consistently** within the document.

- **Place subjects and verbs close together,** and modifying words close to the words they modify.

- **Eliminate complex words where possible** and replace with simple words.

- **Avoid the use of unfamiliar acronyms.** Your reader is likely not as familiar with them as you are.

- Make your organization apparent to the reader. **Use headings, white space, transitions,** and **coherent paragraphing.**

- **Make judicious use of repetition.** (Place your conclusion up front.)

- **Update and document your research.**

- **Run spell-check.**

- **Proofread** your document yourself. Spell-check is not a substitute for proofreading. If you can, have someone else proofread your document as well.

- **Paginate** the document.
- **Date the document.**
- Check for **accurate internal references** to sections of the document.
- **Review for punctuation errors** described in Section B.
- **Refer to cases and courts appropriately** as described in Section C.

B. IMPORTANT AND COMMON ERRORS TO AVOID

1. Do Not Omit the Last Comma in a Series

While the trend in *informal* writing is to omit the last comma in a series, don't do this! In other words, if each word in your list is intended to be a separate item, avoid ambiguity by including a comma before the *and, or*, or *nor*.

a. **Incorrect because ambiguous:** "I leave my estate in equal parts to Adam, Eve, Cain and Abel." (Divide into three or four parts?)

Correct because clear: "I leave my estate in equal parts to Adam, Eve, Cain, and Abel." (Divide into four parts).

Read *O'Connor v. Oakhurst Dairy* (1st Circuit, March 13, 2017), where the lack of a comma before the word "and" determined that the defendants could be held liable for millions of dollars in overtime pay.

See **The Redbook, § 1.3**, page 3.

2. Common Error: Commas, Periods, Quotation Marks

   a. **Incorrect:** He said, "Please turn out the lights when you are finished".

   Correct: He said, "Please turn out the lights when you are finished."

   b. **Incorrect:** Once he'd announced that he "was finished with this **place",** he slammed the door.

   Correct: Once he'd announced that he was "finished with this **place,"** he slammed the door.

   Note: American and British systems differ here; the American system often seems illogical.

   See **The Redbook, § 1.32**, p. 20.

3. Common Error: Confusing "Its" with "It's", and "Their" with "They're"

   a. **Incorrect: Its** easy to make mistakes.

   Correct: It's easy to make mistakes.

   b. **Incorrect:** He grabbed the jacket by **it's** sleeve and ran away.

   Correct: He grabbed the jacket by **its** sleeve and ran away.

  c. **Incorrect:** Good writers proofread **they're** documents.

  Correct: Good writers proofread **their** documents.

  See **The Redbook, § 7.13**, p. 94.

References are to Bryan A. Garner, *The Redbook, A Manual on Legal Style* (West Group 2002).

C.   WRITING ABOUT CASES AND COURTS

- Refer to your case as "this case" or (in an office memo) "our case."

- After you've given the full citation of a case, refer to it by name or abbreviated name.

- Describe the facts and the court's discussion in the past tense. Use present tense for case holdings and to talk about statutes currently in force.

- Compare cases to cases and facts to facts. Example: Don't say "Like *Hill*, Wold was arrested without a warrant." Say "Like the defendant in *Hill*, Wold was arrested without a warrant." or "Like *Hill*, this case involves a warrantless arrest."

- When citing a case, make it clear which court you're talking about. Name the court in full the first time you speak about it, and after that switch to "the court" if the reference is close enough to be understandable.

- When writing about several courts, always specify which court you are referring to. After giving the full name, refer to each court by a short form of its name (e.g., "the court of appeals," "the trial court").

- Don't refer to a court as "the lower court."

- **Remember which court you're addressing when writing briefs.** Example: when preparing an appeal to the Arizona Supreme Court, don't say, "In *Hill*, the Arizona Supreme Court. . . ." Instead say, "In *Hill*, this Court. . . ."

- Be precise in describing what a court did.

- Courts don't have feelings. Don't say the court felt something unless those words were used by the court. Instead, say the court noted, acknowledged, or recognized something.

- Don't say the "case" stated. Instead, say the "court" stated.

From Alan L. Dworsky, *The Little Book on Legal Writing* (Fred B. Rothman & Co., pp 55–63, 1992).

D.   BECOMING A BETTER WRITER

If you want to become a better writer, we suggest that you find out who the best writers are in your office and read what they've written. Then go buy a copy of Terri LeClercq, *Expert Legal Writing* (the University of Texas Press 2002). Work through it methodically, but first look at Chapter 17, which alone is worth the purchase price. A three-page chapter, it features "Quick Tricks for Organization," a primer on **what to do when your deadline is moved up on you expectedly.** It offers concrete steps to quickly ensure that your document is organized, provides the reader with a roadmap, has a conclusion, is coherent, and has been spell-checked. While not a recipe for perfection, it is a handy guide to producing a useful document when you've run out of time and must turn in your assignment NOW.

CHAPTER 14

FEEDBACK

"Feedback is the breakfast of champions."
Ken Blanchard

I would describe myself as overly sensitive to criticism, and too dependent on positive feedback from others.

Student Journal

When I have a question about an issue, or an area of law, it is like pulling teeth out of an alligator to find an attorney for help. They are all so busy.

Student Journal

One of the most frequent experiences of new clerks and lawyers is their feeling of "being in the dark" about their performance. This is usually because they haven't received feedback from the person assigning the work (the "Assigning Attorney") or don't know how to interpret the feedback they are receiving.

This chapter will address when and how to obtain feedback; how to comprehend and accept it; and how to put it to good use.

Before turning to these key issues, we need to stress a fundamental point about feedback: **your reasons for wanting it** and your Assigning Attorney's **reasons for giving it are often entirely different.** Understanding the difference may help you feel better if placed in a situation where you want, but seem unable to get, feedback. It may also help you develop new strategies about how and where to get feedback.

A. THE GIVE AND TAKE OF FEEDBACK

1. Why Do People Want Feedback?

First, we want to know that the job we are working on or have just finished is the one that was expected. We like to know that we are earning our keep, and that our employer doesn't regret providing us workspace, a computer, co-workers, and, perhaps, a paycheck. If you're working in the summer before the third year of law school, you may also be looking for signs that you'll receive a permanent offer at the end of the summer. In other words, we want *basic reassurance*. For many of us, especially at the beginning of a job as we enter a new profession, basic reassurance can be the most important reason we want feedback.

Second, we want to *develop our skills* so that we can do a better job. In other words, *we want to get better at what we do*. There are many other reasons that we want feedback, but these two are likely common to most of us.

2. Why Do People Give Feedback?

People who give feedback don't have as great a need to give it as the people who want it have to get it. For example, the work you produce is often needed for a larger project—work that has a function in a greater whole. You are hoping to receive feedback, but your Assigning Attorney's focus is getting the whole project accomplished capably, on time, cost-efficiently, and with satisfactory results.

The kind of feedback received in practice can differ dramatically, from the kind of feedback received in law school. If you've received extensive written comments on your writing in law school, you may expect the same in practice. Yet few practicing attorneys provide detailed explanations alongside their revisions to a document, since it is not essential to completion of the project. Related to this, the pace of practice and pressure to move quickly to the next case, client, or crisis, conspire against consistent and comprehensive feedback.

Let's look for a moment at a day in the life of a typical Assigning Attorney. We'll call her Judith. Her life, like that of most lawyers and judges, is pressure-and deadline-driven. No sooner is one case completed than the rest of the back-burner cases and projects rear their ugly heads.

Today, because Judith is relatively high in the organization, she is dealing with a tricky personnel issue that has been simmering for a month but has now reached full boil. She has an oral argument tomorrow for which a mooting session is scheduled this afternoon. On her way to the office, she received a call that one of the firm's partners is in the hospital with inexplicable internal bleeding; he was scheduled to argue a motion early this afternoon, so she needs to find someone to cover for him. She arrives at the office without having had time to read her e-mail.

You submitted your first research project yesterday afternoon on time, and are anxious to know what she thinks. She walks into the office and flies by you in the hall. You are sure that she is avoiding you because she cannot bring herself to tell you how horrible your memo was.

In reality, she doesn't even know you've turned it in, and hasn't had time to read it. Once she *does* read it, she will fold it into the document for which it was prepared, and ask a senior associate to put the final touches on the project. She will then turn to the day's next emergency, totally unaware of your urgent need for feedback.

From the point of view of the Assigning Attorney, if the work is good, the project moves along, and no feedback is needed. If it needs improvement, you may, or may not, be the one asked to make the revisions.

In this case, and in general, there is a bit of built-in tension around feedback—the person who wants it feels that he "needs it," and the person in the most natural position to give it may view it as unnecessary or as requiring additional work unrelated to the central task. In other words, as the seeker of feedback, you are focused more on yourself; the provider of feedback is more focused on completing the project on schedule and using it for its intended purpose.

B.   WHEN AND HOW WILL YOU GET IT?

Many firms and agencies have well-developed standards for providing feedback that include guidelines for both quality and timing of feedback. In those cases, the feedback mechanisms, and perhaps even forms and checklists, are set. But let's assume that feedback is not something your firm or agency regularly provides, or that the established methods of feedback aren't being followed or seem insufficient to you.

1.   Preparing the Stage for Useful Feedback

You can prepare the stage for obtaining useful feedback by learning what is expected *before* you begin the project. This is important and independent of any considerations of feedback. **You simply must be sure that you understand the assignment.**

Many of us have endured the frustrating experience of learning, only after we've turned in a project, that the memo we've created was not what the Assigning Attorney expected. Thus, much of what passes for feedback at the *end* of the project is really information about what had been expected—but was either not clearly described or was not clearly understood—at the beginning of the project.

To avoid the frustration of "information-that-could-have-been-very-helpful-if-I'd-only-known-it-earlier, gather it ahead of time." When you receive feedback, you want it to focus the work you did, not the work you should have done. See Chapter 11, "Managing Written Assignments," for specific ways to get the information you need at the beginning of assignments, along with a useful Project Assignment Checklist.

I have learned that knowing how to ask the right questions is critical. If I can get a better sense of what the assigning attorney needs at a project's outset, I can better manage her expectations and mine.

Student Journal

2.   During the Project

Communicate at appropriate intervals with the Assigning Attorney or with others who might be able to help you. For instance, when receiving your assignment, you might ask the best way and how frequently to check in, depending on the magnitude and time frame of the project. If the Assigning Attorney is busy, he may ask you to check in via e-mail instead of an in-person meeting, or may ask you to meet with someone else on the project. In some situations, a legal assistant or other non-lawyer on the team may be the best person to assist you. In fact, as one summer intern learned, sometimes the best help you get is not from the person you thought or hoped it would be.

I have mixed feelings about the associate attorneys' level of experience, because I wanted to learn from an expert. On the positive side, I can learn from two people who are not so experienced that they have forgotten how to explain things to a novice.

Student Journal

In consulting with people other than the Assigning Attorney, **you need to be sensitive to the social and political environment in the office.** While many questions—such as those about document format, office procedures, research resources—can be answered by several people, other questions are more appropriately directed to the Assigning Attorney herself.

Learn the habits of people who have information you'll need. Is first thing in the morning a bad time to call or knock on his door, or is that the best time to catch 'him? Is e-mail the best means of communicating, or does he prefer phone or in-person conversations? Appointments or drop-in? Don't be shy about asking him—and anyone else you work with—for preferences about the best time and manner of communicating.

Before **requesting direction or assistance, first ask yourself whether there is anything more that you can do.** Use your creativity and initiative to obtain all the information you can *efficiently* find on your own before going to someone else. For instance, if you are working on a research project with three relatively independent issues, and you have questions on the first, work on the other two before seeking advice. Efficiency often suggests batching all your questions to ask in one discussion, rather than asking bit by bit.

Once you *do* approach someone with questions, remember that *your* case may not be foremost on the mind of the person you are tracking down for help. **Be prepared to give a quick description of the case (the name, the issue, the pertinent facts) before launching into your questions.**

Before beginning the conversation, formulate the bottom line question or questions you need to have answered and prioritize them. Ask yourself, "What do I need to know before I leave this conversation?" **Make notes, so you'll be sure to cover all your questions.**

3.   When You Turn Your Project In

When turning your assignment in, now would be the time to identify questions you still have about the substance or organization of the project. One of us used this approach when in practice, by providing a brief cover memo identifying areas of concern.

For instance, if you are dissatisfied with your discussion of a certain issue, but feel it is absolutely the best you can do, you might consider saying something like,

- "My discussion of X case is the best argument I can come up with, but I think we could make better use of it." Or,

- "I've organized the memo with A as our most powerful argument, followed by B. This does expose our vulnerability on X fact, but the legal argument is stronger. If you think that we should reverse the order of the arguments, we could do so; it would minimize the emphasis on X fact."

You can also include a short statement, possibly in your cover e-mail or, if you are handing in a hard copy of your project, a handwritten note on a post-it, asking whether there is anything you can do to improve the project or be of further help.

4.   After the Project

When working with attorneys who are not good at giving feedback, or in organizations where the culture does not promote feedback, be **prepared to structure the conversation** in a way that relates directly to the Assigning Attorney's goals for the project. The more specific you can be in phrasing your questions, the more helpful it will be. Here are some examples of specific questions:

- "Did you have to do work that you had hoped I would do? Did I go into too much or not enough detail of the cases?"

- "I was unsure of how to approach X case. It seemed helpful on one issue, but not on another issue. Did you agree with my analysis? Would you have approached it differently?"

- "Was the document organized in a useful order? Is there anything you wish had been included? Would it have been helpful if I had provided copies of the cases?"

5. Never

Finally, **on some projects and with some people, you may never, ever receive useful feedback.** You will learn what Attorney X thinks only when you hear, possibly from a third party, that X thought your project was a disaster or that X thought you'd done something very well. Attorneys like X may be very busy and may not have the time or the inclination to provide feedback. Or they may simply be incapable of or unwilling to slow down enough to teach as well as use. The best way to deal with that is to look elsewhere for the reassurance and skills development that most of us seek from feedback.

"Feedback" doesn't always have to come from someone else. Sometimes the most useful thing you can do is ask for a copy of the final document and review it yourself to see how much of your work was used, and how it was modified. By learning how to extract feedback through observation and inference, you'll be able to do your own self-assessment.

Above all, **don't waste your time wondering or worrying about whether you've received *enough* feedback—find another way to learn.**

C. OVERCOMING DEFENSIVENESS

We often must overcome our natural defensiveness when receiving feedback. That defensiveness most frequently asserts itself when we are *actually* hoping (sometimes unconsciously) to gain reassurance, rather than information about the project or how we can improve our skills. When we are defensive, it is hard to comprehend the feedback.

We peer edit each other's motions. Initially, the comments and corrections bothered me. I told myself that some of them were not based upon an objective standard, but rather on personal choice and style. I decided to just make the "objective" corrections, such as grammar, spelling, and citation and ignore the "subjective" ones. But then I realized that some changes I previously labeled as being subjective actually gave my writing a crisper, more formal voice that was more appropriate for submission to the court.

After that, I changed my view of the comments and corrections and, in the process, became more confident in my legal writing. The comments and corrections were not personal attacks on my writing ability in general, but were improvements upon a specific piece of writing that help shape my legal writing voice.

Student Journal

Especially if what we seek is reassurance, it sometimes takes a while to allow feedback to register. We want to focus more on why we did something than on why someone is suggesting we do otherwise. We resist the merits of the feedback. For a moment (or longer), we don't care about developing our skills or learning from someone with more experience. We want to explain why we weren't wrong, or at least why we were reasonable to have written what we wrote. Perhaps we actually want to convince the other person that no one made a mistake in hiring us.

Sometimes it takes a few hours or a few days to "sit with it" and view the feedback as it relates to *our work* and *not to ourselves*. Once we are ready to accept feedback for what it's worth, we can comprehend it. Ideally, after you receive feedback, especially if written, you'll take the opportunity to talk with the person who gave it, to make sure you understand it completely.

Another useful way to learn from the changes made to your writing is to talk to another attorney or law clerk who has worked with your Assigning Attorney. By learning more about his patterns and preferences in wording, structure, and format, you'll be better able to meet those "unspoken standards" on your next project. It can be helpful, too, in terms of understanding and coping with particularities in editing style. For example, had you known that he was a prolific editor, to the point of making minute changes in wording, you wouldn't have almost had a heart attack when you found a (very) red-lettered copy of your draft memorandum on your desk!

D.   PUTTING FEEDBACK TO GOOD USE

Not all feedback is equal. Feedback can be mined for many kinds of information. **For instance, it can provide information about any of the following, and more:**

1. About the Project

- Purposes of the project of which you'd been unaware;

- Key information (for instance, facts) about the project that you didn't know; and

- Document conventions and styles of your firm or agency.

2. About Your Supervisor's Expectations

- Personal preferences of your supervisor;

- The similarity of your understanding of the project compared to your supervisor's;

- Idiosyncrasies of your supervisor that you didn't know about; and

- Your supervisor's assumptions about your role in the project of which you were unaware.

3. About Skills You Need to Improve

- Aspects of your legal analysis that need correction or improvement; and

- Aspects of your writing that need correction or improvement; and

- Aspects of your communication patterns that can be modified to better suit your supervisor's personal preferences.

4. Information About Yourself

- Assumptions you made that were not accurate;

- Habits in your own work that you had not realized;

- Your physical limitations—for instance, your inability to work all night and function the next day;

- How you deal with frustrations and anxieties, and your emotional responses when in those types of situations, as well as how you would *like* to be able to respond; and

- The difficulty or ease you have in applying to future projects what your supervisor says about your work.

5. General

- Approaches to organization of a document that are new to you;

- Ways of thinking about a legal problem that are new to you;

- Ways one reader (your supervisor) interpreted your writing (either as you intended or as you didn't intend);

- Aspects of your approach to the project that were helpful; and

- General expectations about project drafting, timing, delivery, length, and level of formality.

Finally, of course, **your own response to the feedback you receive is information that will be important.**

As is evident from the previous list, the usefulness of the feedback you receive will vary. Some of it will be useful because it helps you understand more about the culture and expectations of your workplace and some of the people in it. Some of it will be useful because it provides the opportunity to develop specific legal skills of research or writing or organization. **Much of it will be useful because of what you infer from it, rather than because particular words were spoken or points made in the explicit feedback you were given.**

Once you can view feedback as a reflection on your work, rather than a judgment about your worth as a person, you'll learn something that you can put to good use. When you reflect on your own responses to those comments, you'll likely learn something about *yourself* as well.

E. FEEDBACK AND JUDGMENT

As we mentioned, not all feedback is equal. If you show your work to more than one person, you may receive contradictory suggestions. This is because **much of legal writing, and legal work as a whole, is a matter of judgment.** You know from law school as well as from other experiences, that there are many legitimate approaches to most questions, including approaches to the assignments that you'll receive as a law clerk or new lawyer.

At some point, you'll **face the need to deal with contradictory messages, or with messages from supervising attorneys with whom you disagree.** Sometimes you rightly won't want to follow suggestions; at other times, you'll only later appreciate the wisdom of suggested changes. Our advice is to pick your battles carefully: if your disagreements are about style, and your name is not the first one on the document (and it may not be on the document at all), it's almost always best to follow the suggestions of the senior person. Sometimes your disagreement may raise questions of professional ethics (accuracy in statement of facts, in describing what a case stands for, or other matters raising questions of professional responsibility). If so, you need to make sure you understand clearly the points of disagreement before you speak up; and, when you do speak up, explain your concerns clearly and persuasively.

Finally, remember to **think of feedback as a small component of learning how to do your job and improve your performance.** Feedback is only one part of a continuous loop of learning about what your project is, what the expectations are for your part of the project, and who can provide ongoing information as you try to complete your work.

If you focus on learning, rather than on feedback specifically, you can learn in other ways. For example, in general discussion, ask experienced attorneys how *they* best learned when they were new attorneys, what their greatest challenges were in learning to write effectively and efficiently, and how they overcame them. Ask what advice they have for you as a new attorney who is anxious to develop excellent skills. If you ask outside the context of a specific project or assignment, they may feel more comfortable giving explicit advice and discussing problems that new attorneys often face early in their careers.

Eventually, you will become an educated consumer of feedback. You will know what to accept and what to reject. You will develop confidence in making your own writing decisions and will be better able to assess your own work. Feedback will always be useful. Get it, think about it, and exercise your own judgment about when to use it.

That's when *your* name will be going on the letters, the complaint, the brief. Until then, we hope this helps!

CHAPTER 15

IN-PERSON COMMUNICATION

*"There is only one rule for being a
good talker—learn to listen."*
Christopher Morley

Outstanding advocates are, first and foremost, **good listeners.** This is because to communicate effectively, the advocate must *first* understand the questions posed by the judge—this requires good listening.

Not limited to oral advocacy or litigation contexts, good listening skills (and the attitude of openness to what another is saying that goes with it) are vital whenever interpersonal communication is attempted. In this chapter, we discuss other **settings where communication skills, including listening skills, are so essential, yet fundamental, that they are often overlooked.** We'll include traditional, face-to-face communications as well as "real-time" conversations that are facilitated by technology and occur between people who are in different locations.

The qualities we will emphasize are vital to constructive interactions with clients and co-workers and apply as well to *any* situation where people are trying to speak with, understand, and be understood by each other.

The suggestions summarized below reflect our own personal experiences as well as the insights of practicing attorneys and judges we have consulted about the oral communication skills of new attorneys, particularly in the non-litigation context. We posed the question, "What interpersonal skills do you wish you had developed before beginning your practice, and what oral communication skills do you wish new attorneys possessed upon beginning their work with you?"

A. VALUES UNDERLYING GOOD COMMUNICATION

- **Respect** for those who are speaking (especially clients).

- **Honesty,** such as telling your Supervising Attorney that you don't understand an assignment or know how to begin working on it, or telling a client there are limits to what you or the system can achieve, when knowing those limits will disappoint your client.

- **Openness** to receiving new information that may change your original perceptions.

- **Empathy,** particularly with clients, but also with attorneys, non-lawyers, court staff, and others with whom you interact.

- **Preparation,** which should be as thorough as if you were about to attend a meeting. To do otherwise is to risk wasting time and perhaps squandering an opportunity. Ask yourself, "What do I hope to accomplish and what goals do the other parties have? How can I best structure the conversation?"

- **Mutual sharing** of information and points of view, so that all parties feel heard.

- **Clarity,** so that all participants have a mutual understanding of the *information* shared (though they may not agree regarding the facts, application of law, etc.).

B.   IN GENERAL

- **Listening** is key in any conversation. Focus on what other people are saying; try to understand what they intend to say, and the importance *to them* of what they are saying.

- Listening skills are crucial in **teleconferences** and other types of distance communication, because visual cues are absent and maintaining focus is more difficult than when talking in person. Don't be afraid to ask someone to repeat a statement that seems confusing or was garbled during transmission. Also, if you would smile while speaking in person, smile while participating in a teleconference—the same meaning will be transmitted through your voice.

- Both you and your listeners are constantly giving and receiving **nonverbal cues;** learn to "read" them. For example, crossed arms, lack of eye contact, and doodling on a notepad are likely sending a message that you aren't listening when it is the other person's time to talk. Your awareness of nonverbal cues should affect the speed and tone of your voice, your facial expression and body language, as well as what issues you address, how you phrase them, and in what order.

- Overcome your timidity about asking for clarification, and **ask questions.** If *you* have a question or need additional clarification, more than likely others do too.

- **Get to the point early,** unless the conversation warrants a longer, more detailed discussion.

- **Know when a face-to-face conversation is warranted.** Where complex or emotionally charged matters are at issue, especially when the parties have a long-term working relationship, an in-person conversation can help to avoid misunderstandings.

C. COMMUNICATING WITH CLIENTS

- **Establish credibility.** Think about how to do this before meeting with a client. Prepare, listen, respond, ask questions.

- **Give clients your undivided attention.** Avoid multitasking when you are with a client (or anyone else). For instance, clear your desk, take no phone calls, allow no interruptions, and don't check your e-mail while meeting. If your office is a "working" office (meaning very messy), consider meeting in a conference room.

- When speaking with clients, **put yourself in their shoes** and try to see things from their perspective.

- To learn your client's story, **ask open-ended questions as well as specific questions related to specific facts.** Open-ended questions may reveal important information that you didn't know was relevant. When asking questions, learn to tolerate silence, giving others time to think.

- Try to **avoid compound questions.**

- Speak to clients and non-lawyers in **plain English.** When you need to use a legal term, explain it without being patronizing.

- **Don't rush.** Let the client's story unfold at a comfortable pace while at the same time respectfully keeping the client on track. You may learn important facts that you hadn't anticipated.

- Conversation is a two-way street; **converse *with*, don't speak *at*,** your clients.

- **Rephrase the issues** after the client speaks, to verify that you have complete and correct information.

- **Clients may not understand** what you say the first time. You may need to find at least two other ways to repeat it.

- To determine what you can realistically achieve for your client, you need to know the other side's perspective. At some point, **ask your client for the other side's view.** This has the added benefit of helping your client gain a realistic idea of what is possible.

- **Be realistic up front.** Focus on what is possible and tell the client your own and the system's limitations (in terms of your area of expertise as well as your willingness to take, or not take, certain steps).

- **Identify and periodically reconfirm your client's goals.** If your client's goals have changed over time, the action you planned earlier may now conflict with those new goals. Don't make assumptions. Ask questions. Sometimes when asked, your client will articulate a goal that surprises you.

- Don't be afraid to **identify and discuss emotional issues that may accompany legal ones.** Know when to suggest alternative professional consultation. This is part of knowing your own limits and acknowledging them to your client.

- Especially when reporting back to a client, **get to the point early.** Present backup data to support your recommendations, and know when to provide the bottom line.

- **Commit to ongoing communication with your client** and to responding to his phone calls and other communications promptly.

D. LEADING OTHER MEMBERS
OF YOUR TEAM

- Develop **positive and respectful relationships** with members of your team.

- **Take a genuine interest in your co-workers.** When you (and they) have time, interact on matters of common interest unrelated to work—children, sports, snow, heat, or movies.

- **Give clear assignments,** with realistic, clearly stated deadlines and priorities. When on the receiving end of an assignment, make sure that you have the same information.

- **Check in frequently to see if questions need answers.** Initiate interaction.

- **Treat members of your team as if they are your most important clients.** Without your feedback and support, they may not be able to take the next steps on their assignments.

- **Express appreciation and thanks for work well done,** as well as work done under pressure and work done with good humor. Notice details and be specific.

- **Update members of your team,** including those who are not lawyers, on the progress and final resolution of cases and projects.

E.   MAKING MISTAKES

- **Ask questions if you don't understand something and do it sooner rather than later.** It is better to admit ignorance and get more information than to pretend to "know it all," and get it all wrong.

- **Ask lots of questions, pay attention to the answers and remember them,** so that you don't keep making the same mistakes.

- **It is never OK to make up answers** (sometimes they don't exist). It's not a good idea to speculate either.

- Acknowledge and **learn from your mistakes.**

- **Never blame anyone else for your mistakes.**

- Learn how to **deal with someone else's mistake** in a way that acknowledges the error and helps correct it without attaching blame.

F.   CLOSING THOUGHTS

- Your courtesy to colleagues—broadly defined—will determine your professional reputation.

- **Conversation is an *exchange of dialogue*,** where neither person monopolizes the conversation.

- **Silence is an important part of conversation;** learn to be comfortable with it.

- **Avoid making snap judgments** based on someone's appearance, unfamiliar or unique accent, or use of poor grammar and other speech patterns that may not appeal to you. On the other hand, try to become aware of and avoid any habits of speech *you* may have that others may find distracting. Be aware of the possibility of cultural differences. See Chapter 7, "Cultural Differences."

- Be **aware of your unconscious body language** and how it may communicate in ways you don't intend, as well as ways you might use non-verbal cues to place proper emphasis on your meaning.

- **Develop and refine your own unique style.** Watch other attorneys and team members at every opportunity and you will see that many different communication styles can be equally effective.

CHAPTER 16

E-MAIL USES AND ABUSES

*"Everyone wanted to say so much that no
one said anything in particular."*
Rudyard Kipling, from *Captains Courageous*

E-mail has likely saved and has certainly ruined many careers. This brief discussion alerts you to some of the costs and benefits of relying on e-mail in a professional setting.

E-mail is subject to the same considerations of audience, purpose, and context that apply to all forms of communication. But because it combines a number of special characteristics, e-mail can be both more dangerous and more useful than other forms of communication.

The combined characteristics of speed and volume (in all of its senses) are what make e-mail such a powerful tool, for better or worse. It can be produced and sent *very* quickly. It invites immediate reaction, removing the likelihood of reflection that other forms of communication allow. Finally, a single recipient of a message can increase its volume by simply forwarding it to an infinite number of other people. This allows a warm discussion to heat up quickly.

Paradoxically, while the "delete" feature gives e-mails a transitory feeling, they can live forever. Our experience has been that it is only the e-mail you want desperately to find that disappears; the others—the ones you wish you'd never sent—seem to be permanently retrievable from a number of inboxes. Remember, too, that e-mails sent using an employer's server become part of the employer's permanent records, as if they had been printed and saved in a folder in a file cabinet.

Yet none of these concerns adequately addresses the central duty of lawyers to protect their clients' information from both deliberate and inadvertent disclosure. Your employer should have in a place a series of measures to protect client information. We implore you to learn the formal and informal rules, guidelines and conventions used by your organization and follow them. In addition, consider the following tips.

A. GREAT USES FOR E-MAIL

- Seeking and providing information, especially non-controversial information.

- Communicating messages quickly and to many people, so that they can read at their convenience.

- Transmitting documents.

- Conducting straightforward business.

- Scheduling meetings.

- Exchanging ideas, with two caveats: first, some people may be reluctant to participate due to the lack of give-and-take in e-mail discussions and, second, if conversation slows down and/or the process becomes unproductive, you should find a way to continue the discussion using a different medium.

B.   LESS USEFUL AND POSSIBLY DANGEROUS USES

- Settling disputes.

- Sharing nuanced and confidential information.

- Emotionally charged discussions.

- Communicating bad news (unless there is no better way).

C.   GOOD PRACTICES FOR USE OF E-MAIL

- State your subject clearly in the Subject Line.

- Make sure that outgoing e-mails say what you mean them to say before sending them.

- If sending a long message, consider using an attachment.

- Avoid using complicated formatting such as centered lines, excessive tabulation, and graphics that might not be recognized by your recipients' software.

- Be sparing in the use of capitalization and avoid emoticons and texting acronyms altogether (other than those which are very commonly used, e.g., FYI).

- If you use "Reply" to an old e-mail simply to use the address(es), be sure to delete all extraneous information and insert a new Subject Line.

- Read incoming e-mails *carefully* and *completely* before responding.

- If you have an immediate negative reaction to an e-mail, pause before responding. If you decide to respond, consider showing your response to someone you trust before sending it.

- Use "Reply to all" only when the information will be useful to the entire group. For example, the person scheduling a committee meeting may send an e-mail to the committee members asking about available dates. In this case, there is no need for each recipient to "Reply to all."

- Always write e-mails with the unfortunate assumption that they may be forwarded without notice; similarly, forward e-mails of others with extreme caution.

- If you forward a message to someone, make sure it contains no information that would inadvertently embarrass the original sender or the new recipient. Also, consider adding the e-mail's author to the Cc: line.

- If you *do* forward a message, indicate what action you intend your recipient to take, unless you know it is clear to the recipient. If you are sending for information only, indicate FYI in the Subject line.

- **Observe the e-mail habits of those with whom you work** so that, if you need a quick or complete response, you will know when to use e-mail and when to use the phone. For instance, some people respond to only one question sent in an e-mail, even if the e-mail contains three questions.

- An email with phrases such as "could you explain," "what did you mean," and "I'm unclear about" should most likely be handled with a phone call or face-to-face discussion.

- Learn (by observing) the level of formality *and* the norms for salutations and closings used for e-mails in your workplace generally and by individuals specifically, so that you can avoid inadvertently offending your readers.

- **Beware of autocomplete.** Make sure you are sending your e-mail to the addressee you intend. E-mail applications often complete e-mail addresses automatically after the first few letters of the address. Many people in your contact list share the beginning letters of their e-mail addresses. Confidential and sensitive information has been sent to journalists and other unintended recipients because of careless addressing of e-mails, with disastrous results to the client, the attorney, and the law firm involved. **Slow down.**

D. PERSONAL AND WORK E-MAIL
DISTINGUISHED

- Learn your agency's, firm's, or organization's
  e-mail customs. The level of informality used
  in instant-messaging or e-mails for personal
  use is often inappropriate for professional use.
  This sounds a lot like the second-to-last point
  made in Section C. It is. *It's important enough
  to say twice.*

- If your employer has a policy on the use of
  office e-mail for personal conversations,
  adhere to it. Better yet, simply avoid using
  work e-mail for personal conversations. E-
  mails sent from your employer's server are
  never private, regardless of whether they are
  on your personal account or theirs.

- Whether your message is private or not,
  assume that someone who is not the intended
  recipient will read it.

E. ALTERNATIVES TO E-MAIL

- Consider whether a different form of
  communication might serve you better than e-
  mail. If you have not had a face-to-face
  conversation with someone in a while, a walk
  down the hall or a phone call might be a
  valuable way of maintaining your
  relationship. E-mail is efficient, but the give-
  and-take of a conversation often is more
  effective and has benefits that e-mail is
  unable to produce.

- Notice if others with whom you work use different media for communicating—if so, consider following their lead every now and then. If someone only calls you on the phone, consider occasionally calling instead of e-mailing. If you work with someone who clearly prefers face-to-face interaction, make a point of initiating in-person discussions from time to time.

F.   INCOMING E-MAIL AS INTERRUPTIONS

- Because e-mail is ubiquitous, it has become another form of interruption that we must consciously manage. Legal research and writing require intense concentration, which is difficult to maintain when e-mails announce their presence in the very space where we are researching or writing. If you are focusing on each e-mail as it comes in, find a way to structure your e-mail life so that you can focus on tasks that require your full attention.

While e-mail is our focus in this chapter, many of these concepts also apply to other forms of communication. See Chapter 15, "In-Person Communication" and especially Chapter 17, "E-Professionalism," for a discussion of other principles related to communication and technology.

CHAPTER 17
E-PROFESSIONALISM

*"Where is the knowledge we have
lost in information?"*

T. S. Eliot

If you were born after 1985, you're what is referred to as a "digital native," someone who grew up with computers and the internet. In other words, you grew up in the digital culture. Technology is second nature to you, but the rest of us are quickly catching up. According to the Pew Research Center, which has gathered research on the internet for 15 years, **more than 86% of adults in the U.S. now use internet-related technology.** We use it for a growing number of activities—to make financial investments and handle our banking; to research medical issues and find specialists to treat them; to purchase everything from our next vacation to next week's groceries; to stay informed about today's news and tomorrow's weather forecast; to read books, play games, watch movies; and to stay in touch with colleagues, family and friends.

However, to be proficient at something does not always mean to use it wisely. **The qualities that make the internet a valuable tool for communication—speed, immediacy, and the power to reach a broad audience—also magnify its potential for unintended and potentially harmful consequences.**

Because of its implications for law students and new professionals, the responsible use of social media both in the workplace and at home—we'll call it e-professionalism—is increasingly important. In this chapter, we'll discuss: (a) the characteristics of social media that warrant new and different guidelines than those used for more traditional means of communication; (b) ways that law schools, legal organizations, and legal employers might be using social media to monitor the e-behavior of students and new professionals; and (c) guidelines for more professional use of social media.

We'll use the term "social media" to refer to interactive platforms such as Facebook, Instagram, Twitter, LinkedIn, Snapchat, You Tube, Pinterest, online dating sites, blogs, discussion boards and interactive websites, but *not* e-mail. For more information about e-mail, see Chapter 16, "E-mail Uses and Abuses."

A.   CHARACTERISTICS OF SOCIAL MEDIA

1.   Audience—Intended and Unintended

Social media is a great vehicle for staying connected with people. With a single keystroke, you can send a message, a photograph, a video, or a document to a single individual or to a broad, generalized audience. Likewise, **with a keystroke, recipients of your message can share it, re-post it, and re-tweet it to an unknown number of "others," who can indiscriminately pass it on . . . again and again.** Distribution of your message doesn't necessarily end there, either. It may be found by anyone searching for your name on the internet, which might include an employer who is screening your credentials before making a job offer or a client who was impressed by your handling of his case and interested in knowing more about you.

A family member could also share your post with others, not realizing the potentially negative repercussions. For example, a recruiting coordinator at a mid-sized law firm told us about accidentally stumbling on something posted by the mother of one of their new associates. She announced: "We're thrilled to tell everyone that [son's name] has accepted a job offer! The firm was his second choice, but the pay was so high that he couldn't turn it down!"

Even if your original message contained personal, private, and/or confidential information that was not really meant for sharing, it is now out there for all the world to see.

Unfortunately, this kind of thing happens far too often, not only to law students and new professionals. It happens across all disciplines, and to professionals with all levels of experience. **There is something about the immediacy, informality, and seeming-intimacy of social media that causes people to communicate in thoughtless and impulsive ways** that are, at a minimum, inappropriate and, at times, unethical. Thus, we read of the law student whose blog included accounts of confidential strategy sessions that she attended during her internship with a public defender's office. An experienced attorney is disciplined after the judge discovers photos on Facebook that show him at a party, despite having requested a continuance due to a death in the family.

2.   Content

Content found on social media platforms can result in misunderstandings and crossed communications that reflect negatively on the personal and professional images of users as well as on their employers. We'll discuss a few examples below.

- *"Innocent" disclosure of inappropriate and possibly confidential information.* Do you really want potential employers or clients to know about your religious and political views? Or that you had a little bit too much to drink last night? Probably not, yet this type of information can readily be discovered on social media. Other topics to avoid are matters to do with sexual activity, as well as alcohol and substance use and abuse, and both your medical history and that of your family members. Photos of yourself in bathing suits or suggestive clothing are probably not appropriate for mass consumption, either.

It should be obvious that the rules of professional ethics apply to social media, as they do to all other types of communications, and so it is difficult to understand why an attorney would broadcast confidential information about an "unnamed, unidentifiable" client. Usually, because of the high level of detail needed to tell an entertaining story, the posting contains sufficient identifiable information and someone *does* end up identifying the client.

- ***Perceived vs. intended meaning.* Readers of social media must interpret postings without the visual and oral cues such as facial expressions, gestures, and tone of voice, that normally add meaning to our words.** Nuance, too, is lost in translation. For example, something that you meant as a joke and, perhaps, posted with a winking-face emoticon, might be perceived by someone as a statement of fact or, worse, a veiled threat. A sarcastic remark could be interpreted as a form of online bullying. What seems an innocent comment to one person is a demeaning remark to another, and one person's use of slang is another's "bad" language.

- ***Quantity vs. quality of information.* With** so much content flooding into their computers each day, and no time (or, in some cases, no inclination) to thoroughly read, verify, and filter each item, some people have a tendency to forward everything on indiscriminately which, in turn, floods *your* "news feed" with information that may or may not be true. What you may be passing on to others may more and more be based on social media algorithms that populate your view of their sites with one-sided information designed to more closely match your values, beliefs, and preferences.

This means that, if social media is one of your chief sources for news (as it is for almost 60% of the U.S. population these days) and you want to be well-informed and well-rounded, **you must actively reach out for verified news from a wider variety of legitimate sources.** To maintain your personal and professional reputations, be discriminating about what you pass along to others, too.

- *Personal vs. professional representation.* Do you know whether people attribute your contributions on social media to you personally, or to your employer? If you post something about a topic related to your area of practice, might people assume that you have "insider" information? Consider these issues before posting.

3. Permanence

Your post was regrettable and you'd like it to simply disappear. There are ways to remove postings on social media, but the process is lengthy and complicated, can be expensive, and the results are not guaranteed. Moreover, **what has been read and heard and forwarded by others cannot be "un-read and un-heard and un-forwarded";** damaged reputations are hard to heal, and esteem is hard to regain.

4. Discoverability

Not one social media platform guarantees the confidentiality of its content. Like it or not, despite protestation that "what's private should stay private," you must consider everything that you say or pass along on social media as a form of public speech, despite all of the controls that you may have placed on it.

B. ORGANIZATIONAL MONITORING OF SOCIAL MEDIA

We know that many websites, including social media, monitor our online activity for marketing purposes, but you might be surprised to learn that other organizations are also doing so, for other reasons.

1. Pre-Screening

If an applicant's background raises red flags, the Florida Board of Bar Examiners has a policy that allows it to review personal websites and social media on a case-by-case basis. Representatives from several bar associations have also told us that **they consider "all available information that is relevant to an applicant's fitness and character to practice law."** Does this include social media? We think it is highly likely.

Additionally, **bar associations may use social media profiles and postings as considerations in the imposition of attorney discipline.** Your LinkedIn profile could be viewed as a form of legal advertising and, by commenting about a legal issue on a website, you might be seen as holding yourself out to be an expert on such matters. Several judges may be included in your group of Facebook friends, but you, they, and their staff members must establish proper boundaries for communications if you are trying a case before any of them. These are but a few examples of issues that you should keep in mind while participating on social media platforms.

Many employers, including law firms and other legal employers, currently screen job candidates for their participation on social media. The process might be formal (handled by the Chair of the Hiring Committee, someone from the Recruiting Office or Human Resources Department, or a third-party screening company) or it could be informal (the result of "casual" surfing by someone on the Hiring Committee or another employee).

Occasionally, employers find positive information that sways the hiring decision, but more commonly **they find online content, photos, and videos that cause them to remove a candidate from consideration.** Negative factors include drinking and drugs; discriminatory comments regarding religion, race, and gender; badmouthing previous employers, professors, fellow students, and co-workers; sharing of confidential information from previous employers; lying about qualifications; examples of "poor communication skills," excessive negativity; use of "unprofessional" screen name; excessive posting. (It is true that a complete lack of presence on social media could also raise questions, but this is less likely and more easily explained.) Employers who find negative information may or may not give a candidate the opportunity to confirm, deny, or explain what has been found—but even if they do, can you ever completely erase a negative first impression?

2.   Policies Concerning Use of Internet

An **increasing number of employers have written policies governing employees' use of social media,** and many others offer social media education in lieu of a mandate. Employers that *do* have policies may also have procedures for periodic or ongoing monitoring to ensure compliance with those policies. This is especially common in government settings such as prosecutor's offices and in highly regulated areas. Typical policy provisions are attitudinal in nature (e.g., "be respectful, honest, and accurate"), content-related (e.g., "no divulgence of confidential information or private information"), and related to time spent and use of resources (e.g., "refrain from using the internet at work unless work-related").

So-called "cyber slacking" is also of growing concern to employers, with current data indicating that anywhere from 30–40% of an employee's internet time at work is not spent on employer-related matters.

C.   GUIDELINES FOR E-PROFESSIONALISM

- **Conduct an online search of your name to see what information is out there**

about you. Use various platforms (Google, Yahoo, Bing, etc.) and don't stop after the first few screens on each site, even if the information begins to seem redundant. Often new information is buried deeper in the search results.

- **If you find false or damaging information, do your best to have it removed.** Contact the website's administrator, the source or individual responsible for the posting, or even a professional "cleaning company," if necessary. An additional strategy is to post positive content, in hopes of burying the negative posts.

- **Create a "Google alert" and pre-set, ongoing searches on other sites as well,** to receive notice of new postings in which you are mentioned.

- **Adjust your privacy settings,** but be clear about the fact that, no matter how informed you are about the process and how conscientious you are in setting limits, something is still likely to get out there. Don't overlook the possibility that, even if you are not named or tagged, you may still be recognized because of a photo or comment that someone else posts.

- **Reflect on your goals in using social media and think about their implications.** Will it be primarily a means of staying in touch with family and friends, for more professional reasons, or a bit of both? **Would it make sense to use one name and platform for personal use and something different for professional purposes? How will you handle friend requests** from co-workers, other attorneys, clients? **Could you estimate how much time you spend on social networking** and, if so, how does this compare to what you would ideally like to spend? Remember—for everything you add to your schedule, you'll have to forego an equal amount of time that you could spend on something else.

- **If you currently have or plan to have a blog or website, will you have sufficient time to keep the site current?** If so, a blog or website can be a positive reputation builder. One of our students, a gourmet cook, created a blog to share recipes and experiences with her friends; when asked about outside interests during call-back interviews, both her dedication to becoming a good cook and her interest in blogging about the process made a positive impression on interviewers. In contrast, if you don't have time to keep your website or blog current, wait until you *do* have the time; otherwise, it might appear that you are the type of person who doesn't follow through on his commitments.

- **If your law school or employer has a formal policy or recommended**

guidelines for social media and internet use, find out what it contains, ask questions if you need clarification about anything, and then *follow the policy or guidelines . . . to the letter.*

- **Notice how professionals in your field or area of interest use well-considered comments and postings on networking sites** such as LinkedIn, as well as how they use these sites to market themselves and their firms, and to maintain relationships with colleagues, clients, and others. You can begin to emulate this type of behavior by complimenting an effective speaker after attending a conference, or by following up on a posted topic in a professional discussion board with a thoughtful question.

- If you are currently looking for a job, contact your Career Office for tips about how to use professional networking sites to augment your job search.

CHAPTER 18

FORMAL AND INFORMAL PRESENTATIONS

*"Begin at the beginning and go on til
you come to the end; then stop."*
Lewis Carroll, from Alice in Wonderland

You may be asked to talk about your research or
other projects, rather than to write about them.
Sometimes your oral presentations will be planned;
other times, they will be impromptu. In any event,
it's beneficial to think ahead about some aspects of
oral presentations. Many of the considerations, such
as the need to focus carefully on audience, purpose,
and context, are the same as in written
communication, but important differences bear
emphasis.

This chapter addresses preparation, practice, and
presentation when speaking formally or informally.

A. SETTING THE STAGE

1. Determine Your Audience

Who are your listeners and how would they prefer
to receive your information? What do they know or
not know about your topic? Even if *you* have just
learned about the area of law, your listener may
already be an expert and want a narrowly focused
discussion. On the other hand, someone unfamiliar
with the law may welcome a broad overview. In
certain contexts, you'll speak to lawyers who know a

lot about the law, but less about the relevant business; in others, to non-lawyers who know a lot about the business, and less about the law. At other times, you may speak to mixed or general audiences.

2. Identify Your Purpose

What is the purpose of your presentation, and what will the audience do with it once you give it to them? When you are invited to make a presentation, **find out why you were invited and what your audience's goals might be.** Make sure your presentation addresses these goals explicitly.

3. Consider Context and Logistics

Often overlooked until the last minute, logistics can make or break a presentation. Find out the following in time to make the necessary preparations:

- **Where** will you make your presentation?

- **How much time** will you have to speak?

- How formal is the meeting?

- Will you be speaking alone, or as part of a group?

- How many people will be there?

- **What kind of equipment will be available for your use?**

- If you'll be using PowerPoint, overheads, or handouts, what resources (people and equipment) will be on site?

- How far in advance will you need to provide PowerPoint or materials for handouts?

- How early do you need to be there to test the equipment?

- Who is your contact person for IT and other logistical questions?

Even if you make the most elaborate and cautious arrangements for technical support, be prepared for the technology to fail. **Always have a contingency plan if your presentation relies on the use of technology.**

If you are speaking to a group with whom you don't interact regularly, try to get a sense of the **historical context related to the subject of your presentation**—what has happened before that you need to know? For instance, if you're asked to make a presentation on employment discrimination, it would be helpful to know if your talk is part of an ongoing educational series or whether the group is in the midst of defending an employment discrimination lawsuit. To find this out, ask the person who invited you to present.

B.   PREPARATION AND PRACTICE

1.   Prepare a Brief Outline

Prepare a brief outline and establish how long you'll take on each part of your presentation. The outline can take many forms, depending on the purpose and subject area of your presentation. This should *not be a script*, or you risk losing your place the first time you look up from your notes. Use a large font and give yourself enough white space for notes and to keep track of your place. An outline on a legal issue might look like this:

1. Introduction or Overview, including Roadmap of Presentation (5 minutes)

   a. Provide necessary (but *only* necessary) background.

   b. Identify the specific topic to be addressed, including facts if needed.

   c. Provide a brief summary of your topic, so your listeners know where you are going. **Don't leave your listeners in suspense.**

2. Your Discussion (10–12 minutes)

   a. Provide a synthesis of applicable law. Be prepared to give holdings and key facts of key cases **in response to questions,** but don't assume that you should go through them in your presentation. On the other hand, remember that listeners need to be kept engaged, and facts are helpful in maintaining interest.

   b. Use key ideas and make your organization obvious to the listeners by using signposts ("and so," "even though," "next," "in spite of").

   c. Apply relevant law to the situation and explore counter arguments.

3. Conclusion (3–5 minutes)

　　a. State probable conclusion.

　　b. Recommend additional lines of inquiry or actions.

　　c. Call to action: What do you want your audience to do, if anything? Be clear and direct.

4. Questions (5–10 minutes)

2.　Plan for the Unexpected

Think about how to keep the presentation on track if unexpected questions or interruptions arise. Consider preparing a brief handout that hits the highlights, but keep it simple and relatively free of detail that you'll address in your presentation. While handouts can be helpful, they can also distract the audience from your presentation. Unless a handout is vital during your presentation, distribute it at the end or at the door so people can pick up a copy as they leave. Tell them at the introduction that you will do so. For the future convenience of your audience, put the date, name of the meeting, your contact information and name of firm or agency on the handout.

3.　Practice Out Loud

Practice your presentation out loud in a setting similar to the one where you'll speak, with someone who doesn't know the subject matter. Anticipate and ask for questions. Then adjust your presentation based on the feedback you receive. Check your timing throughout. If you haven't done much public speaking, you are probably speaking too fast, as most of us do when we are nervous. **Practice speaking slowly.** If you'll be speaking to a small group, think of your presentation as more like a conversation than like a speech.

Practice again . . . and again.

C.   GIVING THE PRESENTATION

1.   Introduce Yourself

Before the presentation, introduce yourself individually to as many participants as possible to help put everyone at ease.

2.   Get Everyone's Attention

If you are introduced, make eye contact with members of the group before beginning to speak.

3.   Provide a Brief Introduction

The traditional advice works: **Tell the group what you are going to say, say it, and then tell them what you told them.** Mention how long you plan to talk, so your listeners will have an idea of what to expect. Address if, how, and when you will answer questions.

For instance, assume you are speaking to the corporate counsel and administrators, physicians, and members of the board of a corporation that operates urgent care clinics in a large city. You might begin as follows:

> "I'm going to talk this morning for about 15 minutes about the obligation of a health care provider to protect the medical information of its patients. I'll also address exceptions to the general rule that you'll come across most frequently in your work. First, I'll briefly describe the specific incident that prompted the urgency of this presentation. Second, I'll summarize the statutes and regulations that apply. Third, I'll outline areas where you may need to review your policies and practices. Finally, I'll talk about a few cases and tell you what the open questions are that relate to your work.

> "I'd prefer that you hold your questions until the end of my presentation, unless you need clarification to understand what I'm saying. I'll try to avoid acronyms (such as HIPAA, which stands for the Health Insurance Portability and Accountability Act), but if I use them, feel free to stop me. I've provided an outline for you to follow so you can track the main points of my presentation."

Then, pause, make eye contact with a few people to make sure they are following you, and continue.

4. During the Presentation

- **Speak slowly and breathe** from your diaphragm, not from the top of your lungs.

This will help you modulate your voice to its proper level.

- **Avoid reading from a script.** If you must read significant portions of text, do it with expression, looking up frequently from your notes. Be conversational, but professional.

- **Make eye contact with each person at the meeting,** or with individuals in each section of the room. Use your normal facial expressions and gestures; it will make your presentation more natural and enjoyable.

- **Know what and where your authority is,** and be able to support your points, but don't necessarily bring everything in your file to the presentation. You won't have time to consult everything and will do better if you keep your papers to a minimum. If you bring your laptop or tablet, have your files well organized so you can find supporting information if you need it.

- **Be clear and be brief.** Speak in relatively short sentences, and pause between points. It's tiring to listen for a long time, and most lawyers and clients don't have a lot of time to spare. Focus on the most important points and on the facts and aspects of the relevant law that are crucial.

- **Observe your listeners' reactions.** If several people look confused, clarification is probably necessary. Provide it.

- **Stay attuned to the present,** not inflexibly tied to your outline. Be aware of the tension between covering your points and the possible need to change your direction based on your listeners' reactions. Listen, observe non-verbal cues, and adjust to new information. Based on what occurs, you may decide to change the order of your presentation, to skip certain parts, or to otherwise adjust to what you observe.

5.   Conclude Clearly and Concisely

- **Conclude clearly and briefly.** Avoid simply trailing off, with "So, that's all I have, uh. . . ." Instead, try something like this, "In summary, we can confidently say that to protect the medical information of our patients, we must 1). . . ; 2) . . . ; and 3). . . . Before releasing any information, we must be sure to do X and Y. In circumstances A and B, we may share medical information with other health care providers. Now if there are any questions, I'd be happy to take them. Thank you for your attention."

- **If you are new to public speaking, you may be nervous.** If you remember your purpose—to educate, inform, facilitate—in other words, to help, you will be less likely to focus on yourself and more likely to give a helpful presentation.

- **Some speakers are intimidated by offering to answer questions.** Not knowing what the questions might be, they worry about being unprepared. As experienced attorneys know, there's no shame in saying you don't have an answer. **Avoid speculation.** For instance, "That's an interesting question. I don't know how the courts will apply that provision of the statute, but the issue will likely be . . . ," or "I don't know, but I'd be happy to look into that for you." (Be careful here, or you may commit yourself to more than you really should.) You can only answer what you can, and it's totally appropriate to say you don't know.

After the presentation, try to talk to one or more participants to find out what worked well and what could have been presented differently, more clearly, in a different order, or otherwise improved.

CHAPTER 19

MAKING THE MOST OF MEETINGS

Like it or not, lawyers and those who work with them spend an enormous amount of time in meetings. Just say, "Let's schedule a meeting," and watch how fast a group of lawyers can whip out their phones or calendars.

If most people view meetings as unwelcome interruptions, why do we have so many of them? For this chapter, we'll consider a gathering of three or more people to be a meeting. In Chapter 15, "In-Person Communication," we address the more particular aspects of a one-on-one meeting. Some of the **most common reasons for convening a meeting** follow:

- **To solve a specific** problem (e.g., prepare for an appeal, revise conflicts procedures, address public relations crisis);

- **To conduct business** of a group that meets on a regular basis (e.g., Board of Directors, Managing Partners, Weekly Staff Meeting), or for a specified period of time, to accomplish a specific task (e.g., Conference Planning Team, State Bar Task Force); and

- **To strengthen relationships** (e.g., inter-organizational coalitions).

Meetings are more productive and less stressful when conducted according to a few basic principles. New lawyers are also often surprised to find that it can be almost as challenging to *attend and participate productively in* a meeting, as to be the meeting leader. In this chapter, we'll explore how to do both with skill.

Participants know a meeting is successful when:

- Useful information is shared.

- Problems (and potential problems), are identified, examined, and perhaps resolved.

- Everyone understands future actions needed, and agrees on individual responsibilities and deadlines.

- Discussion is thorough, yet business is conducted efficiently.

A. BE AN EFFECTIVE PARTICIPANT

1. Before the Meeting

- **Calendar the meeting,** noting the date, time, name/phone number of the coordinator, and location (or dial-in number and access code). Insert directions to the meeting at the same time you put it into your calendar. Calendar regularly held meetings, too. If you have an assistant, your calendaring system should allow for automatic notification of your assistant of your scheduled events.

- **Prepare well in advance** if you need to take action or perform research to prepare for the meeting, so that you have time to handle unexpected issues that might arise. Even if you aren't chairing the meeting or presenting research, you still need to prepare sufficiently to contribute to the meeting.

- **Review the agenda** at least the day before the meeting, to be sure you've completed your action items from the last meeting and to refresh your memory of the meeting's purpose.

- **If the meeting is not in your office, get directions** (including parking). Plan to arrive a little early if this is your first time at the location.

- **Bring along** your laptop, tablet, or a pad, pencil, and paperwork or files that you might need. Bring your calendar in case follow-up meetings are scheduled.

- If attending a brown bag meeting, take along something that is easy to eat without utensils, or bring your own utensils.

- **Introduce yourself** to people you don't know and **chat informally** before the meeting begins. In group settings, respect and cooperation flourish as people get to know each other better.

- If the group meets regularly, sit next to different people occasionally, to help form stronger individual relationships.

- **Switch off your cell phone** (including the vibrate setting) unless you are on call for an urgent matter. If you must take or make a call, mention this beforehand to the chair of the meeting, and step outside and make it as brief as possible.

- Take your seat before the starting time of the meeting and wrap up conversations when the chair is ready for the meeting to begin.

2.   During the Meeting

- **Listen carefully** to other speakers, instead of focusing on what you want to say when they are finished.

- **Show by your posture and facial expression that you are interested** in what is being said. Try to avoid fidgeting, slouching, or shaking your leg back and forth.

- **Contribute to the discussion,** but don't monopolize it. Don't interrupt, even if the conversation is informal and animated. Instead, wait for a break in the conversation, or raise your hand enough to be seen by the chair but not so much that you become a distraction. When you do speak, maintain eye contact with the entire group. Don't repeat previous comments, even rephrased or summarized, because it wastes valuable time and suggests that you haven't been paying attention.

- **Don't try to bluff** if you are asked for information that you don't have. Say, "I don't know the answer to that question." If appropriate, you can offer to follow up, but only if it is within the scope of your work and general responsibilities.

- **Don't commit your client or anyone else to a point of view or course of action unless you know that you have authorization to do so.** If there is a request for volunteers, do participate—but, don't overextend yourself, or make commitments you can't keep.

- **Don't take personally other people's criticism of your ideas.** It's tempting to "clam up" and stop participating in the conversation, but the best way to avoid defensiveness is to keep participating.

- **Be tactful** in expressing differences of opinion. Avoid raised eyebrows and frowns. Instead of saying, "No, that won't work," try "That might raise the issue of strict liability, and I'm wondering if we might resolve it by changing our approach just a bit."

- **Refer to handouts as needed,** but focus primarily on the discussion.

- **Take notes,** even if minutes are being taken. Jot down your own action items, along with due dates. Follow up soon afterwards, and be sure to update your supervisor and others in your organization as appropriate.

- Avoid side conversations. They are disruptive and rude.

- Don't read your email, texts, unrelated paperwork, conduct online shopping, etc., during meetings.

B.   LEADING EFFECTIVELY

Why do we talk about how to lead an effective meeting when, as a student or new attorney, you will almost certainly be placed in the role of, at most, merely a participant? In your current or "previous life," or through your participation with law student organizations, you may already have gained experience leading a meeting. If not, you may get your chance sooner than you expect.

New lawyers are frequently asked to assume leadership roles on bar committees and in their firms or organizations, and we want you to be prepared if the opportunity presents itself. Moreover, especially if you are the only lawyer or law student in a group, others may assume that you know how to run a meeting. You may find yourself chairing a meeting unexpectedly.

While many of the same guidelines that apply to participating in a meeting are still appropriate, a leader has additional responsibilities.

1.   Before the Meeting

- **Decide whether a meeting is really necessary.** If so, **who needs to be there?** Make sure to invite everyone who should attend. **When and for how long** should you meet? Be considerate in establishing a meeting time. Consider using meeting software to schedule the meeting. Instead of automatically assuming that folks want to meet during lunch or after hours, check with the group. The optimum meeting length is usually $1-1\frac{1}{2}$ hours.

- Depending on the purpose of the meeting, and its geographical location, some people may prefer to attend remotely. This does present challenges, though, so be sure to introduce everyone, and ask participants to say their names before speaking. Remind everyone of lag time when some participate remotely, or people will speak over each other and waste additional time. Remember that, lacking visual cues, people may be unsure about when someone is finished speaking or about to speak. One student pointed out an additional problem:

The teams have members in both locations, and conduct their meetings via speaker phones. This format has been the hardest thing for me to get used to, especially since I haven't yet met the people on the other end of the line.

Student Journal

- Distribute a **well-prepared agenda** several days in advance of the meeting. Include the date, location and purpose of the meeting, as well as a framework for the discussion, and a list of issues and speakers. Bring along copies to distribute at the meeting, too, for those who forget them.

- Along with the agenda, **distribute other documents** that may be useful, such as minutes of the last meeting, past Treasurer's report, and updates from committees.

- A good meeting has few surprises. Talk to key people ahead of time if complicated or potentially controversial issues will come up. This will allow you to prepare as well as to assess how much time agenda items are likely to take.

- **Arrange for water** (and possibly soft drinks, snacks or lunch, depending on your budget and time of day). If the meeting is "brown bag," offer to place an order for delivery from a local sandwich shop, and collect the money later.

- If a whiteboard or easel would move things along in a constructive way, provide them (along with markers), and take the lead in using them.

- On the day before the meeting, send a brief **e-mail reminder,** with the time, location or dial-in number.

2.   **Getting off to a Good Start**

- **Start on time, stay on time, and end on time or *earlier*.** This will require tact and attention on your part, but is worth the effort.

If one part of the discussion takes longer than expected, you may need to move the conversation along, or postpone other agenda items to a later meeting.

- Begin the meeting with a **welcome** (and **introductions** if needed). **Pay attention to new members of the group,** giving brief background to unfamiliar references if needed.

- If the meeting will be unusual in any way, such as a brainstorming or conference planning session, illustrate how the "ground rules" may be slightly different than usual.

- Ask someone to **take notes,** or take them yourself.

- At the beginning of each agenda item, provide the group with brief **background or updates** if needed.

The boss was always calm, friendly, straightforward, and respectful. I would sit in meetings watching her watch everyone else. You could tell that she really had a handle on the group dynamic and the best way to deal with everyone individually. I learned a lot by observing her.

Student Journal

3. Guiding the Discussion

- Do you need to follow *Roberts Rules of Order*? Probably not, unless the meeting is formal.

However, you should become familiar with the rules, because even an informal meeting may unexpectedly require more structure to the process, or a formal vote. In any event, do call on people to speak, so they don't all talk at once. If several people want to contribute to the discussion, indicate an order for them to speak (e.g., "Let's hear from Stephanie first, then Clark and Roberto."). This may feel awkward at first, but will be appreciated by all.

- Listen carefully and **allow the group sufficient time to express their opinions** before offering your own. So that all will have an opportunity to speak, don't allow someone to monopolize the conversation.

- **Give those who have been silent a chance to speak,** without putting them on the spot. For example, "We haven't heard from several people yet, and I want to be sure we hear their thoughts." "Does anybody who hasn't spoken yet have anything to add before we move on to another topic?" We suggest that you wait a few moments before moving on, even if the group is silent.

- **Intervene if tensions begin to rise.** Identify common ground, ask for other opinions, decide a course of action (if necessary), and move the discussion along. The meeting will not only be more productive—participants will also be grateful.

I sat in on my share of boring meetings. I was on a telephone conference between members of several groups who were searching for ways to remove barriers to their collaboration on a project. The meeting mired down into trivial infighting. The lawyer in our office muted the call and shook her head. "I spend more time listening to this sort of thing than doing my job."

Student Journal

- If the **conversation begins to "loop back around"** again and again, it is time to draw discussion on that issue to a close.

- Wrap up each topic by asking whether anybody has final comments. Ask for volunteers for follow-up tasks, and get consensus on tentative date for achieving them. Then **sum up the discussion and announce action items.**

4. After the Meeting

- Promptly distribute a **draft copy of the minutes,** and ask for corrections and comments.

- **Follow up on action items, responsibilities and deadlines.** This will require organization on your part. Consider using an indexed notebook or series of folders to keep track of what needs to be accomplished by each person at each juncture.

- Maintain a **positive group identity** by periodically thanking the group, as well as specific members, for their contributions. Communicate the group's activities to others (such as management, full membership of the organization, etc.), via e-mail or newsletter articles.

C.   LAST-MINUTE LEADING

Sometimes you will arrive at a meeting and find that there is no chair of the meeting or the chair has unexpectedly been prevented from attending. Non-lawyers may assume because you are a law student or lawyer that you know how to run a meeting. Others may judge you to have leadership qualities because of your personality or connection to law. Without warning, you may be drafted to chair the meeting. If there is a written agenda, you have guidance, but you should quickly review it and try to estimate appropriate times for each item. If the meeting has no prepared agenda (for instance, a weekly staff meeting), here are some suggestions:

- Ask for agenda items: Does anyone have an item that needs to be addressed today?

- Ask for someone to take notes. Take your own, but it's hard to run a meeting and take comprehensive notes at the same time.

- Prioritize agenda items based on importance and urgency.

- Establish an end time.

- Summarize at the end; list action items and persons responsible.

- End on or before time is up.

- After the meeting, promptly provide a report to the usual chair. If there is no usual chair, keep your notes handy for the next meeting.

SECTION 3
SELF AND OTHERS

CHAPTER 20

TIME MANAGEMENT AND PROCRASTINATION

"Time is the coin of your life. It is the only coin you have, and only you can determine how it will be spent. Be careful lest you let other people spend it for you."
Carl Sandburg

The need for and challenges to time management come in all shapes and sizes—at the beginning of a job, you may have *too little* to do. Once you've been on the job for a while, you may think you have *too much* to do. Once you *really* have too much to do, you'll yearn for the days when you only thought you had too much to do, but just didn't know what you were doing or how to manage your time.

Let's begin with the short-lived, but often frequent situation faced by people in a *new job: too little to do, and the related problem of boredom.*

Our suggestions for this difficulty—"what do I do with all this time that I have on my hands?"—is to ask for work, to be willing to do whatever work is given to you, and to do a **thorough job** before you submit it. Once you establish yourself as a conscientious and competent worker, you'll be justified in asking for more interesting and challenging work. **Soon you'll have what feels like too much work for the time you have, and you'll be ready for this chapter.**

As with so many things, **time management is a lot about knowing yourself, and then communicating with others about what you are doing** and **what your realistic needs and limitations are.** It's also about comprehending the realistic needs of others and building into your schedule a way to meet those needs. Good time management requires you to anticipate interruptions and unexpected assignments. It also requires you to create and keep a **schedule or calendar** that keeps track of all your work assignments so that you meet all deadlines and appointments. Finally, for many of us, time management includes understanding why we procrastinate, and taking steps to overcome it.

A. MANAGING YOURSELF

When we enter a new job in a new profession, we face new experiences that challenge our ability to predict accurately how long something will take. How can we know how long it will take to research a new legal question in an area of law we've never studied?

A starting point for managing our time is recognizing that **we aren't going to be as good at it today as we may be six months from now,** when we've had some experience with doing the kinds of things that today are totally foreign.

In the meantime, it's crucial to notice our habits. How do you spend your time? Most of us are surrounded by communication tools—laptops, tablets, smart phones, etc. **Take stock of how much time you spend hanging around online— chatting, surfing, shopping, etc. As a**

professional, not only will you need to pay more attention to the substance of your online life, you will likely need to change your online habits as well **so that you can focus completely on the task at hand.**

Managing ourselves requires more than just knowing how long things will take us to do. It requires reflection about our cycles of energy, how we react to stress, and how quickly we can recover from potentially time-consuming responses to stress. We need to examine how we respond to the challenges of being in a new situation. **Finally, we must use productively and minimize the length of the "recovery or transition time" we need between completing one task and becoming absorbed in the next.**

But it's impossible to talk about managing one's self without talking about communicating with others.

B.   COMMUNICATING WITH OTHERS

One of the most challenging aspects of starting a new job in a law firm or agency is the large number of people who can give you work, the unpredictability of when you'll receive that work, and the shock that hits on learning when it will be due. The more you can learn about what to expect, the greater your chances will be of managing your time well. **Especially in the beginning of a job, it's important to gain as much clarity as possible about the demands others have on your time.**

Find out from the people giving you work both **how long *they think* it should take** you **and when it is due.** Keep in mind that even experienced attorneys often underestimate the length of time a task should take. They may not have done this kind of work in a long time. Or they may incorrectly assume that you can complete a project in the same amount of time they would need, despite their having more experience. Most importantly, many experienced attorneys can't always predict accurately how long it will take to do their *own* work, with good reason. In resolving even "minor" legal questions, it's hard to predict what new obstacles or challenges will arise and how long it will take to resolve them. Even so, it's still a good idea to find out the other person's expectations and an absolute necessity to know when the work is expected of you. **In other words, know your deadline.**

A difficult but necessary aspect of communication related to time management is the ability to tell someone that you will not be able to meet a deadline. The ability to communicate this bad news is necessary because you owe your co-workers honesty and predictability— they are relying on you to do your part of the project on time. But it's important for other reasons as well; without the ability to state honestly that you will be late, you will likely avoid the other person, earn the reputation of being unreliable, and generally create a situation of paralysis that almost guarantees that you'll manage your time poorly.

For instance, you may have a project from one attorney due by the end of the day Friday. On Tuesday you receive a new, apparently more urgent project from another attorney and see that you won't be able to meet both deadlines. You should immediately discuss this—ideally in person—with the person to whom you owe the project, as well as with your "boss," if that is a different person. "I realize that I have a project due for you at 5:00 p.m. Friday. I have a new urgent project from Attorney X. I can see that I won't be able to meet both deadlines. May I discuss this with you?"

The key is to communicate the problem as early as possible to the person depending on you once you realize you may not be able to meet a deadline. This is not to suggest that you do this often, but to alert you to the probability that one day, when you may least expect it, you will find that you cannot complete your work on time.

Never miss a deadline. The better practice is to request an extension of time from your assigning attorney, in advance, and explain why there is good reason to do so.

Advice from an Employer

In addition to knowing what others expect of you, you need to let others know what you expect of them. At some point, you will delegate to others, or rely on others to provide parts of a project to you. Communicate clearly *your deadlines* **to others.** To do this, you'll need to **plan so you can give others enough time to meet your timetable.** Otherwise you'll end up having to do it yourself or having a team that resents your lack of planning.

C.   DEALING WITH THE UNEXPECTED

If we think of time management in large part as a state of mind (Is your work out of control? Do you have too much to do and not enough time to do it?), then **a great deal of time management is about managing your expectations about work, and being realistic about what your work is.**

For instance, experience guarantees that something unexpected will come up in most of our work lives as practicing lawyers, and it will come up often. Sometimes it will be in the form of an irritating interruption when you are working on a tight deadline; sometimes it will be more serious than a simple interruption.

You'll be able to manage your time better if you're prepared to face unexpected demands, emergencies, or even minor irritations. If you allot more time for tasks than they are likely to take, your overall plan will be realistic. You will have built in a buffer for the unexpected. You won't be surprised or angered by the intrusion of unplanned demands on your time, and your emotional energies won't be spent responding to the anger or frustration you feel because of them.

People who manage their time well manage their interruptions. Even if you cannot control the *fact* of interruptions—because you are being interrupted by your supervising attorney, for instance—one thing you *can often* do is finish the sentence you are writing, or the e-mail you are sending, or the billing description you were entering before you were interrupted. Taking 10–15 seconds to finish what you are working on before attending to the interruption can save you an enormous amount of time and frustration.

One of the authors realized many years ago that about 60% of her job was dealing with the unexpected. Once she acknowledged this, interruptions simply became part of what she saw as her job. The interruptions were still there; they simply weren't as irritating, and no longer seemed like unwelcome visitors.

Finally, recognize that **you may be able to control some interruptions.** Work with your assistant to protect at least some part of your day from drop-ins or phone calls, except from a designated few. If you don't have an assistant, find another way to save some uninterrupted time for yourself. If you build in time to return phone calls or e-mails, or time to walk down the hall to chat briefly with a colleague, you can "consolidate your losses" and put your time to better use.

Beware of "multitasking." We've talked in this section about interruptions that other people or outside events create. Another species of interruption is the kind that you create yourself. **You may interrupt yourself by jumping from one thing to another with no discernable pattern.** This is sometimes called "multitasking," *as if you can do two things at once,* but it's been well documented that **multi-tasking is generally both inefficient and**

ineffective, resulting in lost time and accuracy. It is certainly not something to try in a new job.

D. DELEGATION

Delegation is another way to manage your time. Early in your career, you may not be able to delegate. When the time comes, though, if there is a task that doesn't require your training or expertise that someone else can perform as well as you can, or better than you can, or as well as it needs to be done, then you probably should be delegating that task to someone else.

Delegation takes an initial investment of time to train and explain; it takes planning ahead; and it takes supervision. In the long run, if you aren't delegating when you can, you aren't managing your time as well as you can. For suggestions on delegation, see Chapter 10, "The Art of Supervising."

E. PLANNING, CALENDARING, AND SCHEDULING

Create a system that works and that is relatively simple. Your employer may have tools for calendaring your appointments and assignments that also keep track of your time spent on each case. If so, master them as soon as you can. Identify your priorities and quickly adapt to the shifts in priorities that inevitably will occur. **Build in buffer time. Don't schedule too tightly.** If your work requires you to bill your time, don't fall into the trap of thinking that the only valuable time at work is billable. Some activities, such as talking to your assistant, keeping your office organized, and keeping up with developments in your field, are as important as billable time. Think of it as building and maintaining the infrastructure for your work. It's not glamorous, but it ensures that you will travel more smoothly and with fewer potholes.

Schedule tasks that require less intellectual energy at a time of day when your physical and intellectual energies are lowest. **Protect the time of day when you are most productive from activities that drain your energy.** Pay attention to your peak times during the day and week. Use them for your most important work. For example, if early mornings are your most productive time at work, don't agree to a breakfast meeting if you have another alternative.

Develop strategies to capture time. Put off unproductive activities if you can. For instance, if you find yourself attending many meetings that are unproductive, but which you are required to attend, if given a choice, select the date that is as far away from today as possible.

Sometimes you'll feel that every project is an emergency; that everything is a rush. **But do whatever you can to approach your work deliberately. By slowing down, you'll do things right the first time and ultimately save time.** In fact, most projects can be slotted into a time progression, and not every project is as important as the next. Of course, for everyone you are working with, *their project* is the most important, and at times you'll need to coordinate with more than one person to resolve conflicting time frames.

You may need to reschedule appointments or rearrange your priorities. The sooner you can do this, the more in control of your time you will feel, and the more grateful people working and meeting with you will be.

F.   PROCRASTINATION AND PERFECTIONISM

The first step to overcoming procrastination is to recognize *when* you are procrastinating. The next step is to identify what is keeping you from doing what you need to do. For some it is indecision: you have so much to do that every time you begin working on one thing, you think of the other 10 things that are more or equally urgent. Others procrastinate to avoid something unpleasant—a phone call, an activity, a discussion with a difficult person, or even a difficult discussion with a pleasant person. Others have such high standards that it is difficult to bring anything to completion because nothing can ever be good enough. This, of course, is the curse of perfectionism.

If you are a perfectionist, the first thing you must realize is that *perfectionism is not a virtue,* but a challenge to be overcome. In the practical world of law practice, where clients depend upon and pay for our work, perfectionism is not an option. Doing a job *as well as it can be done* includes doing it *within a reasonable amount of time,* at the *level of competence necessary to accomplish the task's purpose,* for a *reasonable cost to the client* (whether the client is a private client, a government agency with taxpayers paying our salary, or a non-profit funded by donors). **Perfectionism for its own sake is meaningless; a job well done must be measured against the client's goals, including goals of time and cost.** (If you are not a perfectionist, you must not take this paragraph as permission to do sloppy work, or to ignore the details. Keep working as carefully as you have been, not less so.)

If you are a master procrastinator, you will spend too much time identifying what is keeping you from what you need to be doing. Stop it! Regardless of what is keeping you from doing what you need to do, you need a plan. Any plan. See Section E of this chapter.

Get the little things out of the way first. Or tackle the biggest thing first. Do what's easy first. Or do what's hardest first. Reward yourself. Penalize yourself. Break things down into small steps. Send something out that is less than perfect, but that does the job competently and on time. Praise yourself for taking every little step. Write your mother an e-mail when you finish something. Write your father when you begin something. **Write a to-do list.** Prioritize the tasks in order of importance. **Perform the tasks. Check them off.** As a reward for doing something big on your list, read *The Art of Procrastination* by John Perry. You'll laugh as well as learn something useful about structuring your time.

G. ACKNOWLEDGING OUR LIMITS

Eventually, the self-knowledge required for good time management will include becoming aware of, and willing to acknowledge, our limits.

The ability to recognize our limits allows us to commit only to those things that we can do competently. One of the difficulties many of us face is that modern culture generally, and the legal culture specifically, discourages recognition of limits. In fact, admitting one's limits is often viewed as a weakness rather than a strength. But failure to know our limits is both short-sighted and dangerous. In the long run, knowing and accepting our limits is necessary to our health, both mental and physical, as well as to our integrity. In Chapter 26, "Finding Balance in Your Work and Life," we discuss how to avoid overcommitment, another way of working within your limits.

H. KEEP MOVING AND TAKE BREAKS

From your first days on the job, develop habits that keep you moving. Find ways to incorporate small breaks into your schedule that require you to get away from your desk. Take a real lunch break, preferably one that gets you out of your building. Get up and stretch for small chunks of time. Walk down the hall to ask the question that you could have e-mailed. Get your own coffee. Don't give up your gym membership, but remember to use it. Sometimes the *best* way to manage your time is to get away from work.

CHAPTER 21

MANAGING STRESS

*"Sometimes the most important thing
in a whole day is the rest we take
between two deep breaths."*
Etty Hillesum

Stress has become endemic in the classroom, in the legal profession and, as most would agree, in today's society as a whole.

It can come in the disguise of an unsupportive supervisor, a difficult client, obnoxious opposing counsel, or difficult co-workers. It can also come in the form of long hours, overwhelming workloads, and unreasonable deadlines.

However, before we explore the various stressors in our lives, let's reflect for a moment on some common signs of stress. Some of these signs are so subtle that you might never have connected them with stress.

- Inability to concentrate, forgetfulness.

- Not making time for friends and family, for exercise and other physical activities.

- Both overeating and loss of appetite.

- Irritability, inappropriate ways of dealing with people.

- Difficulty falling or staying asleep; nightmares, grinding teeth.

- Overspending, accumulating excessive debt.

- Dependence on alcohol.

- Inappropriate use of non-prescription, prescription or illegal drugs.

- Gambling, excessive betting.

- Physical symptoms such as headaches, stomach aches, eyelid twitching, sweating, fatigue, heart palpitations, panic attacks, exhaustion.

When we experience stress, our first instinct may be to attribute it to outside factors, such as other people, and to conclude that the situation is pretty much out of our control. Initially, this may be reassuring, because it "gets us off the hook."

But by perceiving ourselves as unable to change a stressful situation, we create even more stress. In other words, how we deal with stress could create another set of stressors. Yet, while it is true that some situations *are* completely out of our control, we *can* change our workplace dynamics—or at least our attitude toward them. Even if a change in attitude changes nothing else, it can have an enormous effect on lowering stress. This puts us back in control of what we can control.

Sometimes outside factors have nothing to do with our stress, because it is self-imposed. In this case, too, reflection is useful.

A. SELF-INDUCED STRESS

1. "Natural Born" Worriers

Some people have always been worriers (or acquired the tendency during law school) and find worrying a hard habit to break. Viewed from the outside, their stress level may seem out of proportion to what many consider appropriate under the circumstances.

If you fall into this category, with attention and perseverance, you can "unlearn" the tendency towards chronic worry and this will relieve much of your anxiety.

It's important to address chronic worry because, if it is persistent or disruptive, your supervisors may also begin to worry . . . about your ability to cope with the stress of practice. Whether as a result of their lack of confidence or from a desire to protect you, they might give more interesting or difficult assignments to others, shield you from client contact, and ultimately pass you up for promotions when the time comes.

An attorney said that a law clerk who just took the bar is obsessing too much over it, and that this is making a poor impression. I can see how obsessing over something you have no control over could be perceived poorly because a key attribute of an attorney is the ability to handle and release stress.

Student Journal

2. Performance Anxiety

Every time I start a new project, I feel overwhelmed. I tell myself that this is just another assignment, but I always feel a pang of self-doubt. There is so much riding on my performance. I am advocating for real people and failure means letting so many others down, rather than just myself.

Student Journal

Most law students and lawyers are competitive, driven, highly stressed individuals. Real "type A" personalities, we set high standards for ourselves, hate to make mistakes, and are accustomed to high achievement.

In law school and on the job, the self-imposed pressure to perform at a very high level is intense. At times, it may seem as if there is little margin for error, and we fear making *the serious mistake* that will finally prove our incompetence for all to see.

Unfortunately, if you buy into it, this attitude is a sure-fire recipe for stress. It would be a shame if you let your own unrealistic expectations, fear of incompetence, or fear of rejection rob you of the learning opportunities and enjoyment you would otherwise receive from your job, clerkship, or internship.

While professors and employers *do* expect you to learn from your mistakes, they don't expect perfection, and will not be upset (or surprised) if you make a mistake or two or have a little trouble juggling assignments. As lawyers, there will be many occasions when we don't know the answer and cannot control the outcome. To expect otherwise is to buy in to a constant, nagging feeling of failure.

> *By realizing that my first year of practice will encompass successes, failures, mistakes, and learning (as opposed to always expecting perfection), I'll be ready for the challenges. If I can use my time to ask honest questions and seek answers from those more experienced than myself, as opposed to pretending to know everything out of the chute, I will be more productive.*

Student Journal

3. Having a Bad Day

Many students wonder how attorneys can deal with so much pain and anger, and yet maintain calm and balance in their own lives.

Unfortunately, some can't—and their negative attitudes can affect others. We all have different personalities, and it's challenging at times to understand and appreciate these differences as we work with our colleagues. Be proactive, find positive role models in your office, and observe how they react and interact with others who may or may not be performing equally well under stress. Similarly, those who are "having a bad day," can teach you a lot, too—about *what not to do.*

> *The legal dispute had been going on for almost 11 years. This is an adversarial process with*

disputes and genuine differences, and that was apparent in the examination of witnesses. Despite this, the attorneys and parties were cordial to each other during the trial and during recess. Civility has not taken a back seat, which I find very rewarding.

Student Journal

4.   Stuck in the "Wrong" Kind of Practice

Students often assume that, by accepting a clerkship in a specific practice or for a certain type of employer, they are committing themselves to a career in the area. This can be a cause for concern because many students and new lawyers are uncertain about their interests, and don't yet know what types of practice they would like to develop. The assumption that you are stuck in a certain area of law can be an even bigger stressor if you accept a job, and then realize that it's not a good fit for you.

Imagine, for example, that you enjoyed Criminal Law so much that you have accepted a clerkship in the felony division of the prosecuting attorney's office. You've landed the ideal job with an attentive supervisor, challenging assignments, and attorneys who take you to court frequently. On the other hand, you have learned that there is a big difference between analyzing fact patterns in a case book and working with real victims and serious crimes. Like the student whose journal appears below, you may not be dealing with it well.

I've felt raw at times, overwhelmed by what poverty, neglect and drugs can do to people. Some circumstances make me question the workings of society and fate ... It seems as though some people are being punished for being born into the wrong families.

Student Journal

Criminal law is not for everybody. Even if you are extremely interested in the law and its ability to influence people's lives, this is a stressful field, the workload can be horrendous, and people may become anesthetized to others' grief and pain. The time and money to prepare for a case is often inadequate and frequently there is a lack of collegiality between the attorneys. And problems with the system are very hard to change. Put in these terms, criminal law sounds downright unappealing. There are some who have a passion for it . . . and these are the people who should go into that kind of practice . . . but maybe not you.

If you find yourself clerking for the "wrong" employer or in an unappealing area of law, remember that your employment setting is temporary. While you are an intern or law clerk, capitalize on opportunities presented in your current position to observe what works for you and what doesn't, what appeals to you and what doesn't. Remember—you aren't boxed into a corner. You don't have to change the world after law school if you don't want to, and you don't have to practice a certain kind of law. You don't even have to practice law at all, and there's no rush to make a decision.

If you're a new professional who shares the feeling of being "stuck," your current situation also need not be permanent. It may take a bit more time, determination, and planning to discover suitable options, but you can make it happen.

B.   EXTERNAL STRESSORS

1.   Challenges to Your Beliefs

In law school, you approached most legal problems and issues from a neutral, unbiased stance. It's different when you're on the job. Depending upon which "side" you find yourself, you might be helping a client to secure zoning for land development, or working with an environmental group to oppose the same proposal. You could be preparing a country study to help prove that a refugee will be persecuted if returned to her home country, or working in a regional office of the U.S. Border Patrol.

If you have very strong feelings about a certain issue, you are unlikely to seek a job that puts you in direct opposition with those convictions. For example, if you vehemently oppose the death penalty, the last place you would probably want to work is the Capital Litigation Unit of a State Attorney General.

Otherwise, your motivation for accepting a position might vary. You may have a real passion for the work, or you might just need a job so badly that you are compelled to take the first offer you receive. You might find a specific area of law extremely interesting and enjoy every moment of your internship. On the other hand, after starting a job that *seemed* to be a perfect fit, you may conclude that you never want to work in the area again.

When an attorney, firm or agency accepts a client's case, they are committing 100% to that client and to handling the matter in the best way possible, within the bounds of the law and ethical considerations. You may be asked to work on cases that you find disagreeable, that require you to take positions with which you don't agree. If this happens, it may be stressful to advocate for your client's position—yet that's what your supervisor expects of you and, moreover, it's what you've agreed to do.

Clients, too, can present an enormous source of external stress. Lawyers don't always like their clients (and vice versa), and don't always agree with them. However, it is unquestionably the client, not the lawyer, who determines the objectives of your representation. This principle is emphasized in your state bar's ethical rules and the ABA Model Rules of Professional Conduct, which outline a lawyer's role, responsibilities and limitations, and give examples of the kinds of dilemmas which lawyers encounter. See Chapter 28, "Judgment, Values, and Professional Ethics," for a more expanded discussion of these challenges.

Ethical rules confirm that a lawyer's representation "does not constitute an endorsement of the client's political, economic, social or moral views or activities." But if you strongly disagree with your client's point of view, this may do little to dispel the emotional stress you feel while representing him.

Sometimes, law clerks and new lawyers work through this discomfort on their own, through a process of self-reflection. Others find it helpful to seek the advice and perspective of attorneys in their office, from a professor who teaches Professional Responsibility, or from a faculty member who supervises for-credit or school-sponsored internships. If you are in this situation and have not developed a strategy for coping with it, you'll find a measure of relief by doing so.

> *I was conflicted about my obligations to our client versus my personal beliefs in the rights of a free press. I spoke to attorneys in my office and found a solution that allowed me to do my job while still keeping my central beliefs intact. They also showed me that an attorney is an advocate for the client, a proxy with knowledge of the law.*
>
> Student Journal

2.   The Emotions of Clients and Victims

In law school, you focused mainly on the intellectual, not emotional, aspects of most cases. Depending on your position, you may not need to change your approach on the job. For example, if you work on a large class action lawsuit, you'll be looking at facts, figures and the law—you may hardly get out of the office (which is not necessarily a bad thing . . . you'll learn a lot).

On the other hand, clients' legal issues can become entangled with other problems, relationships, and emotions that can hardly be ignored. For example, in a prosecutor's office, attorneys have frequent contact with victims of serious crimes, and with facts and materials that are disturbing.

> *I met a woman who was held hostage and tortured for hours, while her ex-husband killed her mother. He stabbed her dozens of times, beat her and cut off her nose—all in front of their toddler son. He was only convicted of one charge of aggravated assault.*

Student Journal (Criminal Prosecution)

Stress is not confined to criminal law. In all types of law firms, government agencies, and public interest organizations, you may suddenly find yourself plunged into the middle of a human drama. Like the student whose journal follows, you might be surprised at the degree of stress that attorneys can experience in worker's compensation, immigration, and even real property law.

> *Every time I meet with a certain client, she cries and then I feel myself tearing up, too. I cry in the bathroom after she leaves, or in my car if it is the end of the day. I worry about her a great deal. She has a significant weakness in her case and, if forced to return to her country, I am convinced she will be killed.*

Student Journal (Immigration Law)

Many law students and lawyers confront conflict and violence for the first time in their internships or law practices. Working with clients or victims in pain and despair can be difficult to handle, even for experienced lawyers. It takes a special kind of emotional strength and perspective to work with people in these settings and it will come as no surprise that some attorneys are better at it than others.

To survive in this type of practice, you need to establish a certain emotional distance between yourself and your clients. This is not to say that you don't care about your clients or the outcome, or that you are an ineffective advocate. By not personally absorbing the pain and trauma of situation, you'll be able to handle the case with greater clarity, purpose and vision, something that your clients may not be able to do.

This is not something you develop overnight or learn from a textbook, so don't be embarrassed or self-critical if you find yourself in tears or experiencing other intense emotions. As you become more experienced over time and build on what you learn from each client, you'll gradually learn to cope more effectively. Otherwise, for now, watch and learn by observing attorneys and others in these settings. You'll notice that those who are most effective in dealing with clients under stress employ some of the following strategies.

- **Allow the client to talk without interruption; then focus the discussion.** Clients under stress want, in fact *need*, to feel that they have been heard. By allowing them to express their anger, hurt, and frustration, you will not only strengthen your attorney-client relationship, but may also learn crucial

facts that might not have been discovered
otherwise. However, set limits on the process.
In the initial interview, you might say,
"During our first 10 minutes, I want you
explain what brings you here so that I can
identify the important facts and legal issues.
Then, I'll ask some questions and we'll talk
more about where you should go from there.
But for now, I just want to hear your story."

- **Learn to distinguish between *empathy***
(imagining yourself in someone's situation, to
better understand their feelings and concerns)
and *sympathy* (being emotionally caught up
in someone's situation and sharing their
feelings to some extent). Your professional
judgment can become clouded if you get too
involved emotionally. For more on empathy,
see Chapter 24, "Emotional Intelligence—The
Key to Excellence."

- **Balance being *supportive*** (emotionally
encouraging) **and *objective*** (able to set aside
emotions and address facts). If you become too
emotionally involved, you risk inadvertently
coloring the facts, incorrectly assessing your
client's case and negative precedents and,
perhaps, going too far in zealous advocacy.
Ultimately this will hurt your client's case,
and threaten your professional integrity.

3. Sometimes Nobody Wins

If you're lucky enough to be on the winning side of a case, everybody goes home and gets the party started, right? Sometimes, but not always.

In many practices, those who win will never be entirely whole. Favorable resolution of a matter may be a cause for relief, but it does not necessarily generate a celebration. A father who is awarded liberal visitation will still miss seeing important experiences as his children grow up. An injured worker who is successful in his worker's compensation claim will receive an amount statutorily capped at an amount that is significantly lower than what he would have earned on the job. Even in business disputes, personal misunderstandings can lurk behind the economics; those issues may be driving the parties towards the courthouse, and may still be unresolved after "resolution" of the case.

In criminal law, too, you could say that most of the time nobody wins. A defendant who is acquitted has still experienced the stress of being accused of a crime, arrested, perhaps jailed, and suffered associated financial costs. A guilty sentence cannot erase the physical harm and/or economic loss suffered by the victims or their survivors; most family members, too, become victims of the situation.

Legal disputes take a physical, emotional and economic toll on *all* participants, winners *and* losers. Even though lawyers do their best to prepare clients for the uncertainties of their cases, they are rarely able to anticipate how draining litigation of any kind will be, and often have unrealistic expectations about their chances of winning, or what a victory will ultimately mean to them.

> *Our client prevailed, but the decision came at a cost to the defendant, who hadn't done anything wrong and yet suffered some pretty harsh consequences. Over 80 years old, she was forced to leave the land that she had lived and grown up on. This could not have been pleasant to deal with during the last weeks of her life (she died soon after the judge's decision). The case set a good legal precedent, but I have come to realize that what looks good on paper does not always have the noblest of consequences in reality.*

> Student Journal (Real Property Law)

C. DEALING WITH STRESS

The following are some practical suggestions for dealing with stress.

- **Acknowledge and try to identify the source of your discomfort, as well as your response to it.** You'll gain valuable insight that can be helpful in other situations.

- **Develop a journaling practice;** it can be a healthy outlet for stress and an effective tool for reflection.

- Do you have a **trusted, confidential sounding board** with whom you can occasionally discuss your problems and worries? If not, who could help in this regard?

- Are there **new activities and hobbies** that could help to relieve your stress? Many people find that meditation, mindfulness, and yoga provide a much-needed respite and, interestingly, advocates of more active physical activities such as walking, running, and bicycling tout these activities for similar benefits.

- **Try to spend more time outside.** Whatever the season and wherever you may live, there's something to be said for the palliative effects of fresh air and Mother Nature's beauty.

- **Realize that you can't solve every problem.** Sometimes, clients will lose cases that should have been won, and vice versa. Harmony will not always reign in the workplace and certain staff members may never get along. It's not your problem.

- Remember—even though you are an advocate, **your clients depend on you to maintain balance and be the voice of reason.**

- **Acknowledge feelings—your own and those of others with whom you are dealing.** Use more "I" statements ("I feel stressed when . . ."), instead of "you" statements ("Why do you always . . .").

- **Use the insight** that you gain from working with one client in your relationships with others.

- **Develop cordial professional relationships with the other side.** Try not to buy into the "we" vs. "them" mentality that may exist in certain legal communities or types of practice. Antagonism can harm your effectiveness in the long run.

- As much as possible, **don't blame, hold grudges, or hang on to negativity.** Medical professionals have been trying to convince us for a very long time that bottling up our feelings is detrimental to our health.

- **Speak with as many professors, attorneys, and other co-workers** as you can about how they deal with on-the-job stress.

- **Sometimes, a "tincture of time" is the best medicine.** Situations have a way of resolving themselves, and intense feelings tend to fade after a while.

- Despite our earlier advice, **realize that we all cope with stress differently.** You may be one of those people who thrives on it, at least to some degree.

- If your stress stems from feeling rushed and never getting all of your work done, **learn how to better manage your time,** possibly with the use of new apps and software. Being prepared will go a long way towards relieving some of your stress. See Chapters 20, "Time Management and Procrastination," and 26, "Finding Balance in Your Work and Life."

- **Learn to recognize the early warning signs of stress.** When you feel them, be careful about sensitive conversations and communications. You could inadvertently display impatience or dissatisfaction, and might make rash decisions that are ultimately negative to your client's case.

- Physical symptoms of stress can also signal minor or serious health problems, so schedule an appointment with your doctor just to be sure.

D.   GETTING PROFESSIONAL HELP

Increasingly, depression has been described as an "occupational hazard" for law students, lawyers and others in high-stress environments.

In these settings, the assistance of a trained, mental health professional can be invaluable in learning to deal with depression and other dangerous behaviors that can go along with it.

However, the perceived importance of our profession can ultimately prevent us from seeking help that we might desperately need. We may worry about the potential damage to our professional reputations and the reactions of family and friends. We worry about having severe depression, alcohol or substance abuse written into our permanent medical records; and fear the possible loss of our licenses to practice.

Law schools and state bar associations are beginning to take notice. Virtually all now provide various type of confidential assistance to law students and lawyers struggling with stress, depression, and the like. They are developing innovative programs to help confront the problem head on, ranging from CLE presentations on topics such as meditation and mindfulness to broad, confidential peer-to-peer support networks. In some cases, peer-volunteers provide very specific types of assistance, for example "I am an ordained minister, and I have experience with . . ." and "I am a recovering alcoholic and understand . . ."

Whether you start with a trusted friend or medical professional or check out your bar association's Member Services website, you'll find that many confidential resources and options are available to you. If your stress level has reached a dangerous level, we urge you to ask for help.

To read more about the topic of stress in the legal profession, see the comprehensive report released in August, 2017, by the ABA National Task Force on Lawyer Well-Being, "The Path to Lawyer Well Being: Practical Recommendations for Positive Change" (www.americanbar.org, search for "lawyer well-being"). The report contains a comprehensive examination of sources of stress in the profession, as well as recommendations for courts and judges, bar associations and other regulators, legal employers, and professional liability carriers.

CHAPTER 22

HANDLING CONFLICTS AT WORK

"A problem is a chance for you to do your best."
Duke Ellington

Conflicts at work are inevitable. Most of us associate the term "conflict" with some level of discomfort, from mild irritation to white-hot anger, resulting from differences or disagreements with others. We don't mean to imply that every conflict, even if uncomfortable, is a bad thing. Many conflicts, when addressed productively, result in stronger relationships and better outcomes generally.

Your exposure to conflict might be peripheral in nature. For example, a dispute between two colleagues may affect you only indirectly, but your awareness of and sensitivity to the situation could be helpful if tensions rise while you're working with them on a big case. Eventually you may be directly involved in or affected by a conflict in the workplace. Regardless of your degree of involvement, you may feel powerless to remedy the situation (for example, because of pre-existing dynamics, or due to your low level of influence in the organization).

> *As a new lawyer, and possibly even as a summer law clerk, you may find yourself in a position where some type of conflict arises. Exhibit maturity and handle the matter with sensitivity and good judgment.*
>
> Advice from an Employer

There *are* positive steps you can take to understand the nature of a conflict and to

minimize your discomfort. Often, the productive resolution of a conflict leads to improvements in relationships and a more productive working environment. In this chapter, we'll discuss how conflicts arise in the workplace and then offer strategies to address them effectively.

A. HOW CONFLICTS ARISE IN THE WORKPLACE

1. Mistaken First Impressions

Frequently the conflicts encountered by students and new lawyers are often the result of our mistaken first impressions of others. Even if we are usually self-confident, the stress of a new job can cause us to be uncertain about how people are reacting to us, leading us to read the wrong thing into someone's behavior. For example, you might get the feeling that your supervisor doesn't like you, or favors a co-worker. You might be unusually resistant to legitimate feedback or be overly sensitive to perceived criticism. Some people unconsciously compensate for their uneasiness by behaving in an overconfident manner, which can in turn put other people off. Add a new or extremely busy supervising attorney or an experienced but often underappreciated legal assistant to the scenario, and the situation is ripe for misunderstanding.

In the following journal, a student describes difficulty "bonding" with a supervisor, even though a co-worker had easily established a positive relationship. Upon reflection, the student decided to ignore the discomfort, offered to help with extra projects (including one that was primarily secretarial), and took both the supervisor and coworker to lunch. The conflict (whether real or imagined) was resolved.

> *I avoid conflict. Once I improved my relationship with my supervisor, I made sure I stayed on top of social AND professional communication—so that I would not slip back to where I had started. I realized it took me too long to try to improve this issue. I experienced so much fear that I would find out my supervisor didn't like me, or thought I was the wrong hire, or thought I was dumb, that I put up with an uncomfortable situation for too long. Really, I think my boss was waiting for a signal that I liked HER, and approved of her!*

Student Journal

2. Personality Conflicts

We all bring unique personalities to the workplace. Personal dynamics affect professional interactions, especially among those who work closely together. We feel more comfortable with certain people than with others. Friendships of varying degrees are established. Personality conflicts occasionally occur, and are difficult to handle, whether we are involved directly, indirectly, or simply feel caught in the middle.

> *Office relationships are an important factor in morale and effectiveness. An office nearby is undergoing many negative personnel issues*

including conflicts between management and subordinates, attorneys who cannot get along with each other, and others whose personal lives adversely affect their work.

Student Journal

Because personal relationships are so important at work, it's worthwhile to explore our own reactions to someone's unpleasant behavior, contemplate reasons why a person might behave in a certain way and what, if anything, we might do in future interactions.

One hypothetical, unnamed attorney seems almost dismissive of the interns and resentful that we breathe the same air, much less are requested to speak at case meetings, or (gasp) are given chances to make input on motions and pleadings. Now that I got that out of my system here in my journal, I suppose I can move on to actual important topics.

Student Journal

The situation described above sounds difficult to deal with, particularly for someone who is very much in the learning mode and needs the help and guidance of attorneys in the office. Even when others are cordial and welcoming, it's hard to feel completely at ease in the face of negative treatment by another person.

There are many reasons why somebody might be unreceptive to a student or new attorney—feeling overwhelmed with his own stress and workload; having a bad day; struggling with a pressing deadline; being a new supervisor and feeling uncertain about supervisory skills—just to name a few. In the situation described above, the student couldn't change the attorney's behavior, but felt much better after venting in a journal.

If you find yourself entangled in a personality conflict, review your assumptions. Try to understand the other person's situation to help pinpoint the potential source or sources of the problem, so that you can consider all possible options for dealing with it. What part, if any, might you be playing in the conflict? If you can't find a way to establish a more positive relationship, consider limiting your interaction with the person as much as possible, and concentrate on those people who are most helpful and willing to work with you. When interacting with the "difficult person," try to lead with positive greetings. In all situations, try to maintain your own positive, professional attitude.

3.   Work and Work Management Issues

From minor irritations to definite challenges, you'll encounter many "learning opportunities" in the workplace. If you haven't yet begun your first legal internship or job, simply scan the Table of Contents and Index of this book to get an idea of the wide range of issues you'll be asked to deal with—including how to conduct yourself professionally, juggle assignments, produce on time the high-quality work that is expected of you, and communicate effectively with supervisors and co-workers. For the most part, the process is both enjoyable and rewarding, and many minor irritations or annoyances disappear with the passage of time. But issues that occur repeatedly, are left unresolved, or are sufficiently serious, become causes for concern.

For example, law clerks collaborating on a joint research project might have incompatible working styles that, if unresolved, could endanger their ability to meet the assigning attorney's deadline. What one clerk views as essential yet meticulous research may delay the process of writing the interoffice memorandum until the very last minute, causing the other clerk to panic and a deadline to be missed. A new lawyer waiting for the assignment may leave for vacation with the project left unfinished, leaving a co-worker with the need to get up to speed rapidly.

A bad experience with one law clerk or new lawyer may leave attorneys and staff skeptical of all clerks or new lawyers. In the following journal, a student describes the efforts she and a co-worker made to overcome the negative impression left by a careless and disorganized student during the previous year.

A supervising attorney accused me and my co-intern of sitting on a case file until the response motion we were responsible for writing was overdue. We listened calmly . . . we agreed filing on time was important . . . we calmly laid out our understanding of what had happened with the file. . . we explained that we had filed the disclosure (which avoided sanctions). Despite our inability to have prevented this, we

*apologized and assured the attorney that we
would continue to be vigilant about deadlines.*

Student Journal

Another problem: One of your co-workers may look
the other way or disappear when routine or tedious
assignments are made, or consistently get the "best"
projects.

*I am co-interning with a law student. After being
here almost two weeks, I'm still waiting to see
what projects are in store for me. My fellow intern
has four research and writing projects going on—
in addition to our client intake interviews. I
wonder why there is such a wide disparity in the
amount and quality of legal work we are
assigned. I'm not sure if I should feel insulted or
not. It's not so much that I'm not given anything
to do, but it's the fact that the two interns are
treated so vastly different. "Does it boil down to
trust?" I ask myself. Needless to say, I start to
doubt myself.*

Student Journal

Uneven work distribution (whether accidental or
by design) can cause concern and, eventually,
resentment, and yet there are many possible
explanations for the problem. For example, where
several law clerks are in the same office, or "pool"
setting, the person getting more desirable projects
may have more legal experience. She may have
worked in the office for a longer period of time, and
the attorneys may have developed confidence in her
work. She may be more assertive and socially at ease,

and more successful at getting work. Instead of waiting for assignments, she may volunteer for projects that she finds interesting. The explanation may also be as simple as the fact that she is the person sitting nearest to the door or to the attorneys' offices. In seeking a more equitable division of work, the student quoted earlier spoke to the managing attorney, asked for more in-depth research projects (as opposed to asking for just "more work," which might leave the door open to receiving more mundane work) and spent the remainder of the summer working on projects that were as interesting and challenging as those being given to her co-worker.

B.   STRATEGIES FOR COPING WITH CONFLICT

Law students and new lawyers often have difficulty finding a balance between avoiding conflicts and trying to resolve them. When does ignoring a situation, instead of confronting it, make sense, and when does it ensure that a problem will escalate? When might assertiveness be perceived as aggressiveness . . . and, for that matter, what is the difference between the two terms? The keys to conflict resolution are openness to the other's position, willingness to take a new look at the situation, the ability to *listen to understand* the other, and openness to seeing the other person and possible solutions more expansively than before. The following strategies may help you deal with the uncertainties and stress that often accompany conflict in the workplace.

- **Before taking any action, first examine your internal discomfort.** When you are upset and uncertain, your feelings are often magnified, sometimes out of proportion to the situation. What exactly is making you uncomfortable or angry or frustrated?

I have experienced personality conflicts before, and learned that patience goes a long way. I don't react to her outbursts and am trying to make the most of my experience here. In the meantime, I don't feel like I have been thrown into the water without a life raft. I really like my peers and the support from them is immense.

Student Journal

- **Look for early solutions that are easy to implement,** before stress builds, before too much time has passed and you feel awkward about raising your concern, or before the situation has spiraled out of control.

- **Don't take someone else's bad attitude personally,** as it most often reflects more about the person living with it than the other people affected by it.

- **Fight the temptation to act based on your knee-jerk reaction, or jump to conclusions, particularly early in your job.** Where conflict is involved, it's tempting to concentrate on the negatives. Balance your focus; try to identify the positives in the workplace or in specific relationships there.

- **Sometimes the best action is not to act at all.** If you are uncertain why, or even whether, someone has a problem with you, by drawing attention to the issue you could create a problem where one never existed. Alternatively, if you actually are in a person's bad graces, by bringing the issue into the open, it can no longer "blow over" casually. If you are a summer intern, as a "short-timer," you are only temporarily involved in the workplace dynamics. The potential negatives of confronting someone about inappropriate behavior may outweigh the benefits.

- Many conflicts are resolved with time and a minimal attitude adjustment. You may never even be able to pinpoint the cause of the problem.

Most problems boil down to personality differences or someone having a bad day. I've found that if I can wait to react, the person in the wrong has an opportunity to apologize before I jump in and make it worse. And as an intern I just don't feel like it's my place to stir the soup. If my job were permanent, I would develop a more aggressive communication style, but as an 8-week intern I don't think it is warranted.

Student Journal

- **Make it a personal rule not to speak ill of anyone,** and not to get caught up in gossip or the personal conflicts of others.

The Talmud tells of a repentant tale-teller who was instructed by a rabbi to repent by tearing open a pillow in the village square on a windy day. He was puzzled, yet complied. Afterwards, he asked why he was told to do such a thing, and the rabbi explained that words are like feathers. Once released, they are impossible to collect.

Student Journal

- **Don't be defensive—even if you think you're in the right.** Ask questions instead. "How could I have done this better?" "Is there anything I could do differently next time to avoid this situation?"

- **Resist the urge to complain or confide to someone in the office.** Find an external sounding board if you must, but be selective in your choice, and avoid disclosing confidential information.

C. CHECKLIST FOR ADDRESSING SERIOUS CONFLICTS

Many of you are familiar with the approaches to conflict resolution set out in *Getting to Yes*, by Roger Fisher and William Ury, the classic work on negotiation used in many law school courses on negotiation. We commend it to you not only in connection with your work with clients, but in addressing your own conflicts. You'll recognize concepts from *Getting to Yes* in the chart below.

We also recommend the principles of conflict resolution set forth with excellent examples and presented in a beautiful visual design, in *Changing the Conversation*, by Dana Caspersen and Joost Elffers. It is well worth reading in its entirety. Many of the ideas in the chart below have been culled from *Changing the Conversation*, supplemented and modified by our own experiences. Language in quotes in the chart are directly quoted from the principles and anti-principles on pp. xviii and xix of *Changing the Conversation*.

For more information about conflicts and how to deal with them, see also Chapter 24, "Emotional Intelligence—The Key to Excellence," Chapter 8, "Working Well with Others," and Chapter 11, "Managing Written Assignments."

Resolving Conflicts: Do's and Don'ts

Do	Don't
Do "Acknowledge conflict. Talk to the right people" about it—the person involved or someone you trust.	**Don't** Avoid serious conflicts or talk to the wrong people about them.
Listen for the other's concerns (what is the other person worried about?).	"Attack the other." Interpret the other's words as an attack (even if it feels like it).
Listen to understand and acknowledge. "Differentiate between acknowledgement and agreement."	Be as vague as possible so the other person isn't sure whether you agree or not.
"Talk to the other person's best self." Assume good faith.	Assume the other isn't interested in a good resolution.
Assume you can have a positive conversation (even if you are skeptical).	Give up before you try to resolve the conflict.
Identify and focus on "needs" and "interests" (there is more than one way to satisfy needs and interests).	Argue about strategy and position (a strategy only allows one way to solve a problem).
Assume you can find a way to solve the problem, even if you don't see it now.	Assume that the only solutions are the ones you can see right now.
Pay attention to the other person's responses. "If you are making things worse, stop."	Make suggestions before you understand the other side.

Resolving Conflicts: Do's and Don'ts (cont.)

Do	**Don't**
Observe. Listen. Again. And again.	"Judge people."
"Test your assumptions." Let them go if they aren't accurate.	Cling to your unproven assumptions.
Consider how you can be flexible and still meet your needs.	Insist on your appoach.
Be curious and open to new information and understandings.	Assume you know it all.
Explore what's going on with a beginner's approach.	Search for blame. Assume you know everything about the situation.
Acknowledge your contribution to the problem.	Assume it's all the fault of the other person.
Be clear and state agrements. Make sure all understand the same thing.	Assume everyone agrees on everything and leave the room as soon as you can.
Re-state your understanding.	Be vague. Generalize.
Listen to the other's under-standing of the agreement.	Rush to agreement.
Expect that similar conflicts will arise and plan together how to handle them.	Avoid all conversations about the future.

CHAPTER 23

HOW ADULTS LEARN—AND WHY IT MATTERS

"I am always ready to learn although I do not always like to be taught."
Sir Winston S. Churchill

By getting into law school, you demonstrated your ability to learn and do it well. So why, you may wonder, have we devoted a chapter of this book to adult learning principles?

You'll face a steep learning curve in the workplace and your employer's training process will likely incorporate many of the key principles that are most supportive of adult learning. But not all on-the-job learning opportunities come in a program specifically created or intended for learning. The following suggestions will help you consciously structure your experiences so that you learn as effectively as possible while managing a new and growing workload. You'll find new contexts for existing skills, more easily assimilate newly acquired skills, and stay more fully engaged while completing assignments that at first glance may look like "busy work."

A. ADULTS LEARN BEST WHEN

- ... they can place new information into their framework of existing skills.

- ... they are in control of their own learning process, or at least know what others expect of them.

- ... they are provided with situations and scenarios that are concrete, rather than abstract.

- ... they are actively participating in the process, rather than merely learning by observation.

- ... they are willing to ask for help when needed.

- ... they are able to vary bursts of activity with brief periods of reflection.

- ... they make the time for realistic and meaningful self-evaluation.

1.   Maximize Your Existing Skills

When learning something new, we want it to have at least some relevance to information that we already have mastered—think of this as the "building block" method of learning.

As a result, when material seems completely foreign, your knee-jerk reaction may be to try to slow things down, so that you can learn methodically, starting from the beginning. In the fast-paced environment of legal practice, new professionals often must "hit the ground running"—and this can feel extremely uncomfortable.

Yet **you do have a solid foundation of skills and abilities,** and **now is the ideal time to take a personal skills inventory.** For example, like most law students, you probably excel at oral and written communications; you also have critical thinking skills and analytical abilities. Through activities such as undergraduate and law school courses, past employment, and participation in volunteer opportunities, you cultivated other unique qualities. Almost all of your existing skills can either be directly applied to your work in law or translated into a useful application in law. You must first be aware of your skills and then consciously consider how they can apply in a new legal setting.

What else can you add to the list? If you find yourself drawing a blank when thinking about your talents and abilities, take a few moments to review the Brainstorming Exercise at the end of this chapter. **If some of your skills are rusty, use this as an opportunity to bring them up to date.**

Once identified and strengthened, your skills base should serve both to reassure and support you while facing new challenges.

2.   Manage Unclear Expectations

Initially, others will have control over your schedule, your deadlines, your workload. Your assignments may come from lawyers with little supervisory experience, who may not even realize that they are being unclear about their expectations. Unfortunately, you can't always depend on senior attorneys to give you as much direction as you would like, either.

You'll find it frustrating when your supervisor is unclear about his expectations. You'll likely feel even more internal discord if you have various supervisors with different management styles, or if multiple attorneys are reviewing the same work product. Who wants what? When? And how can you keep track?

Think of these situations as opportunities to be a bit more self-directed and do your best to seize more control.

- When an assigning attorney gives you a new project, **be as interactive as possible.** Listen closely to instructions, think about what is being requested, and ask for more details or clarification if necessary.

- The **Project Assignment Sheet** in Chapter 11, "Managing Written Assignments," provides a good framework for getting the information you'll need when beginning a new assignment.

- **If you need additional guidance** after starting to work, get in touch with the assigning attorney right away. Don't wait until the last minute, because you never know what both of you might have on your plates later.

- **Keep the assigning attorney informed** about your progress.

- **Ask for feedback** after completing an assignment, both to improve your general skills and to have a better idea of what the attorney expects of you the next time you work together.

- **Your supervisor is not a mind reader.** Be proactive—if you want to work on a certain case, in a particular area of law, or with a specific attorney, ask. You'll still be expected to pitch in on your share of less interesting projects, but attorneys are generally happy to accommodate your interests when possible.

Take responsibility for your own learning experience . . . find a balance between asking and taking the initiative!

Advice from an Employer

As lawyers, there will be many occasions when we don't know the answer and are uncertain of the outcome. Accept the fact that it sometimes goes with the job description and find ways to adapt.

3.   Make "Abstract" Assignments Concrete

It wouldn't be surprising if Torts, Contracts and Criminal Law were among your favorite first-year courses. There, learning occurred in the context of real cases, clients, and problems. Similarly, when you have workplace assignments that deal with real-life situations and legal issues, you'll find it easy to become fully immersed in the facts and their application to law. Time will pass more quickly, and you'll feel that you've accomplished something at the end of each day.

However, an attorney's work is not always case-related. Sometimes **you may be asked to research a general topic, without specific fact patterns, and perhaps without a firm deadline** . . . the so-called "back-burner project."

> *My assignments fall into two categories. One category contains assignments related to matters that attorneys feel are going to be at issue soon. I suppose the lesson here is that you should anticipate and prepare for problems or issues that may arise in your client's future, and determine how you will address them or mitigate them when they occur.*

Student Journal

> *Take control of "non-deadline" projects. Even though they don't have to be completed within a specific timeframe, they do concern issues of importance to us and they offer you the opportunity to begin managing your own workload.*

Advice from an Employer

Without a live issue or "real case," you may feel that your research lacks direction. When you have trouble finding a beginning, middle and end of a project, it seems to drag on forever. And, when the day is filled with "busy work," you'll go home exhausted.

In these circumstances, **try to combat the instinct to feel bored, and look for ways to keep your interest level high.** Here are some strategies:

- To **gain perspective on how a generalized assignment fits into the overall work of your office,** find out how often and **in what context this type of issue might arise.** If time permits, ask whether you can review some case files that provide examples.

- **If you are feeling "unmoored" in your research, ask your supervisor or other attorneys in the office for suggestions** on how to better deal with broad-based research projects. Some attorneys find it helpful to build their own mental fact patterns and stories, to keep the research from feeling so abstract.

- **Clarify your research strategy** and try to distill your broad, generalized research into a few key principles and issues that your audience can more easily follow.

- In your written or oral summary, first state your key findings and principles and then give relevant, specific examples to illustrate how they might arise in various situations. This will help your audience (e.g., supervising attorney or client) better understand how the results of your general research might be applied.

4.   Learn Through Engaged Observation

As a student, and later as a new associate, learning often arises in the context of being invited by someone to go somewhere, to watch something. **As an observer, after anywhere from a few seconds to a few minutes, you'll surely find that your mind begins to wander,** even though the discussion might actually be interesting.

> *In a civil trial, detailed questioning and impeaching based on depositions is common. The process is agonizingly slow, and I often wonder what the point is. I remember watching a civil trial one afternoon. I was bored—and it was a little unsettling when one of the paralegals commented, "This is the high point. This is what we're here for!" If this is as good as it gets, I was wondering why I wasn't having fun yet.*

Student Journal

No one can stay mentally alert 100% of the time, and some situations are particularly challenging. However, **there are a few steps you can take to keep your mind active if you are lucky enough to be invited to meetings, client interviews, hearings, or trials.**

- **Before you go, prepare a list of things to watch for,** such as coverage of certain topics, speech mannerisms, and body language.

- **Sit up** straight, and maintain **eye contact** with the speakers.

- Try to **mentally interact** and have an "internal dialogue" with everything you see and hear. Are comments being made that you don't understand or agree with? Points that you find particularly interesting?

- **When your attention wanders,** bring it back and mentally re-focus. Do this as many times and as frequently as necessary. Based on your observations, make a mental list of do's and don'ts and recall them from time to time.

- **If you find yourself getting drowsy,** do something to wake up. Get a drink of water. Glance around the room. Try isometrics to get your blood circulating (e.g., discretely tighten and then relax your right leg or another set of muscles).

- **Make notes** during or immediately after the event. Notice what the various players are doing that is particularly effective or not. Jot down specific points you found interesting. Later, take a few moments to **reflect** on what you saw.

- Seek out opportunities to **"debrief"** with your supervisor.

5.   Ask for Help if You Need It

How many times have you **passed up an opportunity** to speak in class for fear of looking foolish? Or, after you *did* get up the nerve to make a comment, felt that you'd put your foot in your mouth?

We adults hate to make mistakes. We feel uncomfortable if asked to do something we don't know how to do, or don't know how to do well, and we certainly don't want to do it in front of an audience.

Our hesitation to ask for help is one of the most potentially damaging factors to our professional growth. If you don't conscientiously combat this natural tendency, you'll likely find yourself in trouble on at least one assignment in the workplace. Fear or shyness might also cause you to turn down opportunities, such as an invitation to orally present your research, represent the office at a meeting, or speak in court.

If it helps, acknowledge your fear, then set it aside and move forward. Your supervisor doesn't expect perfection, but does expect you to be fully prepared and give every project 100% of your effort. Experienced attorneys know that law students and new lawyers face very high learning curves; they will celebrate your successes and be supportive when you make mistakes.

6.   Create an Occasional Change of Scene

Although you've only been sitting behind a desk for eight hours, not doing manual labor, **you may be surprised to find yourself totally exhausted at the end of a workday.** Law students and new professionals usually expect to find more action on the job than they get in the beginning. That's the bad news.

*Having to be at the office for 10+ hours a day is
a tiring and wearing schedule. It challenges me
to remain consistent in my level of productivity. I
think being responsible for my own projects
would change this somewhat. Ownership is
motivating.*

Student Journal

The good news is that, once you've been in practice
for a while, you'll find more variety in your work.
Meanwhile, here are a few suggestions to combat the
weariness that comes from sitting behind a desk most
of the day.

- **Set interim goals** to help you work through
  long projects. For example, if you need to wrap
  up your research and submit a memo to your
  supervisor by next Friday, plan to finish the
  first draft by the middle of next week.

- Try to **maintain a high level of
  concentration and work without
  interruption for 20–30 minutes.** Then take
  a short break. Get up and stretch, take a short
  walk, or step outside for a drink of water.
  Move around and relax your focus. Adult
  learning theorists tell us that it is often during
  these brief interludes when "Eureka
  moments" occur and connections between
  seemingly unrelated bits of information are
  made.

*I've learned that my mind works best when I can
break from one project and set into another—
when I get to a sticking point, the ability to place*

that matter on a "back burner" and move to a different subject allows my subconscious to process the first, while I consciously work on the latter. This often results in epiphanies in strange places—realizing a novel new approach while playing basketball, or figuring out the missing piece to a legal puzzle during an episode of Desperate Housewives.

Student Journal

- If your deadline permits, **alternate projects now and then. If your mind begins to wander, use your time working on another assignment** that doesn't take as much concentration. Move around as much as possible during the day, and **get moving after work and on the weekends.** Regular physical activity will help to alleviate stress and help you stay alert during the day.

7.   Assess Yourself Realistically

Many new law grads find themselves floundering without positive indicators such as grades or feedback.

We hope that you will receive feedback from attorneys in your workplace, but that may not always be the case. Chapter 14, "Feedback," may be helpful in this type of situation.

Whether you are receiving feedback or not, as a competent and learning adult, *you must be able to evaluate and monitor your own progress.*

- Learn how to keep yourself motivated and always perform to the best of your ability, knowing that you will continue to reap the benefits of each experience

- Set short-term and long-term goals for yourself; reflect on how you have grown, what you have learned, and areas where you would like to improve. Be concrete so that you can assess your performance.

- Take a long-range view of your expectations, too, because sometimes the full value of an experience does not become apparent until much later.

Listen, observe, and learn—from everything.

Advice from an Employer

B. SKILLS INVENTORY

Initially, law school focuses so much on what we *don't know* that we don't realize we already possess many skills that we'll need as attorneys. Whether you worked extensively prior to law school or came straight from your undergraduate degree, your life skills and experiences provide you with a valuable framework into which you can place new legal and other knowledge.

Moreover, until you acquire more on-the-job legal experience, **employers will make hiring decisions about you based on this "total package" of skills.** These are the strengths and abilities that will set you apart from other candidates.

If asked to realistically assess your strengths and, conversely, areas where you would like to increase your knowledge or ability, could you do so? In our experience, many students draw a blank when it comes to accurately identifying their skills. If you fall into this category, the following brainstorming exercise may help you to better recognize your own unique qualifications. If you are looking for a job, it will boost your confidence and help prepare you to communicate this important information to prospective employers. If you have just started a new a job, this exercise will serve as a reminder that "non-legal skills" are crucial to the tasks that you will be doing as a law clerk or lawyer.

Because I was an English teacher, they give me motions, press releases, and letters for feedback. I feel good that my skills, knowledge and conscientiousness have been recognized and appreciated. This is a reminder that, even though I am new to law, a lot about doing the work of a lawyer is not new to me at all.

Student Journal

C. BRAINSTORMING AND SKILLS INVENTORY

This exercise should take 30 minutes or so to complete. You may wish to do it alone but you might also complete it with the help of a trusted friend or advisor who knows you very well.

To begin, take a moment to review your most current resume. Reflect on answers to the following questions and any other ideas that they generate. This is a brainstorming process, so don't rush, don't be overly analytical, and try not to censor your observations.

- What talents did you develop, both in and out of the classroom, while an undergraduate? What talents had you begun to develop and enjoy as a child? Think of "talent" in as broad a sense as you can.

- What classes interested you the most? Least?

- If you had unlimited time and resources, are there other areas of study and/or career paths that you would have liked to follow and what interested you about them?

- What were your personal interests back then and how, if at all, have they changed?

- What skills are needed for your past and current personal interests? Which of these do you most enjoy doing? Can you identify what it is about them that makes them so enjoyable or satisfying?

- Can you identify any general similarities between your activities and skills and the tasks that lawyers do?

Now, take a blank sheet of paper. Moving down the left-hand margin, jot down the numbers one through ten (or beyond if the questions stimulated a lot of ideas) and leave some space for comments between the numbers. Then, without being overly critical and with minimal editing, jot down reflections about any of the above questions that sparked your interest.

Your general objective is to notice recurring interests and activities, and identify skills and abilities that you employed in the pursuit of them. Ideally, this exercise will give you a better understanding of the "total package" of skills that you have to offer and a more organized way of describing them to a prospective employer.

Following are three observations from students with different backgrounds.

1. From Student with Economics Degree

- *Observation:* "From my background in Economics, I have two different, yet complementary, approaches to research. I can focus on facts, figures and details (the micro view). But I also know how to look for trends, analyze disparate information, and forecast what will happen in an organization's future (the macro view)."

- *Relevance to Legal Practice:* "Both views are relevant to legal research. Lawyers must sift through very detailed, legal and non-legal information, focus on small points, and present them accurately. Yet, they must also be aware of the bigger picture, emerging legal trends, and the potential effects of setting new legal precedent."

2. From Student with Teaching Experience

- *Observation:* "I just realized how much I enjoy being in the role of communicator and teacher. I was a volunteer elementary school tutor, working with at-risk students to strengthen their math skills and help to keep them motivated. Later, as a teaching assistant, I worked with college students (again tutoring, but this time in Japanese . . . a difficult subject). Even my summer jobs in retail and restaurants involved communicating with various audiences."

- *Relevance to Legal Practice:* "Lawyers are fundamentally communicators and teachers, and they work with different audiences from different backgrounds. Whether explaining the results of research to a senior partner, meeting with a client, or standing before a jury, oral communication skills are vital."

3. From Student with Liberal Arts Degree

- *Observation:* "I don't have very much legal research experience, but I did research and write a 25-page paper in an undergrad class called Communications in the 20th Century. I explored the relationship between the expansion of television in the 1950's and emergence of modern advertising trends. It was an interesting project and I had to gather information from books, publications, newspapers and magazines. I analyzed the topic from the standpoint of technology, economics, politics, and behavioral psychology. I got an A, and made an oral presentation on it, too."

- ***Relevance to Legal Practice:*** "The ability to research efficiently, write well, and to speak publicly about your findings is a necessity for lawyers. Research often involves gathering information from various resources (sometimes non-legal), and analyzing topics from different points of view. Maybe I have better research skills than I've given myself credit for."

CHAPTER 24

EMOTIONAL INTELLIGENCE—
THE KEY TO EXCELLENCE

"There are three things extremely hard: steel,
a diamond, and to know one's self."
Benjamin Franklin

Upon entering law school, you and your classmates shared similar undergraduate GPA's and LSAT scores, factors that are considered strong indicators of your potential for success. **In a class of high achievers, you might have wondered if, and how, you could stand out as an excellent performer in school, and later as a lawyer.**

For most of us, law school and the process of beginning a legal career is life-altering. It can be exhausting, exhilarating, and exceedingly difficult . . . all at the same time, with new information to process (the need to learn a new way of thinking, really), the pressure of grade curves, stress of exams and job interviews, and so much more. Many students lose confidence in their abilities and even doubt whether they have what it takes to be good lawyers.

You'll be relieved to know that **there are tangible steps you can take to improve your performance—and they don't involve outside reading, writing assignments, or having your performance evaluated by others.** They also have nothing to do with your IQ (which is fortunate, because research shows there is little you can do to significantly increase it, anyway).

What you *can* increase is your EQ (emotional quotient). This is good news, because studies indicate that almost 90% of one's success in leadership is attributable to "people skills." In fact, EQ may be up to twice as important as your cognitive abilities (e.g., IQ and academic scores). Emotional intelligence has such a powerful effect on performance that the concept is used in a wide variety of settings to enhance management and leadership abilities, employee performance, and team building.

This chapter will explore the elements of emotional intelligence, illustrate how they are directly related to skills lawyers use in their jobs daily, and show you how to increase your own EQ.

A.   DEFINING EMOTIONAL INTELLIGENCE

If we were to suggest that you could resolve many of the problems you encounter in your professional and personal lives by improving your people skills, where would you begin? Just what are "people skills," anyway?

Emotional intelligence explains a nebulous concept like "people skills" in terms of specific, understandable behaviors. It explores the many ways we interact with each other from two distinct, but related, perspectives: "self" and "others." Because our natural inclination is to look for external causes when things go awry, you may find it uncomfortable, yet enlightening, to focus on "self" (your feelings and behaviors, as well as your desire and ability to manage your impulses). After exploring "self," the focus turns outward, to "others," and explores how well you understand and how well you interact with other people.

With emotional intelligence, you will have the tools to design your own, personalized, self-improvement program, and can progress at your own pace, focusing on just one or a few qualities at a time. With each step, you'll notice a tangible difference in the quality of your interactions with others.

B. EMOTIONAL INTELLIGENCE— THE GOLEMAN MODEL

Although there are many people working in the field of emotional intelligence, the model developed by Daniel Goleman offers a user-friendly approach that is easily applied to a variety of settings. The material in this chapter is based on his book, *Emotional Intelligence.*

Goleman's EQ model contains 25 core competencies, along with a framework for measuring and improving your skills in each competency. The framework is presented on the following chart, which we'll use as a guide to explore how these competencies affect your performance at work and your interactions with others.

We'll begin by focusing on the left side, which depicts Personal Competence, with skills and abilities related to *you*, your thoughts and emotions, as well as your ability and motivation to manage them. Then we'll move to the right side of the chart, focusing on your Social Competence, which includes the thoughts, emotions, and actions of *others* (a wide range of "others"), as well as your ability to create positive social interactions with them. We'll discuss most (but not all) of Goleman's 25 competencies.

Emotional Intelligence

Personal Competence

Self-Awareness
   Emotional Awareness
   Self-Assessment
   Self-Confidence

Self Management
   Self-Control
   Influence
   Trustworthiness
   Conscientiousness
   Adaptability
   Innovation

Motivation
   Achievement Drive
   Commitment
   Initiative
   Optimism

Social Competence

Empathy
   Understanding Others
   Developing Others
   Service Orientation
   Leveraging Diversity
   Political Awareness

Social Skills
   Communication
   Conflict Management
   Leadership
   Change Catalyst
   Building Bonds
   Collaboration
      & Cooperation

From **Emotional Intelligence** by Daniel Goleman (1995) Bantam Books

C.   BEFORE WE BEGIN—AN OVERVIEW

Emotional intelligence has many "moving parts," and it is helpful to keep the big picture in mind.

Don't expect to excel in every competency.
We each have particular strengths and weaknesses,
and you'll find that some EQ concepts are harder to
develop than others. If you try to master everything
at once, you'll be frustrated. A better strategy is to
identify key areas that seem most relevant to your
job and/or personal life, and concentrate on a few
concepts at a time.

> *I can be an extreme perfectionist, and it has taken
> time to learn that my strengths differ from the
> strengths of others, just as my weaknesses differ.
> I am learning that a professional does not have
> to be the best at everything. Understanding this
> has been an important lesson for me.*

> Student Journal

**Certain competencies are important early in
your career; others will be more valuable as
you gain experience and undertake more
responsibilities.** For example, for a new
professional, the ability to accurately assess your
work is far more important than the immediate
development of management skills. If you seek
feedback from a more senior lawyer when you need
it, you'll increase the chances of producing excellent
and useful work, of learning how to exercise good
judgment, and, eventually, of receiving positive
performance evaluations. Over time, you will be able
to assess your own work without as much feedback
from others. Once you have developed the ability to
assess your work accurately, you'll be able to provide
feedback to others and focus more on developing your
management and leadership skills. In the meantime,

you can observe how a skilled, experienced attorney provides helpful feedback.

Certain competencies are hierarchical, in that you must have a strong foundation in one area before developing another. For example, to work cooperatively and collaboratively with others, one must first develop self-awareness and self-control.

Certain competencies are most effective when exercised together, such as conscientiousness and trustworthiness.

Finally, **emotional intelligence is not limited to the workplace.** Your family and friends will probably never appreciate your expertise in torts or real property law, but they'll be grateful for the growing insight that EQ gives you in your interactions with them!

D.   FOCUS ON SELF—SELF-AWARENESS

Self-awareness is one of the most valuable areas for inexperienced lawyers to explore. It involves honestly appraising your beliefs, emotions, strengths, weaknesses, and skills, and being self-confident about who you are. It also helps you work through challenges (and with challenging people), be more accepting of feedback, and keeps you from taking yourself too seriously. Self-awareness can guide you towards projects that will help you develop new skills, yet keep you from getting in too far over your head in the process.

Because we are complex individuals, self-exploration can be both illuminating and daunting, but it is ultimately rewarding.

The hardest thing that I've ever done has been getting to know myself on a very intimate level, so that I'm not at the mercy of the world around me. As I say this out loud, it doesn't sound that impressive, but it was a big accomplishment.

Student Journal

Components of Self-Awareness

- Emotional Awareness
- Accurate Self-Assessment
- Self-Confidence

Emotional Awareness. Science confirms what we intuitively already know—**our emotions affect our thoughts and actions.** We have all experienced "knee jerk" reactions that occur so quickly we have neither the time nor the ability to understand or control them. For example, have you ever lashed out at someone in anger, only to realize later that a different underlying emotion actually caused the outburst? Have fear and insecurity ever caused you to be unusually shy or have you ever masked shyness with overconfidence?

During the early days of one's career, and in situations where we feel uncertain, our emotions often get in the way of our learning process. Even worse, they can cause us to behave inappropriately, at times triggering negative reactions from others.

Self-reflection, even if it occurs after your emotions have gotten away from you, can be useful in honing your power of self-awareness. Eventually, you'll learn to better tune into your feelings and analyze their effects (positive or negative) on your behavior, as the student did in the following journal entry.

I didn't realize at first what was bothering me. Emotional awareness and self-assessment would have helped me to more quickly identify the source of my frustration. I was having trouble understanding my own emotions and its causes.

Student Journal

Accurate Self-Assessment. Do you know anyone who takes pleasure in admitting their weaknesses? Probably not, but **in preparing for a new career in law, it is crucial to realistically assess your abilities.** Your supervising attorney won't have a problem if you ask for help when you need it (and, in fact, may be impressed), but will be justifiably concerned if you don't realize that you need assistance, or if you let overconfidence cloud your judgment. Moreover, as discussed in Chapter 23, "How Adults Learn—and Why It Matters," you'll accelerate your pace of learning if you take advantage of every opportunity for self-assessment. Chapter 14, "Feedback," suggests ways of getting feedback from others, as well as ways to develop your ability to provide your own.

Self-Confidence. Law students and new lawyers are in high learning mode, and some may find it difficult to strike a balance between being too confident and not being confident enough. Do yourself a big favor and be clear about your unique skills and abilities. By appreciating your strengths, you can be more proactive in seeking the types of assignments, projects, and feedback that you need to develop new and stronger skills. Chapter 27, "What Skills Do Lawyers Need," provides two useful charts to assist you in assessing your skills and identifying your current strengths as well as future areas for skill development.

Developing self-confidence will make an enormous difference in my personal and professional success. I keep telling myself that I need to work on it, but it is difficult. I often bring myself down, despite the wonderful support I receive in all areas of my life. But, if I cannot be sure of myself, I cannot expect others to be.

Student Journal

To increase your self-awareness, learn to quiet your mind from its incessant chatter and focus on inner calmness. Techniques like meditation and exercise may be helpful, and one of the best reflective tools is to keep a journal. Ask yourself a few introspective questions: "What things make me frustrated or angry, and how do I react when I feel this way?" "In the office, which attorneys do I admire, and why?" Chapter 26, "Finding Balance in Your Work and Life," and Chapter 20, "Time Management and Procrastination," address how to develop greater self-awareness in specific contexts.

E.   FOCUS ON SELF—SELF-MANAGEMENT

For decades, authors have been writing on topics related to self-management. At the bookstore and online, you'll find a wide range of useful articles and books on everything from ethics, to social and moral philosophy, to organization, time management, unlocking your "creative potential," and beyond.

One of the best ways to explore self-management is to observe how attorneys, staff, and interns manage themselves while interacting with each other and with clients. You'll easily find both positive and negative role models from whom to learn. To get the maximum benefit, observe and evaluate your own actions, too.

Components of Self-Management
- Self-Control
- Trustworthiness
- Conscientiousness
- Adaptability
- Innovation

Self-Control. **Have you ever acted out of impulse, only to regret it later? If so, you may have problems with self-control,** which is hard to admit when planning for a career that is inherently stressful. Even those who are adept at controlling their emotions might wonder if they will be able to "keep their cool" under pressure or if confronted by lawyers or others who are rude and behave unprofessionally. Attorneys deal with conflict daily, and those who lose their tempers can negatively affect the outcome of their cases. If you don't learn how to handle the stress, at a minimum you run the risk of going home "mad" on a regular basis. The ramifications for your reputation and health could be even worse. Chapter 21, "Managing Stress," and Chapter 22, "Handling Conflicts at Work," provide helpful suggestions.

Learning to stay calm takes practice, but is worth the effort. First, figure out what makes you angry, so that you'll recognize and be able to control it before it gets out of hand. For example, one lawyer realized that angry phone calls caused her to lose control, so she attached a post-it note to her phone as a reminder to stay 100% present at all times. The post-it is now tattered from monitoring years of phone calls. Regular exercise and behavior modification techniques such as counting to 10, or breathing deeply can be helpful, too. The following journals highlight various aspects of anger.

My supervising attorney didn't seem bothered by opposing counsel's hostility. She seemed cool and unaffected, did not act impulsively, and was able to handle him with tact and diplomacy. I, on the other hand, instantly felt my adrenaline start pumping.

Student Journal

I've found that if I can wait to react, the person in the wrong has an opportunity to apologize, and usually does, before I jump in and make it worse.

Student Journal

Trustworthiness and Conscientiousness. These qualities encompass a range of behaviors, from punctuality and keeping commitments to admitting and correcting your mistakes. **In law, a profession where reputation means everything, people expect a higher level of behavior from lawyers.** Those who are trustworthy and conscientious maintain high standards of integrity, tactfully confront unethical behavior, and give credit to others when due. If you've ever worked with someone who displays these qualities, you may have noticed that they are not only incredibly reliable and easy to work with, but generally inspire those around them to exhibit similar characteristics.

Adaptability. Lawyers should learn early in their careers to expect the unexpected, to handle multiple demands, to be flexible in the face of change, and to shift priorities quickly. **If you become too attached to a specific outcome, you will surely be disappointed.** For example, that case you spent hours researching might change the moment a new court ruling is handed down. The months you spent preparing for trial become nothing more than a billing matter, if the parties settle on the courthouse steps. Chapter 20, "Time Management and Procrastination" offers suggestions on how to manage interruptions as well as competing and changing deadlines.

The following student discusses perfectly the need to let go of expectations at times.

I'll try not to have too many expectations about what the first year will be like. That way I'll remain more flexible and open to new experiences. I think being open to change, feedback, and being able to 'lose' without too much heartache are what makes a first-year prosecutor outstanding instead of just competent.

Student Journal

Innovation. Although much of law practice is based on rules, procedures, form letters, and routine issues, lawyers are fundamentally creative problem solvers. **For those who excel at it, innovation can be one of the most enjoyable parts of a legal practice.** We hope, at some point early in your career, that you'll have an opportunity to observe or participate in solving a unique problem for a client. You'll definitely feel a new level of vitality and excitement in the office.

For those who are not naturally innovative, however, there is a danger. Because law school teaches us to look at opposing views and find fault with every point of view, you may find yourself focusing more heavily on the negatives of a new idea, rather than exploring the positives. If you fall into this camp, study the art of brainstorming . . . and loosen up.

F.   FOCUS ON SELF—MOTIVATION

It's inevitable that there will be times when we feel over-worked, over-committed, and over-stressed. There are steps that you can take to regain control of your life, and we've covered many of them in this book. In the meantime, your ability to maintain the pace and the quality of your work will depend on your mastery of the qualities that Goleman identified under the category of "Motivation." We'll cover those next.

Components of Motivation
- Achievement Drive
- Commitment
- Initiative
- Optimism

Achievement Drive. Most law students and attorneys are highly motivated, have a strong interest in improving their performance, and are results-oriented. It can be challenging, however, to maintain this attitude in the face of external factors such as uninteresting work, too much work (or not enough), problems getting feedback, etc. It is even more difficult to stay motivated in the face of a new challenge that you just can't seem to master, or after receiving serious criticism from a supervisor. For a very few lucky people, motivation skills come naturally. Most of us, however, have to work at it.

I need to make the effort in everything. Nothing will come to me. No one will make me like my job, no one will make friends for me, and no one will write an excellent memo for me. Of course, I ascribe to this—but I have to actively remember it at times.

Student Journal

Commitment. Commitment keeps you in tune with your employer's goals, despite outside factors, such as management practices, salaries, or working conditions that may decrease morale at times.

I knew that I would see red tape in various manifestations, but discovered that attorneys believe it is worth it in the end. They love their jobs, believe in the work they are doing, and admire their colleagues. This is something I will take with me when I leave this internship.

Student Journal

Initiative. Good things don't always come to those who wait—you have to take the initiative and ask for the experiences you hope to have at work. Offer to coordinate a project, or volunteer for an assignment that will be difficult, but that has good learning potential (e.g., would allow you to partner with a respected attorney, or offer good visibility). For example, a young state legislator told law students that, early in her first term and as junior member of the Appropriations Committee, she offered to coordinate an important piece of legislation. As a result, although she was handling basically "glorified clerical work," every piece of correspondence, every document and every idea went across her desk. She became the resident expert on the matter and it was no coincidence that, in her second term, she was appointed Vice Chair of the same committee.

G.   FOCUS ON OTHERS—EMPATHY

The person who can understand and empathize with clients, staff, colleagues, opposing counsel, and others will be a better lawyer. This is true regardless of your practice area and experience level.

When it comes to empathy, attorneys often think it means being a "pushover," someone who is unable to make hard decisions. Actually, it's just the opposite. Empathy, when exhibited in the client's best interests, is what helps a lawyer deal appropriately with the sometimes-harsh realities of practice, including the process of "breaking bad news."

In the following journal, a student illustrates how moments of empathetic reflection can provide much-needed insight to change the course of difficult encounters.

Our clients feel as if they have been wronged in one fashion or another, and want their stories to be heard. The hardest part of my job is telling someone that we can't help them. I have found it is best to listen, then to be straightforward, explain clearly the reasons why we can't help, and wish them good luck.

Student Journal

Components of Empathy
- Understanding Others
- Service Orientation
- Leveraging Diversity
- Developing Others
- Political Awareness

Understanding Others. A lawyer's ability to accurately "read" what is going on under the surface is not just important, but essential. For example, a client may not discuss his true motivations for seeking counsel, his concerns and feelings, and what he hopes ultimately to achieve (and may, in fact, not even be aware of these things himself). In these circumstances, your ability to accurately "read" what is going on is critical, because it will affect not only the eventual outcome of the case, but also your *client's perception* of the quality of representation, and overall satisfaction with our justice system.

Your ability to understand other points of view will be extremely valuable in building relationships with your supervising attorney, coworkers, and other colleagues, and in avoiding misunderstandings. See Chapter 15, "In-Person Communication," for examples.

Service Orientation. **An accomplished attorney learns to anticipate and meet clients' needs almost before they are even aware of them.** You can reflect this attitude with your colleagues, too. For example, you could volunteer to help with an end-of-day rush project that would otherwise keep your administrative assistant working for hours (like assembling trial notebooks).

Your ability to "manage up" by focusing on your supervisors' concerns, stresses, and points of view will enhance their perceptions of you. More importantly, it will improve your own performance and comfort level, as the student who is quoted below found out when working in the office of a busy high-level government official. Chapter 9, "The Art of Being Supervised (Gracefully)," examines some of the challenges and concerns that supervisors face in their jobs.

I need to stay flexible to accommodate the schedules and stress levels of my bosses. Because the job is so taxing, it is hard to gauge their temperaments. I am working to become a bit of a mind reader. If I can anticipate what my bosses need before they ask, it saves everyone time, and creates within them a sense of trust in my abilities.

Student Journal

Leveraging Diversity and Developing Others. **Effective leaders know that projects are almost always improved by the unique abilities and experiences of each member of the team.** They know, too, that taking an interest in the abilities and continued development of employees and colleagues will strengthen relationships and improve overall performance. You intuitively know this, too, if you've ever received guidance from someone who cared deeply about your developing skills. It is a quality that inspires gratitude and loyalty. See Chapter 10, "The Art of Supervising," for illustrations of helping others develop their skills through delegation, feedback, and training opportunities.

Political Awareness. Some people seem to have been born with the ability to read a group's emotional currents and understand unspoken power relationships but, for many of us, this aspect of EQ is a mystery. If you are not naturally a "political savant," **ask someone you trust and admire to show you how to read the nuances in your workplace.** Don't forget to use your powers of observation and reflection, also, to better understand what is happening at a deeper level.

To become a more empathic person, learn to be aware of others' feelings, perspectives, and real concerns. Reach out and take a genuine interest in them. Cultivate active listening skills and the ability to read subtle, non-verbal cues like body language. Your own body language, too, can be a powerful indicator of the undercurrents of an interaction. Finally, be a watchful observer of yourself in social situations. Note what you're feeling, how you behave, and the kinds of behavior it induces in others.

Don't be dismayed to discover that the empathy you display towards others is not always going to be reflected back in their actions towards you (although sometimes it will be). Emotional intelligence is an internal growth process that you undertake for your own benefit. Its greatest value is not what you receive in return or the recognition that you might gain (although these things may come), but in what you learn, and the kind of work you learn to produce.

H.   FOCUS ON OTHERS—SOCIAL SKILLS

As you may already know, **social skills are the key to inducing a desirable response in others.** This is especially true in a profession like law, where communication, compromise, and dispute resolution play such an important role in our day-to-day activities. When meshed with the other aspects of emotional intelligence, your social skills lead to the development of positive personal interactions and rewarding relationships. If you are shy (and many people are), you will be relieved to know that you need not be an extrovert to be socially adept. Social skills encompass communication, handling of conflicts, and many aspects of team building and leadership.

Components of Social Skills

- Communication
- Conflict Management
- Leadership
- Change Catalyst
- Building Bonds
- Collaboration & Cooperation
- Team Capabilities

Communication. Lawyers are fundamentally communicators, as advocates, teachers, creative problem solvers, peace makers, and in the myriad other roles in which they function. They must write and speak well, and be effective listeners. Although you may fine tune and improve your communication skills throughout your years in practice, you must develop them quickly. Often, the first step is taking stock of areas that need attention. To better develop her abilities, the student whose reflections appear below learned that she needed to focus on her audience instead of on her own discomfort, in order to build rapport and find commonalities with them. Chapter 15, "In-Person Communication," discusses values underlying good communication and suggests various techniques for communicating with clients and colleagues.

> *When I am concentrating, I cannot hear others talking; when I am concentrating I sometimes get irritable at interruptions; I need personal space every day or else I become a cranky mess; I feel a bit like the 'weird one' in social interactions; and I have extreme difficulty with public speaking.*
>
> Student Journal

> New professionals often hesitate to communicate sufficiently with their assigning attorneys and, as a result, get overloaded and can't complete their work. You can avoid problems like this by keeping in touch with, and communicating with, those people on your team.
>
> Advice from an Employer

Conflict Management. At its best, effective conflict management entails achieving the correct balance between confrontation and avoidance (depending on the circumstances), and being able to resolve disputes with relationships intact. Knowing how to resolve disagreements is crucial for lawyers, but clearly some people are more effective at it than others (and feel more comfortable doing it, too). Essential qualities here include being able to discuss issues openly and honestly, with tact and diplomacy, and learning to spot and de-escalate potential conflicts. You can often decrease someone's level of aggression by pointing out the common ground that exists and an equitable way to work out differences. This is hard to do when in the middle of a conflict. If you find yourself in this situation, try to calm down, tune in, and express your point of view in a neutral manner. Even for seasoned negotiators, this sometimes takes patience and a willingness to meet again, after emotions have settled. See Chapter 22, "Handling Conflicts at Work," for a more detailed discussion of conflict management.

In the following journal, a student used her powers of observation to note a serious flaw in the problem-solving dynamics of her workplace. In this case, although she had little power to change the situation, it provided her with invaluable learning opportunities.

This office seems to live and breathe politics. My personal disposition is to function as a mediator and find a middle ground to problem solving. Of course, all parties involved must recognize that they are standing on the same ground to find a middle. Some of the folks that I work with are on different continents altogether. I am still struggling to see any efficiency to this system.

Student Journal

Collaboration and Cooperation. Good collaborators know how to balance their focus on a task while paying attention to relationships—*all* relationships. They collaborate, share plans, information and resources, and promote a friendly, cooperative climate. They know how to take credit gracefully for their own performance, and yet are willing to let others shine too.

Building Bonds. People who are adept at building bonds realize the importance of networking to gather the information needed to resolve the day-to-day issues lawyers face. They know how to cultivate and maintain extensive informal networks, and take the time to use occasional e-mails, phone calls, and face-to-face meetings to keep these ties active. To increase your skills in this area, build rapport with others, be willing to keep them in the loop, and develop personal friendships among your work associates.

Team Capabilities. Closely related to collaboration and cooperation is the ability to create team synergy in pursuit of collective goals. Qualities like respect and helpfulness are crucial here. A good team builder knows how to draw all members into a joint effort, build team identity, protect the group and its reputation, and is willing to share the credit. See Chapter 7, "Cultural Differences," for suggestions on how an awareness of cultural differences can help team members work together.

Leadership. A good leader inspires and guides the performance of individuals and groups, while at the same time giving them autonomy and holding them accountable for their performance. It is a matter of knowing when to lead actively, and when to hold back and let others do so. Leaders must be assertive and able to say "no" affirmatively but, because they have created strong relationships and substantial goodwill, people trust them not only to make hard decisions when they must be made, but to make them in the best interests of the group.

As a law student or new professional, you may be already be functioning in a leadership position for a committee or for an organization. You might also receive opportunities to "lead from behind." For example, your excellent input about how to better market the firm's summer law clerk program might lead to an invitation to serve on the recruiting committee. See Chapter 19, "Making the Most of Meetings," for information about how to exercise leadership in meetings, both as chair and participant.

To develop your leadership skills, concentrate on building or strengthening personal bonds with your colleagues, express enthusiasm for shared missions, and volunteer for important projects. You can also learn by observing how experienced leaders interact with and inspire those with whom they work. You'll begin to notice that effective leaders inspire others in part because they have mastered many, if not most, of the competencies on the "self" side of Goleman's chart. As a result, they can be trusted to display self-control, emotional awareness, trustworthiness, conscientiousness, adaptability, and other EQ competencies in their interactions with their team members, with clients, and with others. This is significant for new professionals because it means that every step you take towards developing your emotional intelligence will also be a step towards developing your leadership skills.

I. INCREASE YOUR EMOTIONAL INTELLIGENCE

First, you'll be relieved to know that increasing your EQ needn't be time-consuming. In fact, while it will require attention over a span of time, you can do it on your own schedule, and in whatever way best suits you. There are four basic steps.

1. **Review some of the literature,** to develop a better understanding of EQ principles. You'll find numerous books on the topic, as well as lots of online content.

2. **Take a personal inventory,** to honestly appraise your strengths and weaknesses. Then incorporate feedback from trusted friends or colleagues who know you well and have seen your behavior in various settings. Based on what you learn, and on skills that would be most helpful in the kind of practice you hope to develop, make a preliminary list of areas to improve. For example, if you want to litigate, competencies such as emotional awareness, self-confidence, self-control, communication, and conflict management

might be on your list. If you're going into policy development, you might add skills like optimism, being a change catalyst, commitment, building bonds, and leadership.

3. **Observe attorneys and others you admire,** to notice what qualities contribute to their success. Talk with them about the concepts described in this chapter and ask for their opinions.

4. **Put what you've learned and observed into practice.**

Following are some tips to help along the way:

- **Reflect on your experiences and observations** (both positive and negative). Consider how various facets of emotional intelligence are involved in your interpersonal relationships, and in specific interactions between you, coworkers, supervisors, defendants, victims, witnesses, other attorneys, judges, and others.

- **Identify a situation where EQ skills were helpful, or would have been helpful,** in resolving a problem or issue.

- Prioritize and **focus on a few competencies at a time.** Concentrate on those that are most important, given your current goals. Remember that your strengths in one area can be used to learn something new. For example, if you have strong empathetic skills, you may find it easy to improve your ability to build bonds.

- **Practice, then practice some more.** You may find it helpful to create scenarios and try role playing.

- **Don't expect immediate results.** It takes considerable time to replace "second nature" behaviors with new ones, and increasing your EQ in general requires attention and reinforcement. When your behavior falls short of your expectations (and it will), use your powers of self-awareness to learn what you can from the experience and try to do better next time.

- To better internalize qualities that you are striving to perfect, **acknowledge the positive steps** you are taking to achieve them. Notice how other people respond when you exhibit positive personal and social skills, as well as how you feel when they do.

- **Enjoy the process.** Increasing your EQ will give you the opportunity to exercise an entirely new set of "mental muscles." It's fun . . . and the results will be dramatic.

I learned so much about how to interact with my coworkers and supervisors, and about what I believe to be a good professional personality. I learned how to read people, and adjust to their expectations—even when it was sometimes uncomfortable. My experiences this summer have taught me that I can be someone I am not totally comfortable being—without sacrificing my beliefs, my ethics, or all of my personality.

Student Journal

CHAPTER 25
WORKPLACE DIVERSITY

*"If we are to achieve a wider culture, rich in
contrasting values, we must recognize the
whole gamut of human potentialities, and so
weave a less arbitrary social fabric, one in
which each diverse human gift will
find a fitting place."*
Margaret Mead

There are many ways to describe our differences—
by minority and ethnic status, national origin, age,
sex, mental and physical condition, religion, gender
identity, sexual orientation, veteran status, and
economic background, to name just a few. We are,
indeed, a diverse nation. For example, members of
ethnic minority groups constituted 33% of the
population in 2005 (a percentage the U.S. Census
Bureau projects would grow rapidly).

A. DIVERSITY MATTERS

In the legal as well as other professions, the need
for change has been obvious for decades, and is
intensifying. Fortune 500 leaders such as HP,
Walmart, Home Depot, Morgan Stanley, PwC, and
others, have committed to taking concrete steps
toward diversity and inclusion (search online for
CEO Action for Diversity and Inclusion). In the legal
profession, more and more clients, including in-house
counsel who hire outside law firms, insist that their
accounts be handled by a diverse group of attorneys.

These demands have led to an expansion of recruiting and hiring efforts to include members of groups that have traditionally been woefully under-represented in the profession.

The nature and volume of legal work have also changed significantly. Lawyers are kept very busy these days with a growing body of legislation and case law on a host of issues directly relevant to the diversity of our society, such as those concerning immigrants and immigration; international patent, copyright and trade; and discrimination in all its forms. On an even larger scale, globalization affects virtually every area of business, including the legal world. Many of today's law students will be practicing international law of some kind, or at a minimum, will be working with people, cultures, and issues from around the world. If for no other reason (and there are many other reasons), diversification simply makes good business sense.

Unfortunately, the legal profession has a very poor track record of diversifying its ranks. Minority lawyers are under-represented in the private sector generally earn less (usually much less), and are promoted to partner at a much lower rate than their non-minority counterparts. In addition, minority lawyers are frequently overlooked for networking opportunities and for chances to work with important clients and senior partners on the "best" cases. Today, there is still disparity in virtually every aspect of law, including law school admission and graduation rates; bar exam testing and admission;

recruitment practices; salaries; promotions; and attrition from the practice after admission to the bar.

If you are a member of one (or more) of the traditionally under-represented groups in our profession, or are friends of and will soon be colleagues practicing law with members of an under-represented group, this chapter was written for you. We hope that you are equally concerned with creating a harmonious environment that offers equal opportunity to all its employees and draws on all of the human resources available to build the best possible working groups.

Given our differences, and the strides that still need to be made, **what can *you* expect at school, and in the workplace—especially if you are in one or more of the traditionally "under-represented" groups?**

You know, and we know, that our experiences at work (and in the world, for that matter) will be every bit as unique as we are. In many ways, the attitudes and behaviors we *bring* to the workplace are as influential as the attitudes and actions we *encounter* there. Our own attitudes may help to *shape* the way others react to us. So, in a very real sense, you have some (but not total) control over the nature of your experience.

Because of growing pressure from the outside, you are likely to find a wealth of resources designed to help ensure your successful entry into the profession. Some of these resources address "internal factors" that affect our attitudes toward and behaviors with other people; some encourage "systemic changes," such as the creation of new policies, practices, and procedures for employers. Depending on your own unique situation, and the specifics of what is being offered, you may or may not want to take advantage of some or all of these resources. For example, participating in one program might make good sense politically, because it is encouraged by senior attorneys. You may decide to get involved, at least initially, with another activity and see how it goes, while another may "turn you off" entirely. **The decisions are yours to make, and they may not be easy.**

Our goal in this chapter is to give you a sense of what may be available in your law school, in your place of employment, and in the greater legal community.

B.   AT LAW SCHOOL

Many schools offer special programs, such as **expanded orientation** or "bridge" programs to help entering 1L's get off to a good start, by teaching legal fundamentals (such as briefing a case and conducting research), and introducing 1L's to the study of law generally. Once classes have begun, many schools offer **tutoring** to 1L's in core courses, including research and writing. For 3L's, some law schools offer **bar exam preparation courses** at no cost or at a reduced cost. These programs may be particularly helpful to those with special circumstances, such as those who are the first in their families to get college degrees, and those who feel they could use a little extra help getting started (for example, those who applied several times before being admitted or whose academic credentials are on the lower end of the scale for the entering class).

Many opportunities are offered for networking and building relationships with fellow students, faculty, and members of the legal community. For example, the coordinators of law school mentoring programs are generally able to match students with attorneys based on special factors and interests, including those related to diversity. A wide variety of student organizations are dedicated to diversity issues, not only for students who are members of various ethnic or other minority groups around which the organizations may be focused, but also for those who are interested in promoting diversity-related concerns or working on the related legal issues. These organizations typically host both professional and social activities. The professors and law school administrators who serve as faculty advisors to these groups serve as additional resources. Many law schools also sponsor law reviews and journals dedicated exclusively to matters addressing discrimination and related social justice issues.

C.   DURING THE JOB SEARCH

There are numerous **minority and diversity job fairs around the nation, hosted by law school consortiums, law firms, and bar associations,** and you can find about them through your Career Office. These events are primary recruiting tools for many legal employers, and are not to be missed.

You may be unsure **whether to indicate membership in a minority group on your resume or in your cover letter.** By doing so, you may improve your chances of being interviewed by employers with minority hiring initiatives. A good way to indicate this information is by noting such things as tribal membership, and participation in minority clubs and organizations. Veterans receive preferences in government hiring, and there are special forms to include in the application process to qualify for this benefit. The matter of what to disclose is not so clear cut, however, for people with issues surrounding age, physical or mental disabilities, and sexual orientation. Your Career Office should be able to give you candid advice, including role-playing interview sessions, if you are interested in consulting them.

You may also be unsure about **how to handle questions by employers** during job interviews. Employers are prohibited by federal, state and local laws from asking questions, for the purpose of discriminating based on race, color, national origin, gender, age, religion, or physical disabilities not relevant to the job. Based on our experience, employers usually try to comply with these restrictions but occasionally, in the spirit of casual conversation, they may inadvertently venture into prohibited territory. In that case, you have four options. (1) Confront the employer, refuse to answer, and terminate the interview. (2) Answer the question. (3) Assume that the attorney has an underlying concern, and answer in a tactful way to deal with it. During an interview with a young woman, "Do you have children?" might mean, "Would you miss a lot of work because of day care problems?" She might answer, "I do have one daughter, and am lucky, because both grandmothers live in Tucson and love to take care of her. It's been smooth sailing through law school, and I don't expect any problems when I start working at a firm." (4) Evade the question pleasantly, "You're not really concerned with that are you?"

Before accepting a job offer, you may want to look at the employer's current and past demographics. How diverse are the recruiting and promotion practices, and leadership opportunities? Are there one or more diversity committees? Mentoring programs, training, and other support mechanisms for diverse groups of people? Many employers now provide this kind of information on their websites, and in a variety of employer directories.

Career Office counselors are usually an excellent source of information and advice about diversity in the job search, and the profession. If in doubt about any of the issues raised in this chapter, we encourage you to contact someone in your Career Office.

D. IN THE WORKPLACE AND LEGAL COMMUNITY

If recent diversity initiatives are any indication, **legal employers are getting serious about diversity.** New jobs are being created (such as Diversity Inclusion Officer, and Diversity Manager);

many of the people hired for these **new positions
report directly to top management** and, because
firms are being ranked for their records, they are
being held accountable for measurable improvements
in recruiting and training practices. Diversity
consultants abound these days, and firms frequently
hire them to assist in overhauling their diversity
practices, which may involve conducting confidential
interviews and surveys, providing individualized and
group training, and establishing new policies and
procedures. Firms are establishing Diversity
Committees, and their members are usually
instrumental in creating and monitoring activities
such as: professional development opportunities for
minorities and mentoring programs for groups that
have been traditionally under-represented in the
profession. Many employers have had good success
by providing new minority hires with two mentors—
one mentor of similar ethnicity or minority status,
and another mentor from the ranks of the
organization's traditional power structure (such as a
managing partner).

Legal employers are also increasingly active in
outreach to minority law students. Minority
scholarships provide financial support to students
who could not otherwise afford legal educations.
Through diversity fellowships and scholarships, law
firms hire minority candidates who might not
otherwise have been considered for employment for
summer or school-year clerkships, often resulting in
the extension of offers for permanent employment
after graduation. Special judicial clerkships have

also been developed for minority law students in recent years.

National state and local bar associations are also actively involved in diversifying the profession, with a variety of sections and committees dedicated to this effort. They offer excellent **networking and leadership opportunities;** sponsor activities such as **conferences and CLE programs;** and are quick to welcome law students and new lawyers into their ranks.

Bar associations provide outreach, encouragement, advice, and training to minority attorneys on how to seek political or judicial office, and often monitor the election or appointment process to ensure that all who apply are fairly considered. Specialty bar associations, such as the Minority Corporate Counsel Association, also provide high-level leadership and support to the professional community at large through national efforts, with publication of data and statistics, "best practices" guides, and training, and to individual attorneys more personally, through activities of local chapters. **The ABA provides a Diversity and Inclusion Portal on its website, which has a wealth of information on resources and programs focused on promoting and nurturing diversity.** Many new initiatives are also being developed to feed the "pipeline" into law school, and attorneys are actively working with **high school students in minority and low-income neighborhoods,** encouraging them to consider a legal career as one of their options. Once you are ready to participate in community or pro-bono activities, you may want to consider getting involved in some of these pipeline activities, encouraging high school students to consider a legal career.

CHAPTER 26

FINDING BALANCE IN YOUR WORK AND LIFE

"Congratulations, you've just won the pie eating contest. Your prize is a pie."
One Attorney to Another (on the occasion of making partner)

What important activities have you given up because you don't have time? Working out, or participating in hobbies and sports? Spending time with friends and family? The luxury of reading a good book, instead of a hornbook? Haircuts? Whether you are a law student or new lawyer, you almost certainly feel stretched for time.

Lawyers and future lawyers who strive to have fulfilling professional *and* personal lives face a dilemma. While rewarding, both law school and legal work are demanding. Our workloads and schedules are primarily controlled by outside forces (such as supervisors, clients, and judges) and, as a result, we are frequently over-booked, juggling responsibilities, and "flying by the seat of our pants." It can be both exhilarating and terrifying.

We want to have satisfying lives, but we can't seem to stop overextending ourselves. This raises a conundrum that we'll attempt to answer in this chapter: **Can you have it all? For that matter, what do we mean by "all"?**

By everybody's standards, Kim has solved the problem. A young attorney, she's got a great job at a large regional law firm, is happily married, and holds leadership positions in both the state bar's Young Lawyers Section and the local Women Lawyers Association. At a meeting of a state conference planning team (which Kim attended despite upcoming hearings and trials), one of the authors (who was drafting this chapter at the time) asked her, "I know how busy you are, and yet you seem to accomplish everything effortlessly. How do you stay so balanced?" She responded, "It depends on when you ask, and what you call balance."

Your definition of "all" and "balance" may not be the same as Kim's. But, however you define them, we hope this chapter will provide helpful suggestions about **how to avoid becoming overcommitted and how to achieve balance in your life.** We recommend reading this chapter in conjunction with Chapter 31, "First-Year Career Plan—A Guided Exercise," which goes into detail about how to explore your personal and professional goals, budget your time, and develop a plan for spending it.

A. CAN YOU HAVE IT ALL?

This will be a short section because it primarily requires only reassurance and a bit of a pep talk on our part. We are convinced that, if you seek it with clarity, purpose, and discipline, you can indeed have it all. You are talented, intelligent people. At great expense and sacrifice, you have trained for what can be a very rewarding career, one that offers you flexibility and options. **You can, indeed, have it all.**

But first take the time to figure out what you mean by "all."

B.   WHAT IS ALL?

We have all heard the adage, "Beware of what you ask for, because you may get it." Unfortunately, many of us realize only too late that what we asked for (consciously or subconsciously) was not what we really wanted, or what best served our needs after all. Or we realize that we have inadvertently turned our decision-making power over to someone else.

Knowing what we want in both our personal and professional lives (in the short term, long term, or at any given moment, for that matter) takes thought, reflection and, often, input from others. While you are early in your career as a lawyer, now is the time to consider several important issues. Give yourself plenty of time to reflect on your answers, and answer with specificity, so that you can get a realistic sense of what your "all" is right now.

- What roles do you play at home? At work or school?

- On average, or during various cycles of activity if there is no "average," how much time do you spend in your roles, and on the specific tasks, that comprise your working life? Are there certain areas where you feel you are spending more, or less, time than you should be? Can you figure out why?

- How much control do you have over your workload and schedule? In what ways do you exercise control over them? Who else has control over these areas of your life, and how do they exercise this control?

- Do you have any leisure time? If so, who else exercises control over it? What things are out of your control?

- How are your family obligations handled and who takes responsibility for which tasks? In a perfect world, how would you like these things to be handled, and why? Are there certain tasks at home where you feel you are spending more, or less, time than you should be? Can you figure out why?

- What are your interests? What ideas and activities ignite your passion?

The questions above are designed to help you define, in detail, the existing landscape of your professional and personal lives . . . **your present reality,** so to speak. The questions below will help you define "having it all—for **your future reality—** the one we know you can create for yourself, that we are all capable of creating for ourselves.

- Where do you want to be in terms of your professional and personal lives in one month? One year? Five years? Ten years?

- What things are you currently doing that you would prefer not to do? What would happen if you simply stopped doing them? If this would create a problem, can all or some of these things realistically and fairly be delegated to someone else? If you must continue doing them, would doing them differently make them less objectionable or take less time?

- What kind of career would you like to develop and how would you like to see it evolve?

- How would you like to see your personal life evolve? What sorts of things would you like to be doing, and with whom? Where would you like to be living?

- What kind of lifestyle do you want to create? How much money do you need to earn, and how much time and energy are you willing to devote to earn it?

Many of the people I worked with this summer invest everything in the law, and it makes them great lawyers, but doesn't do as much for them as people. With my first child on the way any day, I am discovering that I want to practice law so that my family and I can live, not live so that I can practice law. Some attorneys never retire it seems; they just have heart attacks and cut back their hours. I don't want to do that either.

Student Journal

C. AVOID BECOMING OVERCOMMITTED

After arguing that you really can have it all, we must interject a note of clarification. **You really *can* have it all ... you just can't have it all at the same time.**

Contrary to popular belief, there really *can* be too much of a good thing . . . too many clients, too many exciting projects, too many leadership opportunities, too many invitations to speak at CLE programs and conferences, too many . . . you get the idea. If you've ever been in this position, you know that being overcommitted is not a pleasant experience.

What makes this type of situation even worse is that **often we ourselves are to blame for being overcommitted,** or at least to blame for not letting those in control of our workload know that we are becoming dangerously overloaded. We tend to be better at knowing our strengths than at acknowledging, setting and respecting our limits. When someone asks for a volunteer, we can't seem to keep our hand in our laps. When someone asks a question, we assume that we must find the answer for them. We need to make everything the best it can be. Because we *can* do something, we volunteer or agree to do it. And it ends up being too much.

While we may be able to maintain a kind of precarious balance despite overcommitting, it's difficult to do in the long run, and eventually we experience negative consequences. Our work may begin to suffer, in terms of timeliness and quality. Our personal interactions and communication suffer as well, because we have less and less time to interact courteously and pleasantly with others, leading to a host of associated problems. Our "professional image" becomes tarnished, as we seem to spiral more and more out of control. Our business and personal relationships suffer, as we don't keep our commitments, and people begin to feel they can't count on us to follow through. Stress, overwork, and lack of sleep take a physical and emotional toll. It's not a pretty picture.

Why do we find it so hard to say no? Here are some thoughts about why and how to avoid becoming overcommitted when you have a choice:

- **Think before volunteering or accepting optional projects. If you accept every invitation to get involved in a project, people may begin to take your participation for granted.** Accept projects selectively, based on factors such as their importance, your interest, and your current commitments (including the ones you are neglecting now). Your contributions will be better, you'll enjoy yourself more, and others will place a greater premium on your participation.

- By overextending yourself, **you may end up spending 90% of your time on low-priority projects.** Complex and possibly more important projects take time and focus. Try to avoid these projects when you're feeling stressed and over-committed—but do your best in the future to block out larger chunks of time for projects that will help you to stretch and grow your professional skills.

- There are only 24 hours in each day. **For every opportunity you accept, there will**

be another that you will have to forego.
Your current workload may suffer as well.

- Avoid committing to an extravagant lifestyle
  that may eventually feel more like a trap than
  an opportunity. Regardless of your current
  obligations, just as we advise in Chapter 36,
  "Money Matters," try to **keep your options
  open.** You may choose to work long hours
  currently, and that may be the right decision
  for you now. However, if you decide to marry
  and raise a family, or train for a marathon,
  you may want or need to reduce your
  schedule.

- Practice saying "no" out loud. It can help you
  find the right words when you are given a
  choice. Saying "I'm not . . ." is better than "I
  can't . . ." Example: "I'm not taking on any
  additional volunteer commitments for the
  time being," vs. "I'm so overloaded right now
  that I just can't help with anything else."

- **Learn when to let go of a project.**
  Perfectionism is a form of overcommitment.
  Sometimes "good" is good enough, and
  sometimes it's time to step back and let others
  contribute their efforts to the process.

*When I finally do find some time that isn't
devoted to doing work of one kind or another—I
spend that time thinking about something I
could be doing. I think this is part of that drive*

for perfection. I need to stop thinking about law and being a lawyer for some parts of my day.

Student Journal

- Take an audit of how much time you spend doing or avoiding household chores. Ask yourself, "Can I do some things differently, have someone else do them, or not do them at all?" **Convenience comes at a cost, and sometimes the cost is worth it.** If you have sufficient income, you may feel that the expense of paying someone to clean the house regularly is money well spent, both in terms of sanity and time management. Hint: Have the work done late in the week, so you'll enjoy a clean house on the weekend.

- **Treat yourself occasionally,** especially when you've been working hard—and **never underestimate the value of humor** to get you through stressful times. Sometimes laughter really is the best medicine, especially enjoyed with good friends. Keep them close and your life will be in better balance.

D. FIND YOUR OWN BALANCE

We've come full circle, back to the question of whether and how to find balance in our lives, and what the attorney meant at the beginning of this chapter when she said, "It depends on when you ask, and what you mean by balance." We'll deal with those issues below and hope that, by the time you have finished this chapter, you will have a better idea about how to define and find the balance you seek in your professional and personal lives.

- Have you ever seen a tightrope artist walk effortlessly across a rope strung hundreds of feet off the ground? Perfect balance in this case, and every case, involves a lot of movement. The artist sways from side to side, correcting the swing when it becomes too exaggerated, and at moments (but only brief moments) is able to poise directly and perfectly over a solid base of support. The tightrope artist knows what you will soon learn—**balance is not something you get and keep forever. It's something that you work at maintaining all the time.** As with any good athlete, some days are good days, and some days are bad days.

- Life is not a marathon. It's a series of sprints. In a sense, **balance can amount to bursts of activity followed by rest.** This is the way top athletes train, and it works well in all types of endeavors. Try to avoid thinking of down time as "doing nothing," because these times can provide your best inspiration.

If I can find a way to spend more time on the bike, I'll be better off in other aspects of my life. The kind of thinking that I do in the saddle can't be replaced or replicated in other ways. Of course, calling what goes through your consciousness while riding "thinking" is often a stretch. Endlessly repeating lyrics to a pop song hardly seems to qualify. However, every thought is indeed true when you are pedaling. Those lyrics become the poetry that describes your life. Moments of clarity abound, only to vanish when the ride ends. However, every so often I'm surprised by a good thought, a solid thought, a thought that still makes sense after the legs stop pumping, the heart slows down, and the epinephrine fades away.

Student Journal

- **Balance is not about trying to be a super hero, figuring out how to do everything smarter, better and faster, and at the same time pretending that it's effortless.** Don't buy into this myth, exhaust yourself, and risk suffering burnout as a result. Most of us are, or will be, in positions that afford us very pleasant lifestyles. If we remember that it is a sign of strength to set limits, we should be able to find a balance between work and pleasure.

- Some choices may require you to work longer or assume responsibilities that are overwhelming at times. For example, you may have accepted a position in a firm with a high billable hour requirement. For the time being, this may suit you very well. You're young and have relatively few family obligations. You've always wanted to live in a big city, in a fast-paced environment, and this type of job may be a dream come true. This leads us to another principle of balance—**your own personal definition of balance will change,**

**depending on your goals and life
circumstances.**

*My mentor was fairly stressed out, having just
come from an interview for a promotion. She had
a hard time focusing. It occurred to me that I
want a career where I am challenged, constantly
learning new things, and not growing
complacent. But I don't care about "climbing the
ladder." I don't think my mentor is unhappy, but
she has definitely run herself ragged and is worn
out at the moment in all aspects of her life.*

Student Journal

- **Realize that balance can take time to
  achieve,** even when you're happy with your
  job, and are doing well on it. Like the
  tightrope artist learning his craft, you may
  feel out of kilter early in your career, and be
  happy at times that you've got a safety net to
  provide support if needed. As you gain
  confidence and experience, what at first
  seemed difficult will get easier and even
  become second nature. As you develop
  stronger relationships with your co-workers,
  clients and others, you'll find more balance
  and stability. You'll notice that projects that
  first took longer than seemed necessary, kept
  you working long after hours, and needed
  extensive editing, are now accomplished in
  less time, earlier in the day, with fewer
  revisions, and with far greater ease. You'll be
  in balance . . . savor the moment!

CHAPTER 27

WHAT SKILLS DO LAWYERS NEED?

"Be committed to a life of learning."
Dean Charles E. Ares

Law students and new lawyers frequently ask, **"What skills do lawyers really need? Does law school prepare us for succeeding as lawyers?** These are natural concerns and they illustrate the difficulty many of us (including experienced attorneys) have in articulating, or even agreeing about, the fundamental skills that lawyers need, beyond those which are obvious, such as legal analysis, research and writing, and oral communication.

Why do we care? Identifying fundamental skills is paramount to law students and new lawyers, as well as to the firms, agencies, and organizations that hire them. Think of the confidence you would gain about your potential as a lawyer, if you knew where to focus your energies, what new skills to develop, and what goals to set. If employers knew how to better screen applicants for the qualities and skills most applicable for their business, they could more narrowly tailor their hiring procedures and offer more relevant and effective training to the candidates they ultimately hire.

If you've read other segments of this book, you already know that we take a broad approach to skills development. Skills traditionally considered "legal" (like legal analysis, research, writing, and oral advocacy) are but the beginning of the story and comprise only a portion of the foundation of skills and qualities that every lawyer, in every type of practice, needs. What are these important skills?

This chapter focuses on two studies that offer useful perspectives on the topic. *Predicting Lawyer Effectiveness: Broadening the Basis for Law School Admission Decisions,* Shultz, M., & Zedeck, S. (*Law & Social Inquiry,* vol. 36, no. 3, 2011, pp. 620–661), discusses an in-depth, 2003 multi-year research project for the Law School Admissions Council ("LSAC Study"). The study surveyed over 3,000 lawyers, law professors, law students, judges and clients with the goal of identifying skills, abilities, and behaviors that were most predictive of lawyer competence. Ideally, this data could be used in developing more effective and accurate tools for law schools to use in screening applicant pools.

The second study, the *NCBE Job Analysis* (*A Study of the Newly Licensed Lawyer,* National Conference of Bar Examiners, January 2013, www. ncbex.org) ("NCBE Analysis"), takes a similar approach, but from the perspective of identifying specific knowledge, skills, and abilities that newly licensed lawyers need to carry out their work.

Both studies distill essential lawyering into fundamental skill sets—26 factors in the LSAC Study and, in the NCBE Analysis, 25 "practical skills and abilities" that were deemed more important than the highest-rated "knowledge area" (i.e., Rules of Evidence, Civil Procedure, and Criminal Law).

We translated the findings of each study into a visual format (see Chart One, "LSAC Study" and Chart Two, "NCBE Analysis," to assist you in seeing the data from various perspectives). For example, you might wish to compare both studies, or focus on "hard vs. soft" skills; "analytical vs. people" skills; "legal vs. general" skills; "basic vs. advanced" skills; or "skills you already have vs. skills you need to develop."

When viewed separately and together, **each chart provides a template of skills and abilities that you would do well to develop.** Skills traditionally considered "legal" appear on the left-hand side of each chart, and you may be surprised to see that, though important, they comprise a relatively small proportion of each overall skill set.

Chart One
Law School Admission Council
Study to Predict Lawyer Effectiveness

	Writing	Problem Solving	Able to See World Through Eyes of Others	Creativity/ Innovation	
Fact Finding	Questioning/ Interviewing	Strategic Planning	Influencing & Advocating	Passion & Engagement	Organizing & Managing Own Work
Researching the Law	Listening	Organizing & Managing Others (Staff/ Colleagues)	Providing Advice & Counsel/ Building Relationships with Clients	Integrity/ Honesty	Self-Development
Analysis & Reasoning	Speaking	Networking & Business Development	Evaluation, Development & Mentoring	Diligence	Stress Management
	Negotiation Skills	Developing Relationships Within the Legal Profession	Community Involvement & Service	Practical Judgment	

Chart Two
Job Analysis Survey Results
National Conference of Bar Examiners
25 Highest-Scoring Key Skill Factors for Newly Admitted Lawyers

Written Communications	Paying Attention to Detail
Listening	Professionalism
Oral Communication	Knowing When to Go Back and Ask Questions
Answering Questions Succinctly	
Using Office Technologies	Organizational Skills
Critical Reading and Comprehension	Working Within Established Time Constraints
Synthesizing Facts and Law	
Legal Reasoning	Interpersonal Skills
Fact Gathering/Evaluation	Decisiveness
Issue Spotting	Diligence
Electronic Researching	Judgment
Computer Skills	Consciousness of Personal and Professional Limitations
Information Integrating	
Planning and Strategizing	
Advocacy	

Both charts will be helpful as you develop your own road map for professional development. We hope it builds your confidence to see that you already possess many of the skills and qualities that lawyers need. At the same time, you may wish to refocus on various chapters in this book that discuss each of the skills represented on the charts in more detail.

For example, using Chart Two as a reference, you may be competent in many of the skills related to legal research and writing, but have difficulty organizing your work and meeting established deadlines. Chapter 20, "Time Management and Procrastination," offers specific suggestions to help you regain control of your schedule.

Chapter 34, "How to Get Practical Skills in Law School," offers suggestions on law school courses and activities that focus specifically on practical skills training, often in settings that allow you to work with actual clients.

Finally, you may want to review Chapter 24, "Emotional Intelligence—The Key to Excellence," which expands upon many of the concepts identified in the LSAC Study and NCBE Analysis, especially those critical "soft skills" that populate the right-hand side of each chart.

CHAPTER 28

JUDGMENT, VALUES, AND PROFESSIONAL ETHICS

"Character is like a tree and reputation like its shadow. The shadow is what we think of it; the tree is the real thing."
Abraham Lincoln

A great deal of the stress associated with the practice of law arises from **tensions between the various roles we undertake as lawyers and the personal values we bring to our professional lives.** In a sense, this entire book is designed to underscore the importance of identifying and living your values and exercising your own judgment, rather than allowing predominantly external forces to determine your path. How can you do this in light of the professional responsibilities you knowingly undertake as a lawyer?

As you know, **a lawyer's overarching obligation is to serve as a fiduciary for our clients, putting the interests of our clients above our own.** In short, as lawyers, we commit to working with our clients in good faith and with honesty and trustworthiness. The *Rules* of *Professional Conduct* cited most frequently in connection with our fiduciary duty are the duties of competence, communication, confidentiality, and avoidance of conflicts of interest. (References to the "Rules" are to the ABA Model Rules of Professional Conduct as amended through August 2016.)

In this chapter, we'll briefly explore some of the ways you might think about your personal values, and their relation to the ethical requirements and professional expectations to which lawyers are subject. **Become familiar with the specific rules of professional conduct under which you are practicing.** Not only do states have rules governing the professional conduct of lawyers, but various state and federal courts and agencies before whom you may appear have **rules that affect your professional conduct as well.** Specialized bar associations also have published standards of practice that, while not necessarily binding, often reflect a **consensus of the group of practitioners on what constitutes ethical behavior in more specially defined circumstances.** (See, for example, ABA Section of Family Law Standards of Practice for Lawyers Who Represent Children in Abuse and Neglect Cases on ABA website, under Sections, Family Law, Legal Resources; ABA Criminal Justice Standards for the Prosecution Function and ABA Criminal Justice Standards for the Defense Function on ABA website, under Sections, Criminal Justice, Criminal Justice Standards.)

Often, when faced with a difficult decision, there will be no "perfect," and sometimes, no "good" option. You will face choices between conflicting values and duties—values of confidentiality and candor; loyalty to your client and fairness to others; and duties to your client, society, the court, and your own sense of morality. These conflicting values and duties will sometimes point you in different directions, but there is more guidance in the Rules than you might realize.

For ease of discussion, let's break potential concerns down into two categories:

1. Concern that you may be *required* by the *Rules of Professional Conduct* or professional ethics to take actions that may conflict with your fundamental personal values.

2. Concern that you may be *expected* by your employer, client, or professional peers to take actions that conflict with your personal values.

A. THE RULES

It's important to **test your assumptions** against what the Rules in fact acknowledge, require, and allow. It's no accident that the first Rule addresses **competence.** When faced with any ethical or moral dilemma involving what you believe your professional responsibilities to be, **read the relevant rules—all of them.** In fact, the Rules explicitly recognize the difficult moral and ethical decisions faced by lawyers. A very quick review of the Rules reveals relatively few places that might *require* you to take actions likely to directly conflict with your personal values.

Take a look at a few provisions of the Rules to get your bearings. Read the "Preamble: A Lawyer's Responsibilities." **The Preamble recognizes the role that personal conscience plays in a lawyer's actions.** At the same time, it acknowledges that almost all "difficult ethical problems arise from conflict between a lawyer's responsibilities to clients, to the legal system and to the lawyer's own interest in remaining an ethical person while earning a satisfactory living."

At times, these conflicts may *seem* insurmountable to new lawyers. **Many fear that the answer to the question, "Is it possible to be a good person and a good lawyer?" is "No."** They often put their fears into the following categories, which we address, in very broad brush, under the Rules.

1. *"I am afraid I will be required to lie to others or mislead them because of my obligation of loyalty to my client."*

If you are afraid you'll be required to lie, it won't be because the Rules or professional ethics require *or* allow it. **To the contrary,** both *require* honesty and candor, and dishonesty is one of the worst ethical violations a lawyer can commit.

- See Rule 3.3, **Candor to Tribunal** (prohibiting a lawyer from knowingly making false statements to the court or failing to correct a false statement, as well as addressing related issues of candor).

- See Rule 4.1, **Truthfulness in Statements to Others** (prohibiting a lawyer from knowingly making false statements of material fact or law and from failing to disclose a material fact if necessary to avoid a client's criminal or fraudulent act unless disclosure prohibited by Rule 1.6, **Confidentiality of Information**).

- See Rule 8.4, **Maintaining the Integrity of the Profession: Misconduct** (providing that dishonesty, fraud, deceit, or misrepresentation constitute professional misconduct).

2. *"I am afraid I will not be allowed to reveal information when I feel that I should because of prohibitions on disclosure of confidential information, even when I think I need to disclose information to protect some higher good."*

Many requirements of client confidentiality that have prompted these concerns have been addressed explicitly in Rule 1.6, **Confidentiality**, which now allows for limited disclosure where prohibitions against disclosure were criticized in the past. **Some states allow, and others** *require,* **greater disclosure than those provided for in the Model Rule.** It is true, however, that the requirement of client confidentiality continues to pose some of the greatest potential conflicts between one's personal values and one's obligations as a lawyer.

The requirement of confidentiality at times appears to conflict with other obligations under the rules. Careful reading of the apparently conflicting rules often reveals where one overrides the other.

- See Rule 1.13, **Organization as Client** (providing for a lawyer's disclosure of certain information within the organization, and in limited circumstances, disclosure outside the organization, if certain well-defined and narrow circumstances exist).

- See Rule 1.14, **Clients with Diminished Capacity** (acknowledging that in protecting the interests of a client with diminished capacity, the lawyer is impliedly authorized to consult with others who have the ability to protect the client, while at the same time noting the requirements of Rule 1.6, **Confidentiality**, continue to apply).

3. *"I am afraid I will be required to act in ways that conflict with how I think people should be treated, or required to take positions with which I disagree, because of my obligations to my client."*

Ambiguities abound when trying to make decisions that are subject to the provisions of several rules. But in the presence of ambiguities, it's often difficult to say what the Rules *require*. It is precisely when ambiguities or conflicting instructions present themselves that lawyers are required to exercise discretion and judgment. **That's where the real action is—where lawyers have no clear rules, but uncomfortable decisions in the face of very strong expectations.**

- See Rule 1.2, **Scope of Representation** (noting that a lawyer's representation of a client does not constitute endorsement of the client's views or activities).

- See Rule 1.4 (a)(5), **Communication, Client Lawyer Relationship** (requiring a lawyer to "consult with the client about any relevant limitation on the lawyer's conduct when the lawyer knows that the client expects assistance not permitted by the Rules of Professional Conduct or other law).

- See Rule 1.16, **Declining or Terminating Representation** (explicitly providing for withdrawal from representation of a client if the client "insists upon taking action that the lawyer considers repugnant or with which the lawyer has a fundamental disagreement.").

- See Rule 2.1, **Advisor** (providing that a lawyer, in advising a client, may refer to relevant non-legal factors such as moral, economic, social, and political factors. Comment 2 notes that it is appropriate to refer to "relevant moral and ethical considerations in giving advice.").

- See Rule 3.1, **Meritorious Claims and Contentions** (prohibiting lawyers from bringing or defending frivolous lawsuits, with relevant exceptions in criminal cases allowing defense counsel to require the prosecution to prove each element of its case).

- See Rule 3.4, **Fairness to Opposing Party and Counsel** (addressing, albeit narrowly, issues of fairness in litigation).

- See Rule 3.8, **Special Responsibilities of a Prosecutor** (requiring prosecutors to refrain from some actions, and to take others, in order to protect the rights of the accused).

- See Rule 6.2, **Accepting Appointments** (allowing a lawyer to refuse appointment to represent a client if the client or cause is "so repugnant to the lawyer" that it would likely make adequate representation impossible).

B.   EXPECTATIONS OF OTHERS

Many of the difficult value-laden decisions that you'll be faced with will be in this category—**the Rules don't require you to take a certain action, or refrain from an action, but you think someone else expects you to take a step or make a decision that goes against your values.**

As a law clerk or new attorney, you will likely face challenges to your personal values in the categories of overzealousness in procedural matters, misstatements about the law, and cultural expectations against civility and courtesy to opposing parties and others. For example, *you may feel that you are expected to be unreasonable* **in responding to discovery requests and requests by opposing parties for extensions of time.** *You may feel that if you notice a misstatement* of law in a document prepared by your firm or agency, you should not point it out. *You may feel that you are expected to be unreasonable* and uncivil, to show that you are zealously representing your client.

First, be sure that you aren't operating under false assumptions. If you believe your supervising attorney expects you to take or not take a certain action that goes against your values, **make sure that your perception is accurate.** Many law clerks and new lawyers are reassured when entering practice to learn that the ethical standards of the judges, firms, or government agencies for whom they work are extremely high.

Second, **speak up if you disagree with a proposed action.** Before judging and speaking, though, **be sure that you understand what is proposed and the reasons for it.** If you disagree, be prepared to give your reasons and to suggest an alternative course of action. One student was reassured after having the courage to raise a point of concern with his superiors:

> *It is easy to have a lapse of integrity when you're so anxious to please. After reviewing the police report, and interviewing the officers, I believed that the evidence should be suppressed. The Deputy DA disagreed, which presented the dilemma I feared I would encounter as a legal professional: "Do we rely only on the power over things we CAN do, or are we to be guided by the things we believe we SHOULD do?"*

> *Feeling a little conflicted, I asked the District Attorney himself what he thought. He said, "I think we lose. This is the kind of motion we want to lose on. Would you want that to be the law?" His response assured me that being who you are, and being the kind of attorney you want to be, not*

*only is possible but sometimes is the only thing
that may promote "justice" over "victory."*

Student Journal (Criminal Law)

You will face challenges to your efforts to maintain a respectful and civil attitude toward others. You may experience pressure, both subtle and overt, to adopt more of an adversarial approach than may be necessary to get your job done. Sometimes these pressures will come from external sources, such as your client or supervisors. Just as often, though, you may experience internal pressure, such as your effort to prove that you are a capable advocate, that makes it difficult for you to interact respectfully with others.

Reach out to trusted colleagues, inside and outside of your office, to discuss and explore ways of resolving your concerns. Many state bar associations have Ethics Hotlines, allowing attorneys to call for confidential, oral advice on their prospective actions. State Bar Ethics Committees will generally provide both formal and informal written opinions.

You are not alone in struggling with the difficulties presented by your various roles as an advocate and efforts to be a person of integrity. By consulting with others, you'll often find unexpected resolutions. At times, an ethical problem that seems overwhelming can be managed by applying the same legal skills of analysis and research and thoughtful exploration of alternatives that solves legal questions. Make sure you understand all the facts. Precisely what is the issue you are grappling with?

Over time, and with experience, you'll see that the most capable advocates take ethical issues seriously, and treat everyone with courtesy and respect. Let their examples help you resist both external and internal pressures to act otherwise. You'll become more confident in your judgment as you gain more experience. Ultimately, if your individual values are important to you, expect to take some risks and make some sacrifices to honor them.

CHAPTER 29

FOR LAW STUDENTS—
PERSPECTIVES ON
RETURNING TO SCHOOL

*"Education is not the piling on of learning,
information, data, facts, skills, or abilities—
that's training or instruction—but is rather
making visible what is hidden as a seed."*
Sir Thomas More

A central theme of this book has been ongoing reflection in the workplace—on your own thoughts, behaviors, and performance, and on what you observe by watching others. Learning a new skill or profession is like other types of growth—a gradual and subtle process that can happen almost without notice.

Just as a child shopping for back-to-school clothes may be vaguely surprised to find he's "grown a foot in height," students often have similar "a-ha" moments upon returning to the classroom after a summer on the job. When viewed retrospectively, they are shocked at how much they've grown and learned.

Here, students speak about making the journey back to the classroom. We yield the floor to them, and to their journal entries.

A.   ON MAKING CHOICES

Every day we make choices. Some can be trivial, while others can turn out to be life-changing experiences. Law school is no exception. Students make choices. One of the most important is how much time to spend studying. Sometimes this is an easy choice. A student has a reading assignment, and studies until he completes it. But what if he completes it and doesn't quite understand? Should he go back and re-read it? Should he try to outline the reading or take better notes? How much time should he spend on that one reading assignment? As a law student, I am faced with this scenario almost every day.

My first two years of school, I was always holding back. I was not giving my best effort. I am not entirely sure why. I believe it had to do with the fact that I wanted to keep balance in my life, instead of becoming one of those people whose life revolves around studying. In trying to keep this balance, I often limited my studies. I would say that I was going to study for x hours and after that, time was up.

This summer, I simply decided that I was tired of holding back, tired of not reaching my full potential. I decided I would put forth my best effort, and that is exactly what I did. I stayed until I was satisfied with the quality of my work. It felt good to do something and do it right. I wanted to produce quality work for the office but, even more important, prove to myself that I could succeed in that environment. During law school, there is so much emphasis placed on grades that, when my grades suffered, my self-confidence also suffered. I had begun to doubt my legal research and writing skills.

Now that I am beginning my third year, I have this new sense of confidence. I know that although I might not have the best grades, I can do quality work, and I will be a good attorney. Also, I want to put forth my best effort in school, just as I did this summer. I want to hold nothing back. I want to prove to myself that I can get good grades. I am determined to do well. Even if this is my last year, it does not matter to me. I guess all I can say is that it is never too late to start, especially when it comes to giving your best.

Student Journal

B.   ON GAINING CONFIDENCE

I will have a different perspective when I return to classes this year, because I am much more confident in myself and my skills. Although I still have a lot to learn, I now know that I am capable of being very good at the practice of law. This is significant for a couple of reasons. First, because I am not at the top of my class for the first time in my life, I had begun to question how good I could be as a lawyer. Secondly, because jobs have been scarce, I wasn't sure that I could compete for and secure employment that would make me happy upon graduation. I believe my new level of confidence will translate into better performance in the classroom.

Student Journal

C. SIMPLE RULES

*1. Show up every day on time and stay all day—
even if you do no more than count the ceiling tiles.
If someone comes looking for you, you need to be
there.*

*2. Smile and be happy to perform ANY task. You
love to copy files. You are thrilled to attend a
hearing on the terrorism threats posed by the
introduction of a non-native species of snail into
a pond in Montana.*

*3. Do the task assigned to you. Don't rush—the
project was probably assigned to keep you busy
for a good amount of time and you don't want to
be heading back in six minutes with hasty work
that has to be redone—the equivalent of another
project.*

*4. Get along with everybody. No matter what it
takes.*

*5. Figure out something that you can do quietly
in your head that makes you look busy for the
times when you have nothing to do and learn to
wait. (Note: This is not the same as surfing the
internet or playing solitaire.)*

Student Journal

D. ON BEING THE RECESS MONITOR

*After being back in school for over a week, I am
realizing that I need to think differently about
school than I did last year. Then, I was still
thinking of this as "school." As much as I wanted*

to learn, I "had" to go to class and I "had" to read. I was treating this experience as if I were still in elementary, junior high or high school—forced to plod through uninteresting subjects.

I inhaled reality during the past summer. I dreaded coming back to stifling classrooms and tedious lectures. These were my thoughts in the week before school started this fall. This, even though I actually enjoyed most of last year. My characterization of school conflicted with my actual experiences—as with much of life I suspect.

So, my burst of understanding came after one week of this "stifling" atmosphere. Law school most definitely is not "school," not in the way elementary school or high school is. Here, there are no chains of anxious, hand-holding students, no whistle-blowing recess monitors, no identification checks in the parking lot when leaving for lunch. No one is watching me here.

I don't mistake that for, "no one cares." Many people care. No, the true difference, the one that raises law school above mere "school," is the gaping void where someone's eyes used to perpetually be. Because I am an adult now. Make that, I am attempting to be an adult now. I am now my own recess monitor, and when the bell rings, I have to take my seat.

Student Journal

E.   ON A BALANCED APPROACH TO WHINING

I guess it just became a practice during the first year. I went to lunch with some other 1L's and, about 30 minutes in, we were heavy into a critique of the law school experience on a variety of issues. I think that this practice stems for the most part from anxiety—everyone has their own way of dealing, and once you sort of have a certain habit of discourse, well, it's easy.

That having been said, the challenge is controlling this practice because, while on the one hand you may come up with a variety of constructive criticisms, there is a point at which you've convinced yourself that everything is a certain way and you fit all your facts into that particular mold. That is not the model of good lawyering.

Some complaining is good. I am not one who goes in for the "no whining" mantra—I believe that some whining is occasionally justified and necessary. That too is part of what I am coming to believe is good lawyering. Accepting things as they are doesn't keep the creativity going. As with all things, you've got to have balance.

Student Journal

F.   ON GRATITUDE

The most important perspective I gained this summer is that being a lawyer is a very powerful thing to be. Of course, I knew this, but have now realized that the desire to give voices to those traditionally silenced is not just a pipe dream. Having the privilege of witnessing firsthand the power that comes from legal knowledge, I feel excitement along with a great deal of responsibility that I never had before. What I will do differently is not take my education for granted; it is truly a gift that I will spend a lifetime giving back.

Student Journal

SECTION 4

PRACTICAL TOOLS FOR
CAREER PLANNING

CHAPTER 30

GET A MENTOR—EXPAND YOUR WORLD

*"If you would know the road ahead,
ask someone who has traveled it."*
Chinese Saying

Find and establish a relationship with a mentor, someone who will be interested in you and your professional development. This is the single piece of advice most often given to new professionals by leaders in almost every field, including law. We couldn't agree more—if you are fortunate, you will have many mentors throughout your life. On occasion, you'll be lucky enough to have several at once.

The concept of mentoring goes back to the ancient Greeks, when Odysseus put his son in the care of a trusted friend, Mentor, before leaving for the Trojan War. The process is still the same—a more experienced, trusted individual shares advice with a less experienced person.

This chapter will explore some of the ways that mentoring occurs in the legal community. We'll discuss how formal and informal programs work as well as the roles of mentors and mentees and suggestions for deriving maximum benefit from a mentoring relationship.

A. FORMAL MENTORING PROGRAMS

1. In Law School

Most schools offer voluntary or mandatory mentoring programs for incoming first-year students. Several also provide mentors to third-year students, whose needs and concerns change as they approach graduation, the Bar exam, and the impending realities of practice.

Volunteer mentors come from every segment of the legal community. At times, mentoring "matches" are made on a random basis, but an effort is usually made to pair them based on shared interests. Factors used to facilitate mentoring matches include practice interests, professional goals, undergraduate major and institutions, previous employment, personal interests such as sports and hobbies, and special requests (e.g., to be paired with a single parent, someone with a disability, a second-career professional, or an attorney with a particular cultural background).

Once mentors have been assigned, participants may be encouraged to meet and form relationships on their own, or they may be introduced at a welcoming event such as a reception or continuing education program.

How the mentoring relationship proceeds beyond the first meeting is generally left up to the individuals. For whatever reason, some relationships never progress beyond a few meetings (although we'll offer suggestions later in this chapter to avoid that scenario). In contrast, some mentors and mentees form long-term friendships; most mentoring relationships fall somewhere in between. Regardless of the relationship's nature, by the program's end, the mentee will have met a future colleague—and this is always beneficial.

2. In the Workplace

A growing number of employers offer mentoring programs to get their new lawyers off to a good start. New attorneys may be paired with mentors inside or outside of their practice areas, with peer mentors (attorneys close in age and/or experience), with senior mentors (more experienced attorneys at higher levels within the organization), in mentoring teams (comprised of a small number of new, mid-level, and senior attorneys), or with special interest mentors (based on factors such as minority status, first generation professionals, gender, disabilities, and practice areas).

When you're ready to consider a job offer, you may want to ask whether your prospective employer provides mentoring for new lawyers. If they do, discussion points could include how long the program has been offered, who coordinates it, and whether it has formal goals. Ask newer attorneys in the office about their experiences with being mentored and more experienced attorneys whether they serve as mentors. How often do they meet and what kind of contact do mentees have with their mentors? What advice might they share about how to get the most value from the mentoring program?

3.   Through Bar Associations

More than half of state bar associations offer mentoring programs for new lawyers; in a handful of them, the programs are mandatory. For example, in 2005, the State Bar of Georgia made an unprecedented commitment to mentoring with its Transition into Law Practice Program, which is mandatory for new attorneys. TILPP offers formal mentoring with required activities and an extensive curriculum of practical and ethical training.

A greater number of bar associations provide "situational," short-term mentoring. This is often in conjunction with a member assistance program, where attorneys seek help dealing with a specific problem. For example, an inexperienced lawyer might ask to consult with someone about the advisability of going into solo practice. Another might seek help in preparing for his first court-mandated settlement conference. Many bar associations also offer mentors in conjunction with drug and alcohol diversion programs.

The American Bar Association maintains a list of mentoring programs by state on its website.

B.   INFORMAL MENTORING

Some of your mentors will come from formal programs (e.g., in your school or workplace), but we hope that you will also develop informal mentoring relationships on your own.

The first step to finding a mentor is to **put yourself in as many situations as possible**

where you can meet and talk to lawyers. See Chapter 6, "The Art (or Horror) of Networking," for suggestions on how to do this, and Chapter 5, "Overcoming Shyness," if the idea of talking to so many people makes you nervous. Summer employment and school-year externships and internships are good settings, because of the close and continued contact you'll have with attorneys. Attorneys are also involved at the law school as adjunct faculty, Moot Court judges, writing instructors or coaches, supervisors in clinics; most are happy to meet with students.

Specialty bar associations (such as for specific practice areas, women, and minority groups) offer a safe environment to interact with attorneys. If possible, attend a few meetings, CLE programs (often free for students) or social functions. Is there someone with whom you shared a good conversation? Someone who seems particularly interesting or who has similar interests? If so, ask for a business card, and follow up to see if you could get together and chat again over coffee or lunch. *You* must usually be the one to take the initiative here—although many attorneys enjoy talking to students, it may never cross their minds that you would like to meet again. If you think someone has "mentoring potential," try to get together periodically and see how the relationship unfolds.

C.   WHAT TO EXPECT

Ideally, your mentor will provide you with the support and guidance that best meets your

needs. However, each mentoring relationship will develop in its own unique way, depending on the needs and personalities of both parties. Outside of mandatory, well-defined programs, there are no specified number of times the parties should meet, no required activities, and no expectations about what will develop. You will get the greatest benefit from mentoring if you enter it hoping to build a relationship, but without fixed expectations.

With this in mind, your mentor might do some of the following things:

- **Offer support and encouragement concerning your law school experience or integration into practice as a new lawyer.** This might include insight about how to survive exams, handle projects, or juggle family and personal issues. Don't expect your mentor to provide extensive counseling on personal matters unrelated to law school or the profession.

- **Answer "dumb" questions** (the ones you would be afraid to ask a professor or supervising attorney). But, don't ask your mentor for assistance or research on substantive courses or legal issues.

- **Help you find your own way,** and figure out your strengths and weaknesses.

- **Help you gain new perspectives on the profession,** by sharing details about their own practices, as well as the difficulties and satisfaction they experience in their careers.

- **Make it possible for you to better understand the practical aspects of being a lawyer,** by inviting you to visit the office, or attend a meeting, court appearance, or social event.

- **Provide general information about legal careers and career planning.** Some mentors will be willing to look at your resume, and even talk to friends about your interest in a summer or full-time position. But, let them make the offer and under no circumstances should you expect your mentor to provide job placement services.

- **Introduce you to other attorneys and help you get involved with the legal community.** This could give you a valuable head start on the process of networking which, indirectly, could lead to job prospects.

The best way to prepare for mentoring is to **spend time reflecting on what you hope to gain from the experience.** Do you hope to make a friend in the legal community, get a better idea of what attorneys do, and/or learn more about a specific practice area?

Whatever your goals may be, you'll need to **be proactive** and communicate them. Your mentor is not a mind-reader, so you should be the one to initiate the conversation. Your mentor will also appreciate knowing how you would like to structure your time together. If you want to shadow your mentor for a day, or tag along to court, ask!

Here are additional suggestions for getting the most out of a mentoring relationship.

- **Express yourself.** Take some time to develop rapport and get to know each other, both personally and professionally. Let your personality shine through and enjoy yourself. This is not the time to be timid.

- **Share responsibility for making contact.** Don't cancel at the last minute and don't be late to scheduled meetings.

- **Offer to be the host occasionally.** Your mentor may invite you to lunch or dinner, sporting events and the like and, while it may not be financially feasible for you to respond in kind, you could occasionally invite your mentor to meet for coffee or bring some home-baked cookies into the office the next time you meet.

- **Don't be too demanding of your mentor's time.** Be sensitive to your mentor's busy schedule and time limitations that may be placed on your meetings. If you suggest a meeting, always ask if the time is convenient.

- **If your mentor shares personal and professional information with you, remember it** and follow up occasionally on the specifics. For example, remember his daughter's name and, in September, how she's doing in first grade.

- **Show your appreciation.** Mentors almost always say they feel they gain more from the relationship than the mentee. However, be sure to express your thanks occasionally, perhaps with a thank you card or e-mail.

- **Re: social networking.** If your law school doesn't have guidelines on this topic, the decision of whether to "friend" your mentor on Facebook, follow her on Twitter, etc., is yours to make. However, if you do decide to connect, you must always maintain a high level of professionalism. You should already be doing this anyway, but see Chapter 17, "E-Professionalism," for more information on this topic.

- **Don't just drop your mentor at the end of the year.** Even if you don't anticipate an ongoing friendship, do your best to maintain the acquaintance on a cordial level. Make it a point to exchange greetings at bar functions, find a way to make occasional contact by e-mail, etc.

D. WHAT TO DO IF THE RELATIONSHIP STALLS

If you have serious concerns with the mentoring match (for example, your mentor hasn't been in touch at all, even though you've made several attempts to make an introduction), by all means get in touch with the mentoring program coordinator. It is uncommon, but things of this nature occasionally happen. The coordinator will either have some good advice to share with you and/or will assign you to a different mentor.

But hang in there if the relationship merely seems to stall. Some relationships take longer to develop than others, and this might be the case with you and your mentor. Occasionally, close friendships develop through mentoring, and you may see this happen with some of your classmates. However, don't take it personally if the primary focus of your mentoring relationship seems confined to the professional sphere. Learn everything that you can from your mentor, continue to participate in the program until its designated conclusion, and let go of any other expectations.

After you've been in practice for a few years, **you may be recruited as a mentor yourself.** We hope that you'll view this moment as a landmark of sorts, an illustration not only of how far you've come in your growth as an attorney, but also a recognition that you could be a good role model for someone new to the profession. What benefits can you hope to gain from the switch in roles? As a Superior Court Commissioner and long-time mentor commented, "Participating in the mentoring program has been a great opportunity for me to remember the struggles of law school, and be a support system for a young person embarking on that journey. It has also been an opportunity for me to connect with the law school. But, most of all, it has been an opportunity for friendship."

We hope you will take advantage of and enjoy the opportunity to be mentored and later, when you're ready, to step into the role of a mentor yourself!

CHAPTER 31

FIRST-YEAR CAREER PLAN—
A GUIDED EXERCISE

"Give me six hours to chop down a tree and I will spend the first four sharpening the axe."

Abraham Lincoln

In many aspects of your life, **you've already executed at least one long-range plan,** but may not have called it that. For example, **you had a goal in coming to law school** (perhaps to secure a certain lifestyle, get a specific type of job, address a social issue, or find a way to use a unique skill or talent). Your first step towards achieving that goal was getting admitted, and that took determination and planning. Once you were admitted, it involved getting your personal and financial lives in order, and perhaps even relocating to another city or state.

As a law student, you may have felt more like a circus juggler than a master planner. Multi-tasking, however illusory, appears to be the rule of the day. You pared down your schedule to the bare essentials, and much of it was probably dictated by your professors and the law school. If you are like most students, you expected that school would be time-consuming and made allowances for the strain this would put on other parts of your life. But you thought things would return to normal after graduation. You expected to regain a certain degree of control over your career and your life.

In many ways, the move from school to work is liberating. No classes to prepare for, papers to write, exams to take. Especially in the early years though, many lawyers are uncertain of what they hope to accomplish in their jobs and in their personal lives. Even those who *do* want to exercise control and who spend time thinking about their plans often resist putting them on paper, preferring instead to keep them "in the back of their minds."

We encourage *you* to think differently, and to view career planning as an active and conscious process, not something that "happens to you." One of the most positive steps you can take in that direction is to create short-term (0–5 years) and long-term (5–10 years) plans. By setting goals, you can retain a degree of control in the early years of your career—years when many new attorneys feel relatively powerless, at least professionally, and often personally. By keeping your goals in focus, you'll be able to maintain enthusiasm and see each small step as a move toward what you hope to accomplish. You will know how to best direct your efforts, make decisions more quickly, and view setbacks as merely temporary.

> *We encourage our summer law clerks to think about how their experiences with us will change their approach to the coming academic year. We also encourage them to begin thinking about their short/long-term career goals.*
>
> Advice from an Employer

Whether you are a law student, new graduate, or attorney (with or without a job),

it's not too early to make a career plan. This chapter explores two key facets of career planning:

- **How to develop professional and personal goals, and**

- **How to translate these goals into a specific course of action.**

A.   SETTING THE SCENE—A JOB

If you've already accepted a job after graduation, your career plan will at least be based on an initial reality—a job. A growing number of legal employers provide their new hires with various levels of career-planning support. If you are fortunate enough to be in this situation, you'll have extra resources to help you with this process.

Otherwise, we ask you to *imagine* that you are about to take a job as a new lawyer in a firm, agency, or other work setting of your choice. The job should fit well with your working style and practice preferences. Be as realistic as possible in completing this exercise; it will be a valuable point of reference as you near graduation. Even if the employment setting is imaginary, much of what you'll learn from the exercise will be useful for your first "real" career plan and "real" job.

B.   EXPLORE PERSONAL AND PROFESSIONAL GOALS

In surveys, lawyers in overwhelming numbers, of all experience levels, and in every type of setting, report a desire to find more balance in their lives.

One way to achieve better balance is to be more holistic in your career planning and reflection about your values and goals.

During law school, you have likely been narrowly focused on mastering the skills of legal analysis and writing, ways of interpreting and applying cases and statutes, extrapolating legal principles from a variety of legal sources, and otherwise focusing on the "law." Law school is in many ways an exercise in focusing on the trees, with many of us missing the forest. Now is the time to pull back, and **think more broadly about what you hope to achieve, and how much time it might take for you to do so.** This calls for reflection on both your professional and personal goals; answers may not come easily, or at all in some cases. You'll also encounter more general, overarching issues that don't at first seem appropriate for something as narrow as a career plan. **In fact, any career plan must be a "life" plan as well. Career questions can't be answered in a vacuum, out of the context of your life, and all that that entails.**

For example, you may wonder why a professional career plan should include personal goals. Consider for a moment that how well you plan and spend your personal time will affect the energy and time you can devote to your professional life, and vice versa. Your professional and personal lives are intrinsically interwoven; to craft a plan for better handling one aspect without doing so for the other is a recipe for chaos. As you move through the entire exercise, you'll begin to see how everything fits together.

Set aside some time to reflect upon and answer the questions posed here. Write them down! Don't be afraid to think big. The idea is not to restrict your thinking or make you feel pressured, but to engage in self-exploration, think broadly, identify the things that are most important to you. You may never have thought about exactly how you are spending your time, so the process should be illuminating.

- If you are married or in a committed relationship, you'll want to involve your partner in the process at some point, to identify shared goals, and to discuss as well individual goals that require each other's cooperation. You may want to incorporate input from others in your community of professional colleagues and friends. **The goal is to identify the relationships and activities that are important to you and, later, find a way to set aside time for them as you begin your new career.**

- **What are your personal roles?** Are you married or in a committed relationship, or do you hope to be soon? Are your parents living? Do you have children of your own? Do you have a large circle of friends? Are you involved in religious or community groups?

- **What do your personal roles entail?** Describe the activities involved in each of your personal roles, and estimate how much time you spend (or would ideally spend) maintaining them.

For example, how much and what kind of time do you spend with your parents? (If they live out of town, this may involve telephone calls once or twice a week, and a visit of a week or more each year. If they live in town, is dinner on the weekend sufficient to maintain the relationship?) If you are newly married and expecting a baby, your personal time together may have a different quality and intensity than if you have been together several years, with well-established home and daily routines. What does it take to maintain your friendships? Would you need to set aside a couple of lunch hours each week, plus some time on the weekend for golf or a movie?

- **Are you involved in hobbies or other activities and, if so, what do they involve?** Too frequently, the first thing busy people cut from their schedules are personal activities and private time. As a student, you may be all too familiar with this reality. And yet we know that enjoyable physical and mental activities help reduce stress, keep us healthy and enrich our lives. Our goal is to help you find time for them. Think about hobbies, sports, and other activities that you enjoy as important commitments, and estimate both the amount and nature of the time that they require.

In your "new" life after law school, you may want to work out regularly. Would your ideal schedule involve an early-morning hour at the gym three times a week, a morning run, and/or a weekend yoga class? For an avid reader, for example, 30 minutes before bedtime each night to catch up on the latest novel may suffice. Golf, on the other hand, might entail a longer, but perhaps less frequent, time commitment.

- **Do you remember why you wanted to become a lawyer? Have your ideas changed?** People decide to go to law school for a variety of reasons, ranging from things like a desire to create large-scale social change, a passion for political affairs, the need for intellectual stimulation, desire for respect in the community or to earn a good living, and everything you can imagine in between. With your overarching goals in mind, you may be able to identify specific skills and abilities you'll need to achieve those goals, and will need to incorporate sufficient time to develop them in your career plan.

- **Are your technological skills up to date?** Proficiency with technology and computer software consistently appear in lists of "critical skills for lawyers in every type of practice." **If your skills are not up to par, training in this area must be given top priority in your short-term career plan.** Regardless of your skill level, we recommend that you incorporate additional time for staying up to date in both your short-term and long-term career plans.

- As a related issue, **what are your strengths and weaknesses?** Include opportunities in your career plan for experiences that are suited to your strengths, and time for additional training and education to address your weaknesses. (If you're not sure which are which, try the exercise beginning on p. 260 in Chapter 23, "How Adults Learn—And Why It Matters.")

  For example, if one of your weaknesses is a fear of public speaking, you could join Toastmasters this year. If you came to law school to make a difference in people's lives, you could take a step in that direction during your first year of practice by getting involved in a pro bono project in your practice area or in another practice area that can be mastered fairly quickly. You'll reap the additional benefits of learning more about your legal specialty or meeting people in a completely different area of law.

  If you want to remember what life is like outside of law, you may want to volunteer in a totally non-legal context, such as Literacy Volunteers or Big Brother-Big Sister.

- **What personal goals would you like to set for your first year after graduation? What steps would help you achieve those goals?** Be expansive in considering these questions, and incorporate what you learned about yourself from other questions in this section. Are there specific skills that would enrich your personal life?

For example, you may want to create and maintain a savings and investment plan. Or you may decide to focus on your most important personal relationship and consciously commit time and energy to maintain and nurture it. Whatever your personal goals may be, they share equal importance in the career planning process.

- **What do you hope to achieve as a lawyer in your first 5 years? 10 years?** Short-term career plans must also take into account goals that require more time to develop. Should those goals change, you can always adjust your plan; but there is no remedy for a short-sighted plan that does not reach beyond what can be accomplished in the near future.

- **What are your most significant professional and personal accomplishments?** You want this new career of yours to be rewarding, and your career plan should include some time for those things that bring you satisfaction. This question will help you identify activities which are "non-negotiable" when your schedule becomes crowded (as it surely will be).

- **What could you do differently this year that would make the biggest difference in your professional life?** A good time to ask this question is just before the new academic year, a short time after graduation, or at another milestone (such as a six-month evaluation). Answers frequently fall into two categories. The first concerns balance of life, with plans to exercise regularly, spend more time with family, get involved in extracurricular or volunteer activities. The other category deals with quality of learning, such as a vow to "stop comparing myself to others," "ask more questions," "get to know professors or attorneys better," or "take on more challenging projects."

- **What do you believe are the attributes of an outstanding first-year lawyer, and how do they differ from a lawyer who is competent, but not outstanding? What motivates people to want to do their best?** Entering the legal profession doesn't necessarily mean entering a competition but, in seeking role models and in setting goals for yourself, you should know the difference between those who are striving to perform to the best of their abilities and those who are merely "marking time" on the job. In considering this question, you may reflect on different qualities including "confidence," "dedication to even the smaller points," and "treating absolutely everyone with insight and courtesy."

- **What else comes to mind?** The questions posed in this section are quite broad. Have they raised other issues? If so, make a note of them and spend some time considering how they might relate to your career plans.

C. CREATING THE "PLAN"

The first part of this chapter guided you through the process of reflecting on your skills, abilities, and motivations. Next, you'll use what you have learned in creating a career plan. There are three basic steps:

1. Craft a "mission statement" that reflects your aspirational goals in the short and long term.

2. Create a "budget" for your time, based on the realities and demands of your real or imagined workplace.

3. Develop a schedule for your waking hours.

A word of advice before you begin: Take this process seriously, but realize that your plan will be based on many "unknowns." You will likely revise it many times, particularly in the early stages of your career. Your plan is a work in progress, not a piece of sculpture carved into marble. The most valuable part of the plan is your conscious reflection about and attention to what is important in your life.

1. Craft a Mission Statement

The mission statement should reflect your purpose for being a lawyer, and describe how you hope to grow professionally and personally in the next year, five years, and ten years. Following are several examples of mission statements:

- ***Prosecutor.*** "I want to become an outstanding prosecutor, starting with misdemeanors and moving to major felonies by Year Three. From Years Three to Ten, I'll fine-tune my skills, and establish a reputation as an ethical, disciplined and talented lawyer. In Year Ten, I hope to have gained sufficient experience and standing in the community to run for public office. On the personal side, I want to marry my girlfriend in the next couple of years, reduce my student loans, save enough to purchase a home a few years after that, and then begin a family."

- ***Small Firm.*** "I imagine that I'll start working for a small or medium-sized firm, or public agency, and get some experience that I can use. When I can qualify for a small business loan, I want to start my own solo practice, with plans for eventually expanding. By Year Ten, I hope to be managing my own firm and have the freedom to create the kind of firm culture that I want. Alternatively, I'm open to all kinds of entrepreneurial adventures such as opening a small business. Personally, I am already married and have two children (three and five years old). I am willing to work very hard, but my family is important and I want to be a good wife and mother."

- ***Large Firm.*** "I was at a large firm my second summer, and accepted an offer for a job after graduation. Before I start, I want to secure a one-year judicial clerkship at the federal or state supreme court level. Afterwards, at the firm I want to work in several areas of civil law. Eventually, I hope to settle into a practice in real property law. The partnership track at my firm is seven years, and I do intend to make partner. Personally, I'm not currently involved in a relationship, but enjoy working out at the gym, golfing and participating in various sports. I hope to meet that "special someone" within the next few years."

- ***Process Based.*** "I hope to work with individual clients on matters that can be resolved over a relatively short period of time—such as Social Security or Worker's Compensation or Immigration matters. I want to be able to understand what my clients' concerns and goals are and be able to explain to my clients in words they can understand what I hope to accomplish for them. I would like to improve my communication skills (both listening and explaining) as well as become more efficient so that my fees are reasonable. I hope to be able to live on a relatively modest income so that I can spend the time I need to work on client matters without having to charge more than they can afford to pay.

2.   "Budget" Your Time

Develop a monthly or weekly schedule for spending your time, like you might create a household budget.

There is one crucial difference, however. With the help of charge accounts and credit cards, you can overspend without negative consequences (at least in the short term), but there is no such thing as "buying" more time. Each day is limited to 24 hours and, although you may be able to put things off (at least in the short term), you can only do so many things during that time. For example, there are 720 hrs. in every month—how will you spend them? Go ahead and subtract a good night's sleep, then calculate how much time you'll be spending at work. Depending on the setting, your efficiency level, the attorneys you work with and the cases you handle, you'll probably work between 50 and 70 hrs. per week. This leaves between 200 and 280 additional waking hours per month. How will you spend them?

3.   Develop a "Spending Plan" for Your Time

Now, translate your mission statement, along with the personal and professional insights you gained earlier in this chapter, into measurable goals and specific action items. For example, if you want to become an excellent prosecutor or defense lawyer, you know how important it is to master the rules of evidence. Here's how one student described the steps he plans to take to do this.

My experience in the district attorney's office convinced me that it is not the evidence a prosecutor has that matters; rather, it is the evidence he can get admitted. I remember one attorney saying, "If I can master the evidence code, I'm sure I can own the world." To master the evidence code, I need to become more proficient (and faster!) with legal research. I plan on doing research exercises on Lexis and Westlaw, and becoming competent in multiple areas of research. I hope to learn more deeply how electronic research relates and interacts with those books on the library shelves. I plan to invest as much time as necessary to learn these skills—not only to learn them, but to hone and refine them.

Student Journal

Your personal life deserves equal reflection and planning, and can be even more complex because of the often-competing roles and responsibilities it entails. Family, friendships, household tasks, hobbies, physical fitness . . . so much to do, yet so little time! Set aside specific "appointments" for the relationships and activities that you feel are important, and you'll find that you are better able to keep these commitments. If you don't schedule them, you run the risk of never getting around to them. Of course, we all benefit from some unstructured time now and then, too, so don't feel that you must account for every hour and minute in your day.

Once you've created a plan you can live with, refer to it frequently to gauge your progress. You may want to keep a personal calendar as well as a work calendar and may be comfortable using software and technology to help keep track of your time in various activities.

Despite the care and reflection with which your career plan was created, consider it as a guide only. Revise it when you need to (and there will be those times). Adjust and revise it based on your changing experiences and priorities. Every now and then, revisit the fundamental questions and see if your answers have changed. What are the relationships and activities that are most important to you? What, if anything, can you do differently that would make the biggest difference in your personal life? Have your professional goals changed? If so, what might you do to accommodate those changes?

CHAPTER 32

DECIDING WHETHER THE JOB IS RIGHT FOR YOU

"Choose a job you love, and you will never have to work a day in your life."
Confucius

Whether you are a law student, new lawyer, or even a prospective law student, you might have already begun to think about (and possibly search for) your first legal job. You may have gotten a jump on the process because you're just a natural planner. For others, the impetus to begin thinking about a career comes later and more suddenly. There is a point when law school, which initially seemed endless, suddenly begins to accelerate, and the necessity of finding a job begins to loom on the horizon. Panic may set in at this point . . .

Whether you're an early bird, late bloomer, or somewhere in between, it's normal to have a certain amount of anxiety while planning your career. After all, you have a lot at stake in your first legal job after graduation. You may be asked to make this important decision without being 100% sure of what you want to do with your law degree, and without knowing whether a particular employer would be the best fit.

One of our primary goals in writing this book was to help calm those fears by providing many of the tools you need to succeed in the legal profession which, of course, includes getting that first job. **This**

chapter is devoted to encouraging you to explore more subtle aspects of career planning that you may not have considered.

At the end of the day, I find myself faced with a series of questions. Do I look forward to work, so that I have no trouble getting to bed at a reasonable hour, so I can get up and go to work in the morning? Does it pay a living wage? Will the pressures of work bleed over to color my personal life? Will the job land me in a geographic area I like, with friends and family I can call on for support and entertainment? Will the other personality types I can expect to work with drive me completely crazy in the long run?

Student Journal

Developing an awareness of the culture where you work is very important. This is true not only so you can "fit in" once you have been hired, it's also crucial to be aware of your own values before you accept a job. Otherwise, you could easily find yourself in the very stressful position of being in a workplace whose culture totally disregards your own values.

Student Journal

If you ask a number of people how they ended up in their jobs, many (maybe most) would reply, "I just fell into it." Now, we'll grant you that wonderful things have sometimes come about by accident—corn flakes, the popsicle, post-it notes, and Velcro, for example. However, **do you want to entrust your career to a stroke of luck?**

Probably not, although at times you might feel as if things are going that way. For example, imagine that you receive a job offer from your second-favorite employer, but your first choice won't make hiring decisions for a couple of months. Who could have imagined that receiving positive news (a job offer!) could cause such anguish?

Even if there are no guarantees, **when it comes to planning your career, you want to gather as much information as possible** to help plot your next move. A good starting point might be to find out why so many new attorneys decide to leave the jobs they worked so hard to get in the first place. Given the time, energy and worry they put into the process, why didn't they "get it right" the first time? And once you have that job, what can you do to avoid having to make another move before you are ready?

A. WHY DO NEW LAWYERS QUIT THEIR JOBS?

The numbers of new attorneys who leave their law firm jobs within the first five years is surprisingly high. Most studies estimate that upwards of 46% of new associates leave within the first three years; the number climbs to 81% by year five.

Certainly, some moves are positive, such as leaving a job for an advancement opportunity or moving to a different part of the country. More worrisome are situations in which new attorneys leave (or are asked to leave), because they are unable to meet their employers' performance standards or due to billable hour pressures and lack of work-life balance. And what of those who leave for reasons that cannot be articulated (e.g., "just not what I thought it would be" or "just not a good fit")?

Whether due to pleasant or unpleasant circumstances, job changes come at a cost for all who are involved. For the job seeker, searching for another job requires significant time and effort, and the process is not necessarily easier the second time around. There still are inevitable uncertainties about whether a prospective job will be a better fit, and whether one's performance will make the grade. There are financial costs, too, especially if there is a lengthy gap of time between leaving one job and starting another. If the length of time at one job is relatively short, there are sure to be questions about why the job ended so soon. Employers bear costs as well. On average, it takes four to five years for a law firm to recoup its investment in a new lawyer (including organizational costs such as recruiting, hiring and training, and overhead).

How could so many misjudge so badly? More importantly, what can *you* do to improve the likelihood of making wise employment decisions?

We suspect that at least some of those who leave their first jobs failed to consider a less obvious, yet critical, issue in their career planning. This step involves reflecting on the future you hope to develop in the profession generally and, more specifically, in your place of employment. It also involves identifying workplace factors that will be most supportive of your professional and personal goals.

B.   WHAT MIGHT YOU DO DIFFERENTLY?

It's easy to get so enmeshed in *learning the law* that you forget to relate what you are learning to the actual *practice of law*. If you can, try to resist the tendency toward "tunnel vision," and pause occasionally to measure your developing skills, envision how you will use them as a lawyer, and view them in the context of your long and short-term career goals.

While participating in an internship, externship, for-credit judicial clerkship clinic, or summer job, "try out" those settings and legal specialties, and think about how well they mesh with your interests and preferences. Treat each experience as a long job interview—but with a twist. Imagine that the decision to choose the position is *YOURS alone*. If you had many options to choose from, would you want the job? Why or why not?

C.   INQUIRING MINDS WANT TO KNOW

Eventually, the decision *will* be a real one. **The questions below will get you thinking about the kinds of things to consider before accepting a job offer.** Some are appropriate to ask during your first interview; others would be better to raise during a call-back interview or through your own observation. When you ask them, pay close attention not only to the *content* of the answers you receive, but also the *manner* in which they are answered.

At first glance, you might feel that some of these issues are not appropriate for an entry-level attorney to ask. However, if you are serious about a position and "fit" is important to you, regardless of whether you end up staying for the short term or long haul, you owe it to yourself to learn as much as possible about your prospective employer.

You may want to supplement the answers you receive through your own powers of observation, or by talking with contacts in the legal community, such as mentors and previous employers.

The main point here is that **we hope you will look before you leap, instead of just falling into your career.** As you read these questions, some will resonate with you more than others. Pay attention to your reactions to the questions themselves to learn more about your own values and preferences.

1.   Nature of Work

- What kinds of legal work does the organization handle? How has the mix of practice areas shifted and evolved (if at all) over time?

- How much of the work is handled individually? In teams?

- How varied are the projects, both in subject matter and experiences offered?

- Would you be assigned to one department or area, or have the opportunity to explore many specialties before committing to a particular area?

- Would you primarily work with one or a few attorneys, or be introduced to the practice on a broader scale? How would your input be considered when this decision is being made?

- Who are the clients? How much and what kind of client contact would you have? How would this change as you gain experience?

- Would you have opportunities to network with other professionals in the community?

2.   Office Environment

- What are the firm's philosophy and goals? Do the people you meet during your interview process look forward to going to work in the morning?

- What administrative support is available and what assistance do they offer? Who makes up the team of non-lawyers and how are they treated by associates? By senior attorneys?

- What resources are available in terms of computers, computerized research, software and other programs, and IT staff? Are books and other reference materials readily available? Is there a law library on site or nearby? Is there a librarian and, if so, what kind of support is offered?

- What office equipment and supplies are provided?

- What is the level of formality in the office, in relationships and dress?

- What opportunities do new attorneys have to socialize with partners and senior associates?

- Are social events structured to be inclusive to all?

3.   Work-Life Balance

- Do attorneys bill hours or have flexible schedules?

- If they bill hours, what is the minimum billing requirement? Are even higher hours required to receive bonuses and/or promotions?

- Are attorneys required be "on call" at all times, or just for emergencies? Is there internal pressure to be available 24/7, despite a policy that might say otherwise?

- Do attorneys actually get to use their vacation time? If so, do they get away for only a day or two at a time, or are they able to leave for one or more weeks at a time? Does this differ according to practice area or seniority?

- Are flexible work schedules offered? If so, are they offered to all, or only to those with young children? Are men included? Do people actually use them, or do they exist in name only? How are people who use them viewed by firm management?

- In terms of tenure, is there more than one partnership track? Can you remain on partnership track while on a reduced or flexible schedule? Has anyone made partner while taking advantage of this benefit? How long did it take them compared to the typical route to partnership? What options are available for those who do not wish to be on the partnership track?

- How many attorneys in the firm have children, and what are their ages?

- Is travel involved in the position? If so, ask for specifics about how often you would be expected to travel and for what duration. Do certain areas of practice entail more travel?

4. Professional Development and Training

- How are new attorneys supervised? Closely, as-needed, or not at all?

- What feedback do they receive on each assignment?

- Are annual or periodic performance evaluations conducted? If so, what input is sought, and who contributes that information? How are evaluations given? What feedback, if any, would you provide to the process?

- Is ongoing training provided? If so, is it just for new attorneys, or are programs offered for all levels of experience?

- Is someone in the firm formally charged with attorney professional development and, if so, what percentage of their time is spent on this aspect of their responsibilities?

- In what format are training programs offered (in-house, video/web/pod-based, via outside programs, or some combination)?

- Is training offered on non-legal but essential topics, such as law firm economics and time management?

- Is there a formal or informal mentor program? If so, how are matches made and how is the program supported by the organization? What kind of contact is typically offered and how frequently?

- Are the attorneys involved with pro bono work? If so, are the cases of their own choosing, or does the firm sponsor specific pro bono activities? Do the attorneys participate in bar activities? Does the time spent in pursuit of these activities count towards billing requirements?

5. Salary and Benefits

- What is the starting salary? Is it a lockstep system (with all attorneys of similar experience earning the same amount), or is there a "closed compensation system" (where employees are not allowed to share information about salaries)?

- Are bonuses typically awarded? If so, how often, and on what basis? Is this information public?

- Are raises given on a lockstep basis, in equal amounts to all attorneys with the same length of employment? If so, at what times? If raises are tied to other factors such as billable hours, performance evaluations, or work assignments, how are these factors determined, when, and by whom?

- In addition to salary, what other benefits are offered? Benefits packages may include relocation expenses; medical, dental, vision, and short- and long-term disability insurance; loan repayment assistance; vacation; sick leave; retirement plan; supplemental savings plan; bar memberships; and reimbursement for CLE expenses.

6. Size/Scope of Office/Firm

- How big is the office? Is it divided into sections or divisions? If so, how many and what types?

- Does the firm have offices in other U.S. cities and/or around the globe? If so, are they independent, or are certain services more centralized? Would you have the opportunity to move to a different city at some point, if you desired? Would you have an opportunity to work in some capacity with one of the overseas offices?

- What kind of communication, if any, occurs between sections/divisions/offices and at what levels?

- How many partners, associates, and law clerks are there in each office? What is the ratio of partners to associates? Has the ratio changed over time and, if so, how?

- What practices are represented in each office? Look at each area in terms of number of attorneys and associates, as well as historical, current and projected growth. Where are the growth areas?

7.   Firm Governance

- What is the mix of clients and practice areas? How are these decisions made, and has this changed over time?

- What is the firm's management structure? Is it governed by a managing partner, management committee, professional manager, some combination, or something more unique?

- How much do attorneys in the office know about management decisions? Do they have a voice in those decisions?

- If the firm has multi-office settings (domestic and global), what effect does this have on management structure?

8.   Long-Term Prospects

- Is there a clearly defined career path and, if so, what would be required to receive greater responsibility, promotion, or partnership?

- What other career opportunities are available in this field of law? In this firm?

- How are attorneys recruited and what is the average length of time they stay? Why do they leave?

- What is the mix of new attorneys vs. lateral hires?

- When are attorneys expected to begin client development (bringing in new business)? What kind of support and training is offered?

- What is the firm's partnership structure and process for making partnership decisions? What percentage of associates are on the partnership track? What percentage of this number makes partner, and when?

- What happens to those who are not on the partnership track, or who are unsuccessful in their attempt to become a partner?

CHAPTER 33

SALARY NEGOTIATIONS

*"You don't get what you deserve;
you get what you negotiate."*
Anonymous

At some point, whether as a law student or new graduate, you'll have found a job. Depending on the situation, salary negotiations may be in your immediate future.

The very prospect of negotiating a salary with an employer would make most of us extremely nervous, even those who have taken courses on negotiation and are actually very good at it. For some reason, we feel like supplicants, with little room for bargaining. In fact, your ability to negotiate for yourself, with accurate research, good business sense, and a good attitude will help you gain your employer's respect, because it serves as an indication of the professional manner in which you'll handle matters for your clients in the future.

Here are some thoughts to consider about salary negotiations.

A.   BEFORE NEGOTIATIONS

- Sometimes, perhaps even during the initial interview, an employer might surprise you with an awkward (but likely well-intentioned) question, such as "If I were to make you a job offer, what kind of salary would you need?" We have known startled students who responded with a random dollar amount, and afterwards called the Career Office in a panic, to see whether their guess was anywhere close to the mark. **Never allow yourself to be rushed into accepting a job offer or negotiating a salary without taking time to reflect and gather the data you need to do so skillfully.** If you were sufficiently interested to pursue an offer, the appropriate answer to an unexpected question like the one above would be: "I don't have an amount in mind that I can give you with certainty now. I'd need a little bit of time to do some market research."

- Carefully review your finances, and **calculate your realistic bottom line,** which would be the minimum salary that you could afford to take, given your other obligations, including a set-aside for savings. Your goal, of course, is to negotiate a salary in excess of this amount.

- **Research the market for starting salaries in your region, in jobs similar to the one you plan to accept.** Several resources are available to help you estimate an appropriate amount. Your Career Office probably has similar job postings (some with salary ranges), as well as salary surveys, including those published by the National Association of College & Employers; NALP, the Association for Legal Career Professionals; and possibly even your state bar association (which would be helpful in calculating salaries for smaller cities and towns). You will more easily find data for employers that hire on a regular basis, such as large firms and government offices; however, with patience and possibly through the process of extrapolating from other data, you should be able to arrive at a reliable estimate.

- Don't undervalue your worth, because **you will never be in a better position than you are right now to negotiate an excellent salary and benefits package.** The employer has an immediate hiring need and, after what was probably an extensive interviewing period, has decided to hire *you*. Negotiate wisely, because future increases, based on factors such as tenure, growth in business, promotions, and cost-of-living may be smaller than you might anticipate.

- **Despite how it may *feel*, you are not going into battle with your future employer.** You are entering into a reasonable discussion about your salary, with someone who very much wants to hire you. The employer has experience dealing with salary negotiations; if you are unable to come to terms initially, the employer will make a counter-offer or identify the bottom line.

B. DURING NEGOTIATIONS

- **Salary comprises only a portion of your total benefits package,** although certainly it is the primary factor, and likely to be determined first. **Other monetary and non-monetary benefits can also be negotiated, and will add to the total value of your job offer.** While some employers have no discretion over base salaries, such as those that have lockstep salary systems (with pre-established salaries for all new hires within a certain time period), they may be able to negotiate other benefits.

- Factors to consider in your benefits package include: (1) a signing bonus (taking into account things such as previous work experience; significant and relevant law school or related experiences, such as moot court and publications; time already spent with the employer, working on a part-time or hourly basis; other graduate degrees; and completion of a judicial clerkship); (2) tenure and salary credit for post-graduate judicial clerkships; (3) retirement benefits, including availability of an employer match and details regarding vesting and portability (the length of time before the match is partly or 100% your property and options to move it elsewhere, should you decide to leave); (4) tuition reimbursement or credit; (5) educational loan repayment; (6) health insurance; (7) bar preparation and exam fees and/or a stipend while studying for the bar exam; (8) annual bar dues, expenses for bar conferences, CLE programs, in-house training and professional development; (9) relocation and moving expenses; (10) vacation time and holidays; (11) year-end bonuses; (12) free parking or stipend for transportation costs; (13) equipment such as a laptop and cellphone; (14) office decorating fees; (15) child care; and (16) gym memberships. However, use your judgment in asking, prioritize the order in which to ask, and don't waste your negotiating capital on minor issues.

- Inquire about the **policy regarding performance reviews and salary adjustments,** including whether increases are standardized, based on cost-of-living, or based on merit. For example, in return for a slightly lower starting salary, you may be able to negotiate a three-month performance review, and significant salary increase for high marks.

- Expect the employer to be fair and honest in negotiating; however, **it is up to you to negotiate the best benefits package available.** What you don't ask for you may not get.

- There is no rule that a job offer or salary negotiation must be settled in the first discussion; it is customary to take time to reflect. **If you feel that you need more time, ask for it,** and specify the desired time frame. For example, "That's an attractive offer. I'd like a few days to consider it and discuss the matter with my family. May I get back in touch with you on Friday?" It goes without saying that, if you promise to respond by Friday, be sure to do so—and don't wait until 5:00 p.m. to make the call.

C.   AFTER REACHING AGREEMENT

- Be absolutely clear about all the terms to which you and your employer have agreed, and **clarify any issues if necessary.**

- In a timely manner, **accept the offer in writing** and restate the terms of your agreement, including salary and start date. In your excitement about the new job, you may not realize (or have forgotten to mention) that you want to take a couple of weeks off after the bar examination, before starting to work.

CHAPTER 34

HOW TO GET PRACTICAL SKILLS IN LAW SCHOOL

"I never let my schooling interfere with my education."
Mark Twain

Some students can hardly wait to finish law school and begin seeing clients on their own. At the other end of the spectrum are those who feel that three short years of training (or even less, for those in accelerated JD programs) are not nearly long enough to prepare them for practice. If you fall into the latter category, there's no need to panic.

It's true that you'll face a steep learning curve during the first years of practice. However, **you can more easily adjust to life as a new professional by beginning to develop "lawyerly" skills and abilities as a law student.**

In some classes, such as Negotiating, the connection between what you're learning and how you'll use it in practice is very clear. There are also other valuable, but perhaps less apparent, opportunities to learn skills such as time management, general communication skills, and creative problem solving. We encourage you to be proactive in identifying and taking advantage of as many of these opportunities as possible. The alternative—realizing just before graduation that there are courses you would like to have taken, experiences you would like to have had, and people you wish you had established relationships with—is not a risk worth taking, as the students whose journals appear below have realized.

As much as I love my classes, I would give some of them up to have three or four more summer experiences. I need to clerk for a trial judge. I need to work in a government position (public defender, prosecutor, AG, etc.). I need time working with a law firm. But the reality is that I have only two summers, so I'll need to fit more internship-like experiences into my academic schedule. This is less than ideal, but it'll have to do.

Student Journal

Legal studies should be broken into academic and vocational departments. Thus far, my summer internships, the judicial clerking program, and the law school's skills courses have provided me with what I believe to be my most valuable educational experiences.

Student Journal

This chapter will explore the evolution of practical skills training in U.S. law schools. It also will take a closer look at both curricular developments (such as practical skills courses, clinics, and programs) and extracurricular opportunities for students to gain practical skills, and explore how you can craft a plan to incorporate more of them into your law school schedule.

A. THE CHANGING FACE OF LAW SCHOOLS

Years ago, new lawyers honed their skills by serving as apprentices to experienced attorneys. However, that practice faded in the early 1900's and, for almost the next century, legal education focused more strongly on academics than on practical skills. Things began to change dramatically in 1992, with the American Bar Association's (ABA) publication of its "Report of the Task Force on Law Schools and the Profession: Narrowing the Gap" (aka, MacCrate Report).

This report was the catalyst for the integration of practical skills into the law school curriculum. The ABA's revised accreditation standards now require instruction in practical skills for all students. (See "2017–2018 ABA Standards for Approval of Law Schools, Chapter 3: Program of Legal Education, Standard 303, Curriculum" available on the ABA's website, under Sections, Legal Education, Standards. See also *A Survey of Law School Curricula: 2002–2010*, Catherine L. Carpenter, American Bar Association, Section of Legal Education and Admissions to the Bar, available on the ABA's website, at Shop ABA).

These days, to receive a JD degree, you must complete courses in "professional skills," as well as substantive and procedural law; traditional skills such as legal research, analysis, and reasoning; and professional and ethical responsibility. While each law school has broad discretion in identifying and creating "professional skills" courses, topics generally include abilities such as interviewing, counseling, fact development, document drafting, collaboration, and managing legal work. **Students also must satisfactorily complete at least one "experiential course,"** such as a law clinic, field placement, or simulation. Pro bono participation is another way of developing practical skills. Some law schools require it, while others set aspirational goals; virtually all schools make pro bono opportunities available to those who wish to participate.

Given the ABA's mandate and a growing body of research that shows the measurable benefits of practical skills training, students can expect to be offered more varied, creative opportunities to prepare them for their careers. But the ultimate test of whether, and when, you achieve competence in these skills is one you will need to assess for yourself. Completion of a course can serve to introduce you to the kinds of skills you need to develop, but the attainment of competence will require you to continue to develop the skill through as many opportunities as you can find or create, inside and outside of formal course offerings.

B. PLANNING

The required law school curriculum is designed to give you a basic understanding of substantive and procedural law; traditional analytical and problem-solving skills; legal ethics; and how to research and write about the law. **A certain number of credit units must be devoted to mandatory core**

courses but, otherwise, *you* can design your own academic strategy.

A few students know exactly what courses they wish to take, and before their first day of law school have already mapped out the areas of law they want to explore. On the other hand, some don't have a clue about their interests. Most students fall somewhere in the middle.

With so many courses and practical experiences to choose from, what steps can you can take to identify those that will best mesh with your interests, abilities, and future career goals?

- First, **find out what courses will be offered in the coming semesters,** by reviewing your course catalog, academic schedules, and student handbook. (This seems obvious, but you would be amazed at the number of students who avidly read these materials just before beginning law school, and then never give them another glance. This is unfortunate, because they are valuable tools in planning your education.) Look at least a year into the future, because some courses are only offered on an annual or irregular basis and it would be a shame if you missed out on a course you wanted badly. If you're interested in a course taught by a specific professor, note the time(s) and semester(s) that the professor will teach and find out if he will be on sabbatical during your law school years. Finally, jot down any *course* *prerequisites*, so that you can slot them into your long-range academic schedule.

- **Talk with professors about your interests,** especially those whom you respect or who teach in subjects you particularly enjoy. Solicit their recommendations concerning courses you might take and experiences you should consider. Professors can also be a source of valuable contacts in the legal community, and may help connect you to experiences such as pro bono projects and clerkships.

- Ask **upper class students** about courses and instructors they have enjoyed.

- Course planning requires quite a bit of juggling, given the number of options available to you and the fact that your time is limited. If your school has an **academic counselor** and you are still uncertain about which courses you'd like to take, make an appointment to discuss your goals.

- The **Career Office has resources** to help you research practice settings. Counselors are available to discuss general and specific skills required in those areas and, later, help you secure jobs. If you are unfamiliar with the services offered by your Career Office, Chapter 35, "Career Office Resources," provides an overview.

- **Mentors and attorneys in the legal community** will be happy to suggest courses and practical skills that would be helpful in preparing for careers in their areas of practice. For more information about finding a mentor, see Chapter 30, "Get a Mentor— Expand Your World."

C. PRACTICAL SKILLS COURSES

Law schools offer an increasing array of courses that are specifically designed to teach skills such as how to communicate effectively in the workplace, juggle competing projects and deadlines, consistently produce high quality work, seek feedback, and perform the myriad of other tasks that lawyers regularly accomplish in their jobs. "Traditional" law school course may also be revamped to incorporate practical skills training. For example, an Estates and Trust course might include components such as simulated client interviews and the drafting of wills and trust agreements.

Following are examples of the practical skills courses you may find at your own law school.

- Alternative Dispute Resolution
- Law Practice Management
- Interviewing
- Mediation

- Pre-Trial Litigation
- Trial Advocacy
- Appellate Advocacy

- Moot Court or Mock Trial
- Statistics for Lawyers
- Negotiation
- Transactional Drafting
- Estate Planning
- Business Planning
- Lawyering

D. CLINICS

Clinics are viewed by employers as some of the very best law school experiences, even if they are focused on an area unrelated to your career goals. By shedding light on the realities of practice and giving students a chance to practice law under the supervision of an experienced attorney, clinics offer highly valuable, confidence-boosting experiences.

The ABA *Survey of Law School Curricula* indicates that 85% of U.S. law schools offer in-house, for-credit clinical courses, generally beginning in the first or second semester of the second year; about 30% also offer off-site clinics. Most clinics are in litigation-based practice areas, but the number of transactional clinics is steadily growing. Examples of clinical practice areas include Alternative Dispute Resolution, Child Advocacy, Criminal Prosecution and Defense, Domestic Violence, Environmental, Immigration, Landlord-Tenant, Tax, and White-Collar Crime. The list is not inclusive; you'll find almost every type of law represented in a clinic somewhere.

Students participate in an educational classroom component, which focuses on such things as the topical subject matter, procedural aspects of representing a client, and ethics. They are then certified under their state's Student Practice Rule and work as student lawyers, usually with attorney supervision. They interview clients, prepare legal documents, and represent their clients in court. Except for the heightened supervision, students are usually treated as "real" lawyers for all intents and purposes, as noted by the following student.

I feel as if this year will be a transition time between being a student and a lawyer, and this impression is enhanced by my participation in the Child Advocacy Clinic this semester. We have real cases, and are real representatives for our clients for the first time. I've been impressed and a little surprised by the level of respect afforded student lawyers from all parties involved. The lawyers don't seem to take a "you're just a student" attitude, and I can see that this experience will be a really important feature in making this a transition year, instead of just another year in school.

Student Journal

E.   JUDICIAL INTERNSHIPS

Post-graduate judicial clerkships are highly recommended by professors and employers. But, why wait until graduation? Most schools offer for-credit judicial internships, and the benefits are numerous.

Obviously, you would learn your way around the courtroom and courthouse. Working closely with the judge's law clerk, you would read case files (seeing persuasive documents filed by both sides, presenting the issues in a way most favorable to their clients), research unsettled issues of law from the perspective of an unbiased yet precedent-setting decision maker, and, in many cases, get to try your hand at drafting rulings and opinions. You would also see lots of lawyers in action and, afterwards, be able to speak with the judge (and, depending on the court, perhaps juries) about what was most effective, and what mistakes were made.

One of the best parts of a judicial internship is experiencing first-hand the close working relationship that exists between the judge and staff. And finally, if you decide to apply for post-graduate clerkships, you would have the added advantage of being able to demonstrate your understanding of what a clerkship involves and how a clerk can most effectively work with a judge.

F.   EXTERNSHIP PROGRAMS

Externships offer for-credit experiences working as law clerks, legal interns, or research assistants in a variety of government and public interest settings. In addition to local placements, some schools have established relationships in other locations throughout the state and nation and, sometimes, even internationally. Programs are carefully designed to give students specific experiences and responsibilities, as well as close feedback not only from a supervising attorney on site, but also from a faculty externship supervisor.

G.   PRO BONO OPPORTUNITIES

By participating in pro bono projects, students get to work alongside lawyers on real cases in a broad range of areas. Depending on your interests, you could have significant client contact, or you might prefer a project that requires more legal research and writing. Activities range from conducting intake interviews, making legal referrals, working on criminal appeals, assisting with legal work related to disaster relief, conducting research on DNA for post-conviction relief cases, and beyond.

Many schools require pro bono work for graduation but, even if yours doesn't, you'll gain valuable experience by participating. Depending on your school's circumstances, your pro bono connection could be through the Public Interest Center, Career Office, or a designated faculty member. Some firms offer what is called a "public interest split summer," where students work in the firm's office for part of the summer, and with a public interest organization for the remainder, often doing pro bono work. Ask the Career Office to provide you with a list of these firms. You might also check Pro Bono Net (which maintains a database of lawyers and law students), the ABA's National Pro Bono Opportunities Guide, and PSJD (Public Service Jobs Directory), a clearinghouse with public interest job listings and career-building resources, all of which maintain websites.

H.   RESEARCH ASSISTANT POSITIONS

Many professors hire law students to serve as research assistants. Projects often include helping with books or publications in development, or preparing course or conference materials. In addition to developing your research skills while exploring a newly developing area of law, you'll have the chance to establish a close working relationship with the professor. The professor may also serve as a valuable professional reference for you in the future. Openings for research positions may be announced by the professor during class, published in the student bulletin or newspaper, and/or posted in the Career Office and other areas of the law school. If you're interested in working with a particular professor, by all means stop by her office to inquire about the possibility.

I.   PUBLICATION EXPERIENCE

Law Reviews, Journals and other publications offer much more than the obvious in-depth development of research and writing skills, and a notation on your resume (all of which are valuable). You'll also increase your organizational and communication abilities, and develop close working relationships with fellow writers and faculty advisors.

There are other options for those who do not apply for, or are not selected for, these publications. A variety of legal writing contests, often sponsored by bar associations or sections, offer cash prizes, as well as the possibility of having your article published. Your school undoubtedly posts these opportunities in a number of locations; if you are interested, you might also look at the website of the ABA's Law Student Division under "Writing Competitions and Contests."

J.   SEMESTER AND SUMMER ABROAD PROGRAMS

More than half of U.S. law schools offer the option of studying in a foreign country for a semester. There are costs and benefits to be considered in making the decision to study abroad. **For those who plan to practice international law, a semester abroad may fit perfectly into your academic strategies.** If you decide to enroll in such a program, you may be able to combine it with other opportunities, such as foreign language study, an externship or other practical skills component, and activities that put you in contact with lawyers in the community. The ABA maintains a list of Semester Programs and Foreign Summer and Intersession Programs on its website.

K.   CERTIFICATE AND SPECIALIZATION PROGRAMS

Certificate and specialization programs require taking a certain number of courses in a well-outlined formal course of study and completion of a variety of other requirements. Over half of law schools offer them in one or more specific areas of law, and they are becoming increasingly popular. For students who already know what type of law they plan to practice after graduation, a certificate program might be a good strategy. After graduation, you'll have a certificate of specialization that demonstrates to employers your expertise and commitment to a certain kind of legal practice.

The most popular programs are in International Law, Business Law, Intellectual Property, and Litigation, but you'll find programs ranging from relatively broad topics like Constitutional and Criminal Law, to more specialized areas like Food and Agricultural Law, and Environmental Law.

L.   JOINT DEGREE PROGRAMS

An overwhelming majority of law schools allow you to **earn an additional graduate degree in combination with your JD** (thus saving time and money). The JD/MBA is one of the most common joint degrees, but the JD/MSW is gaining in popularity. Law degrees can be combined with many disciplines, some of which are highly specialized, such as finance, women's studies, psychology, and public policy. Although there is no data indicating that joint degree graduates earn higher starting salaries than their JD counterparts, there are other benefits to consider. Many graduates find their joint degrees extremely helpful in getting their foot in the door in competitive fields such as academics, business, and policy.

Typically, students complete the first-year curriculum in both fields consecutively, and then meet other joint requirements concurrently. If you think you might be interested in such a program, it is best to inquire early in the admission process; students often must qualify for, apply to, and commit to both programs at or near the same time.

M. COURSES OUTSIDE OF LAW SCHOOL

Most law schools allow students to take at least a couple of graduate or upper-level undergraduate courses on Main Campus; some of those courses may even be cross-listed with the law school. Depending on your career plans, there might be very good reasons to explore course offerings outside of the law school. For example, if you plan to work in environmental law, a course on Agricultural Economics or Environmental Statistics could be very helpful. If your technological skills aren't up to date, you could benefit from a course on the basics of computer software.

If you hope to develop a certain level of expertise in an area, but not to the extent of a certificate or joint degree, the ability to take one or more courses outside of the law school could be very appealing. Consult the course catalog on Main Campus or speak with an academic advisor about your options.

N. POST-GRADUATE PROGRAMS

Graduation comes too soon for some students, before they've had sufficient time to specialize in the area of law in which they wish to practice. If you feel the same way, **you may want to consider pursuing a post-graduate degree, such as an LL.M.** More than a third of American law schools offer full-time, part-time, and online programs and they are also offered internationally. Taxation, Corporate Law, International Law, and Intellectual Property are some of the most common areas of specialization, but there over 100 areas from which to choose. See the ABA's website for a list of accredited programs and areas of specialization offered.

CHAPTER 35

CAREER OFFICE RESOURCES

"The greatest thing in this world is not so much where we stand, as in what direction we are moving."
Oliver Wendell Holmes

The professionals in your Career Office have significant experience working with students and alumni; some may have practiced law at one time. Most Career Offices offer an assortment of career planning services, professional development activities and online resources. Which resources will be useful to you will depend on your stage of development—from a 1L needing help with your resume and interviewing skills to a post-graduate wanting information about current job opportunities.

We hope you won't wait until just before graduation to take advantage of this valuable resource. Here are some of the services that may be offered:

A. CAREER EXPLORATION

- Personalized **career counseling.**

- **Presentations** on various areas of law practice and alternative careers, where attorneys and other professionals discuss their career paths and day-to-day experiences, and respond to students' questions.

- **Career Library,** with print and online materials to help you learn about various careers, and how to locate jobs.

- **General resources** on topics such as interviewing skills, networking, stress management, and work/life balance.

B. SKILLS BUILDING

- **Professional development training** such as time management, organizational and problem-solving skills, professional etiquette, and oral communication.

- Information about **summer and semester abroad, joint degree, and post-graduate LL.M. programs.**

C. INTRODUCTION TO LEGAL COMMUNITY

- Assistance in **developing networking skills and opportunities to use them.**

- Coordination of **formal and informal mentoring programs.**

- **Links to alumni** who practice in specific areas of law and geographic locations.

- **Referrals to local attorneys,** capitalizing on the office's strong connections with legal employers and bar associations.

- **Employer receptions and other special events,** often in collaboration with other areas of the law school.

D.   JOB SEARCH

- Instruction on how to prepare a **resume and cover letter,** often with editing assistance.

- General advice about selecting **a writing sample** (but generally not on editing, because employers want to see a representative sample of your own work).

- Feedback on **selection of professional references.**

- **Mock interview programs,** to help fine-tune your skills.

- **On-campus interviewing programs,** local and national **job fairs** and consortia.

- **Job postings,** job search resources, and on-line resources.

- Coordination of **internships and externships** in a variety of employment settings, including courts, public interest organizations, state and federal legislators, and government offices.

- Information about **fellowships and post graduate government hiring programs.**

- Coordination of **post-graduate judicial clerkship** applications.

- Information about **principles and standards of receiving and accepting job offers.**

- Access to **salary surveys** and advice about **salary negotiations.**

- **Access to law school Career Offices around the nation** (called "reciprocity"), for job searches in other geographic locations.

- Information about **cost of living and housing in other geographic locations.**

- For experienced lawyers, information about **lateral hiring and legal search firms.**

E.   ADMISSION TO PRACTICE

- Information about **registering for and taking the bar examination** in your own state or others.

- Information about **background checks.**

- Information about, and sometimes coordination of, **fingerprinting** for employment applications and bar examination Character & Fitness Reports.

CHAPTER 36

MONEY MATTERS

"Never anticipate future income."
Anonymous

*"There are people who have money
and people who are rich."*
Coco Chanel

**What place does a discussion on budget and
debt management have in a book about
excellence in the workplace?** You may be
surprised to learn that your finances and how well
you manage them are directly related to several
aspects of your professional life.

We are not financial advisors, and do not intend to
provide financial counseling here. However, provided
below are general observations about managing (and
mismanaging) money, based on our own experiences
and on what we've learned over the years from
students and young lawyers. Our reflections are
designed to get you thinking about what money
means to you, how you handle it, and **how it can
shape your life choices.**

First, on your application for admission to practice
law, you'll be asked to provide information about your
financial history. **The care with which you
manage your money is considered a good
indication of how you will manage your
professional fiduciary responsibilities,** such as
helping your clients make financial decisions, and
managing trust accounts for which you may have

primary responsibility. **Unresolved debt problems and their consequences present a red flag that may delay or even prevent your admission to the bar.** After admission, they can result in discipline or even disbarment of practicing lawyers.

Consider how money relates to freedom and choices. We have all heard of someone bound by "golden handcuffs," who earns a very high salary but depends on every penny of it to support the lifestyle he has created. The problem is not making, or spending, a lot of money—it comes from spending beyond or barely within his income.

One of the best pieces of advice we can give is this: **if you live well below your means, you will always have the luxury of greater freedom and more choices.** By being prudent with your finances, you'll have a full range of choices, both professionally and personally.

After spending so much time in school, having to live on a budget and do without many of the things you'd like to have, you may be tempted as you near graduation, or after accepting a job offer, to "cut loose" a little. For example, we have seen new graduates overspend on such things as clothing and vacations. Almost immediately after beginning new jobs, in anticipation of future income, many new associates invest in new homes and new cars that are well beyond their current reach. They may not realize that, by accumulating significant monthly payments and long-term debt, they are committing themselves to the need for a high annual salary, even though, so early in their careers, they may not be entirely certain what will happen or what they might want to do in the future.

Many of us resist acknowledging what salespeople, money managers and mental health practitioners have known for years—**at times, our feelings of self-worth are tied to our earning power, what we spend and what we buy.** Comparing our financial state to that of others who are better off may make us feel inadequate. As a result, to "keep up appearances," we may spend more than we can afford on meals, clothing, and gifts for our children or other loved ones. Luxuries can slowly become necessities to support a lifestyle that we feel we need to accommodate. If this scenario sounds familiar, here are some tips to help you readjust your thoughts.

- **Somebody is always going to have more money** (usually a whole lot more) than you do, and **most people will have less than you.** This is just a fact—try not to read any more meaning into it, and try to work as best you can with what you have (at least until you earn more).

- **Remember that you have likely made, or may want to make, career choices based on factors other than the compensation (in all forms) that your employer provides.** This is not to say that you shouldn't expect a fair salary and benefits package. But the compensation that you and your friends receive will vary tremendously, depending on where you work and where you live. For example, large firms often provide attorneys with luxuries like expensive meals and tickets to the theater, whereas those in public interest positions may have to pay for their own bar memberships and contribute to the office coffee fund. On the other hand, public interest lawyers may be able to eat more often at home and have more time to go to the theater than their large-firm counterparts. Everything is a matter of choice.

- **Try to break the connection between socializing with your friends and co-workers, and overspending.** You probably have friends who earn less than you do, and those who earn more, yet you would all agree that the value of getting together socially comes primarily not from the activity that brings you together, but from your enjoyment of each other's company. There are many things you can do together that need not revolve around spending a lot of money, such as pot-luck dinners, an evening playing board games, sports and other outdoor activities, and matinee movies or video nights.

- **There may be a big difference between the style in which you were raised and the style in which you can now afford to live, or in a few years will be able to live.** If you grew up in a family that was financially comfortable, purchases that used to be second nature to you may now be beyond your means as a student or new attorney. On a limited budget, one purchase usually means foregoing another and, when you're struggling to pay for the necessities, expensive haircuts and mocha lattes may have to go by the wayside.

- **On the other hand, if you were raised in a family that had difficulty making ends meet, you might have trouble spending money that you can now well afford.** Despite making a good income and having sufficient savings, you may never feel that you have quite enough money. At times, you may even forego the purchase of something you actually need, but consider a luxury.

- **Impulse buying is often tied to your mood.** When you're tired, stressed, or overworked, you may be tempted to overspend or make inappropriate purchases. If you find yourself in this position, resist getting out your wallet; instead wait a few days and carefully consider the purchase. You may find that the item you "just had to have" is no longer important, or that you have forgotten about it altogether.

Don't bury your head in the sand. **If you get in financial trouble, seek credit counseling immediately.** There are many nonprofit agencies who will help you review your finances, intervene for you with your creditors, renegotiate interest rates, and consolidate and prioritize payments. Don't forget to work with your school's financial aid advisor on student loan consolidation, best interest rates, and possible loan forgiveness programs.

CHAPTER 37

LAW FIRM ECONOMICS: UNDERSTANDING THE BUSINESS SIDE OF THE PROFESSION

"Never invest in a business you cannot understand."
Warren Buffet

While it is true that law is a service profession that revolves around relationships, it is also a business. Attorneys provide something of value for which "clients" must be willing to pay. (In firms, clients include individuals, organizations, and corporations. For government and public-sector attorneys, the client base is more varied, and can include other government agencies or departments, the general public, individuals, private donors and grant funders, and other organizations.)

Understanding the business side of the profession is important. It will help you see a direct correlation between your own performance and your employer's profitability. If you work at a law firm, it will also give you a better understanding of how your billable hour goals were determined, and how your firm measures and rewards success. In this chapter, we'll explore basic economic concepts governing law firms, discuss various ways that firms measure profitability and set lawyer compensation, and identify key decision makers in firm management structures.

Because attorneys sell services instead of widgets, placing an accurate value on what is sold can be difficult, yet critical, especially in law firms. A small but growing number of clients ask for alternative fee arrangements and, while the majority of them are amenable to traditional hourly billing, many want itemized invoices and will ask to renegotiate if the total cost seems out of line with what was expected. In both cases, even though it is almost impossible to do so, the firm must estimate at the outset of the case how complex the matter will turn out to be or how much time it may take to resolve.

Managing partners and business managers face a delicate balance in making the financial and administrative decisions needed to keep a firm on solid economic ground. They must focus not only on the efficient production of work, but also on factors both in and out of the firm's control, such as its marketing strategies, short-term and long-term goals; employee health and morale; current and projected client base and demand for services; as well as domestic and international economic policy and trends.

Many legal employers are candid in providing some or all of their attorneys with financial information about the firm as well as about individual attorney performance; in other settings attorneys' knowledge may be limited to their own billing and collections. Whether your employer (or future employer) provides you with more—or less— financial information, **the information in this chapter will enable you to better understand**

and evaluate the organizational factors that bear directly on your workload and compensation.

A. KEY DECISION-MAKERS AND STRUCTURE

1. Management

Who makes financial and administrative decisions in a law firm? Most firms still follow the traditional practice of appointing a Managing Partner, who may or may not work with an Executive Committee. Others have replaced the managing partner structure with a Management Committee. A less-common, but growing practice in large firms, is employment of a non-lawyer Executive Director or Chief Operating Officer, whose education and experience are more suited to handling the firm's increasingly complex management needs. Depending on the firm's size and needs, it may employ other professionals such as a Chief Financial Officer and Chief Information Officer. Regardless of which individuals comprise management's "upper tier," almost everyone in the organization contributes information to help set and meet the firm's financial goals.

2. Partnership

For many new lawyers, partnership represents the ultimate career accomplishment. In its *traditional sense*, equity partnership offers them a percentage ownership in the firm (both assets and liabilities), the knowledge that their work measures up to the firm's standards, and the security of knowing that their positions are secure. Associates are typically considered for equity partnership after a certain time (ranging from seven to ten years, with seven or eight being most common). Generally, but not always, the new partner must make a significant capital contribution to the firm. In return, the partner receives some degree of voting power on firm governance and partner compensation, along with additional perks and bonuses, and may take on a greater share of responsibility for marketing. In this type of setting, associates who do not make partner may or may not leave the firm.

In a majority of law firms, however, the two-tier (or a multi-tier) partnership model affords associates with other options. At or around the same time that equity partnerships are offered, those who are deemed "not ready" for or not interested in equity partnership may be offered non-equity partnerships (also called income partner, non-share partner, junior partner, special partner, or participating associate). Non-equity partners have no ownership in the firm, nor do they have a vote in how it is operated, yet they enjoy the prestige of being known as a partner and may be given the option to be considered for full equity partnership in a few more years. The option of a permanent non-equity partnership is usually available.

There are a number of reasons for the existence of non-equity partnerships, in addition to providing additional time to an associate who has not developed the entire skill set expected of an equity partner. First, they offer an alternative for associates who wish to remain with the firm and whose performance otherwise measures up to partnership quality work but who does not wish to (and never will wish to) be a rainmaker, share the firm's liabilities, or bill the required number of hours to make equity partner. From the firm's perspective, there is a strong business case for non-equity partnerships. Partnership standards are tougher than they were 20 years ago, in part because most firms' economic business models cannot sustain the high level of growth that would be required if equity partners were added at the same rate, year after year. Accordingly, some associates who would have made partner in the past are simply unable to do so now. Non-equity partnerships offer firms a means by which to keep these valuable employees, thus retaining the resources already invested in their training, and the benefit from future value of the work and intangible contributions they will make to the firm.

Less frequently, non-equity partnerships offer a mechanism by which to withdraw the equity partner status of underperforming attorneys, perhaps encouraging them to leave the firm.

3. Of-Counsel

In many firms, this option provides flexibility for those who are valuable to the firm but who don't want to make a full-time commitment. An attorney wishing to work reduced hours (for example, during early years of child rearing) might seek an of-counsel position, and might opt back onto the equity partnership track at a later time. Many attorneys making the transition from full-time practice to retirement choose the of-counsel route as well.

B. BASIC ECONOMIC CONCEPTS

Although there is no "one-size-fits-all" formula to profitability, financial reports and statements are important tools in making decisions about a firm's business. Some of the concepts involved in a firm's financial health are explained below, in a way that illustrates more clearly the complex nature of the business.

- **Operating Expenses:** These are day-to-day costs incurred in running a firm, and include such things as recruiting expenses; lawyer and staff compensation and benefits; costs of bar memberships, CLEs and other training; rent, utilities and other building expenses; equipment maintenance (think "IT") and office supplies; copying charges; and insurance.

- **Leverage:** This indicates the ratio of associates to partners (i.e., the extent to which partners delegate their work) and can be calculated on a firm-wide or practice-specific basis. There is no "magic" ratio for leverage, and many factors affect the calculation. Firms with a sophisticated or specialized practice or clientele may have a relatively low leverage, indicating that senior attorneys perform most of the firm's work. Those with a broad range of practice areas or in high-volume practices where much of the work is routine and/or standardized and can be performed by associates, e.g., insurance defense, may have a higher leverage ratio. In the past, leverage could be used as an economic tool by firms that could use lower-paid associates and paralegals for a higher percentage of the work. However, corporate clients are increasingly resistant to this practice and may instead have a higher leverage rate for their share of the firm's work by moving routine, less difficult work in-house and enlisting firms only for more difficult, highly-specialized work.

- **Fees:** Clients may be billed on an hourly basis (at a rate that varies, depending on who is working on the project); at a fixed rate (for an amount pre-set for a specific period of time); on a per-project rate (a specific amount established for each matter, or type of matter); on a contingency fee basis (where attorney fees are collectible only if the case is successfully resolved); at a rate set by the court; or, in the case of pro bono clients, not at all. Fees tend to be higher in premium practice areas, such as mergers and acquisitions, and intellectual property litigation. The process of billing and collecting for legal services has perhaps been one of the most significant areas of change in the industry in recent years. Today it is estimated that 80–90% of legal work is conducted outside of the standard, fixed billable-hour basis, due to clients' insistence on write-offs, write-downs, and various types of alternative fee or fixed-rate arrangements. Clients with a high volume of business may negotiate for services at a fixed rate and, during economic downturns, the shift of market power makes it possible for an even greater number of clients to demand fixed fees.

- **Utilization:** Used in calculating net income, this refers to total billable hours (which is almost always less than total number of hours worked), without regard to amounts collected. Many firms have uniform billable hours requirements for attorneys. In some firms, partners set their own billable hours, taking into consideration their other activities for the firm (such as mentoring new attorneys, training, and rainmaking).

- **Realization:** Realization measures, in a broad sense, how legal work is billed and collected. In a narrow sense, it measures the relationship of what is billed to what is collected, and how quickly. Attorneys receive various ongoing and monthly reports, showing accounts receivable, the rate of collection, and a record of write-downs and write offs. Firms carefully monitor how many months of work are tied up waiting to be billed, as well as the average length of time between billing a client and receiving payment (as many as five or six months can elapse, but a better average is two months). Realization can be calculated on a firm-wide, practice-based, per-attorney, and/or per-project basis and, as with leverage (discussed above), there is no "magic" number. Many factors influence realization, such as whether billing procedures are cumbersome or streamlined, how promptly bills are collected, and who plays what role in collecting them. Firms may opt out of unprofitable practice areas; for example, there may be a limit to the number of hours that can be billed in some areas, such as probate, where the court closely monitors and often marks down large bills. A firm might search for ways to work more efficiently, or may allow a segment of the practice to operate at a loss, if the work is deemed sufficiently important (e.g., related to an influential and otherwise profitable client). Realization can also be improved by more effective client screening, better client understanding of billing procedures, and better attorney monitoring of total number of hours spent and billed on projects.

- **Debt Load and Capitalization:** Firms require a minimum monthly cash flow to sustain operations (such as salaries and operating expenses, debt payments, payments to retired partners, contributions to pension and profit-sharing plans, costs advanced on behalf of clients, and a reasonable draw for partners to live on, as well as cash flow including cash balances on hand, collections from previous bills and costs advanced). Business managers have several tools to measure this ability. Only a few examples are offered here, as the financial formulas and calculations are certain to cause all but the most business-oriented readers' eyes to glaze over: the ratio of debt and depreciation to equity (permanent capital and undistributed earnings); the ratio of outstanding debt to net fixed assets; the debt coverage ratio (indicating how long it would take to fully retire the firm's debt); and permanent capital per partner.

- **Measures of Productivity:** Typical calculations of productivity are (a) the ratio of average hours billed vs. average collected revenue, and (b) average operating cost vs. average revenue. Both can be determined on a firm-wide, partner, associate and/or fee-earner basis.

- **Measures of Profitability:** Two ways of measuring profitability are "average profits per partner," and "revenue per lawyer" (used in many surveys on law firm profitability). Another is "average net income or revenue," which can be calculated per lawyer, per partner, and/or per fee earner. This is a complex calculation that takes into account the associate/partner ratio, billing rate, hours worked vs. hours billed vs. hours collected, and ratio of net income vs. gross fees. The benefits of using net revenue per lawyer as a measure of profitability is that it gives early signals about whether the market for legal services is softening or clients' fee-resistance is stiffening, and gives insights needed to make educated and profitable staffing decisions firm-wide as well as by practice area. "Partner value" calculates the economic value of revenues generated by a partner's own work on behalf of clients, plus profits generated by associates working on matters managed by that partner, minus the partner's individual overhead. In most measures of profitability, uncollected billing is not figured into the equation, nor are non-revenue generating activities (such as community service or client development), unless the firm has developed a model for taking these into account.

C. INCREASING FIRM PROFITABILITY

The many measures of gauging a firm's increased profitability include: (a) increased average revenue per lawyer, and per fee earner; (b) increased associate productivity (e.g., average hours billed or average collected revenues); (c) lower operating costs; (d) improved profitability (e.g., average net income per lawyer or average profits per partner); and (e) improved associate retention. To achieve these results, a firm might:

- **Decrease overhead and operating costs.** This is usually one of the first areas to be addressed by management in response to factors such as an economic downturn, increased client pressure to reduce rates, decreased client demand, and increased competition from other providers. Cost-cutting measures might range from big changes such as centralizing functions, decreasing staff, or instituting tougher guidelines for making permanent offers to 2L summer associates, to smaller yet profitable economizing measures such as decreasing copying or telephone charges. To save attorney travel time and expenses, for example, a firm might cut back on the number of law schools visited during On-Campus Interviewing season and increase its use of telephonic or video interviews. Similarly, although multi-office firms have unavoidable duplication of certain expenses, many firms are taking advantage of technology and other means to share costs where possible. Although decreasing operating expenses and overhead is often a first response to economic challenges, it will rarely be the last, because expenses can only be cut so much. Afterwards, to increase profitability, the firm must look to other profit-growing measures, such as those discussed below.

- **Change recruiting strategy.** The firm might recruit and retain experienced laterals, increase or decrease the number of entry-level associates or size of the summer clerking programs, economize on costs of running the clerking program or change the focus of training.

- **Strategic use of technology.** Technology is changing the nature of legal services delivery, just as it is changing so many other areas of our economy. Some expenditures on technology, cybersecurity for example, may be viewed as mandatory rather than optional. Law Practice Management Systems can standardize and expedite tasks such as calendaring, expense and time tracking, case filing, document sharing, legal invoicing, online payments, creation of financial performance reports, etc., thus freeing attorneys to spend less time on administrative matters and more time on billable client services. Technology can assist with and decrease processing time for routine matters, e.g., contract review, patent filings, and settlement of lower-level cases, for example— though this development brings other challenges, in that it "commoditizes" those services and could lead to client demand for volume pricing and/or client's entertaining other firm bids for this type of work. While technology has broad potential to decrease operating expenses, it can also require significant up-front expenditures such as purchase cost; training, operating, and maintenance expenses; and replacement costs, as technology becomes obsolete more quickly these days. These expenditures can temporarily decrease the firm's net profits and, depending on the amount of capital that is available, the firm may ask equity partners to contribute funds for these expenditures.

- **Alter firm structure; diversify the practice.** Increasingly, firms are merging, to maximize factors such as size and scope of practice areas, as well as regional and global coverage. This has resulted in creation of numerous "mega-firms." To better withstand economic downturns, a firm might increase the percentage of work that commands higher billings (e.g., IP and technology litigation), and phase out other areas. A firm might also form peripheral business groups (e.g., electronic discovery or accounting services).

- **Increase attention to collecting receivables.**

- **Change the partnership structure.** For example, some firms have decreased the number of equity partnerships or de-equitized partners who are underperforming, so that fewer attorneys are sharing in the firm's pool of profits.

D. COMPENSATION PLANS

1. Associate Compensation

As a new attorney, you will have access to salary data and trends through numerous local, state, and national surveys as well as from other resources (check with your law school Career Office). However, many new associates lack understanding of how salaries are set, and who sets them.

In government settings, local, county or state agencies may compensate employees based on a uniform salary scale, sorted by job classification (e.g., Law Clerk, Attorney I, Attorney II) and years of employment. Salaries may be adjusted via annual cost-of-living increases, and bonuses. Compensation practices are more varied in other public-sector employment settings, ranging from standardized salary structures to structures that allow more room for negotiation.

In law firms, associate compensation is generally established by a firm's Compensation Committee. Factors considered in establishing compensation can include individual performance, unique firm values and practices, as well as the firm's current and projected finances. Market forces significantly drive the process as well; if one firm in a geographic market raises salaries significantly, other firms of similar size are likely to follow suit. Salary trends on the East Coast can be expected to move westward, too. Here are several typical associate compensation plans:

Closed compensation plans. In many firms, associate (and even partner) compensation is confidential and, although the grapevine may provide a certain amount of information, no details are released by the firm.

Lock-step compensation plans. Here, the salaries of all associates who bill a required number of hours and perform satisfactorily are advanced in synch. These plans are easy to administer but provide little motivation for top-performing associates and no enticement to work efficiently.

Bonuses. Some firms deal with problems of a lockstep compensation plan by tacking on incentives like associate bonuses, but this can create a different set of problems. If linked to billable hours, they can invite partner favoritism in allocating work at end of year, create unhealthy competition for projects, and send a message that long hours billed and collected are more important than expertise and relationships developed. Bonus systems also do not adequately address associates who fall in the middle or low performing end of the spectrum.

Performance-based (benchmark or competency based) compensation plans. These plans analyze an associate's performance in a manner similar to the way partners are evaluated for compensation. Many firms are interested in performance-based compensation plans, but are wrestling to decide what factors to consider and how to measure them, for example, requiring a first-year litigation associate to have mastered the Rules of Evidence; worked with a certain number of attorneys on a specific variety of projects; and observed certain events, such as client meeting, deposition, pre-trial motion hearing, trial and settlement conference. At a minimum, this type of compensation requires thoughtful evaluation procedures, as well as provision of opportunities for professional training and development. Additionally, practice group leaders must be willing to provide detailed input on all members in the practice group.

2.   Partner Compensation

The spread in terms of partner salary can be quite wide—with highest-paid partners earning as much as 20 times more than the lowest-paid partner. There are several possible mechanisms for determining partner compensation.

Performance-based compensation plans. By recognizing the value of non-billable time that firm leaders devote to creating and managing the business plan, these plans create incentives for partners to contribute more actively to the group's infrastructure and activities benefitting the whole. An evaluation of the attorney's rate of collection and write-offs may also be included in the calculation.

Unique partner compensation plans. Many firms have procedures for rewarding partners who have unique practices and bring business that the firm would not otherwise receive. Compensation varies, with the partner generally receiving a percentage of the fee generated by the business brought in (varying, depending on amount of client service the partner provides) or an agreed-upon rate.

Open, participative compensation system. A few firms have fully open and participative compensation system, with partners actively involved in the process of determining partner compensation.

INDEX

References are to Pages